S0-BIK-375

Jerry J. Bigner, PhD
Editor

An Introduction to GLBT Family Studies

Pre-publication
REVIEWS,
COMMENTARIES,
EVALUATIONS . . .

"This book represents a much-needed addition to the field of family studies and should be required reading in undergraduate and graduate family studies degree programs—no other book pulls together this much information about these families. It will be of interest to family studies instructors, researchers, and students as well as clinicians working with GLBT families.

Bigner has drawn together respected authors in the field and the book is well written and very interesting to read. It pulls together theoretical, research, and clinical information in a comprehensive introduction to the field of GLBT family studies. One of the most important contributions of this book is that the lives of GLBT individuals are contextualized within a comprehensive family systems framework."

Kevin P. Lyness, PhD
Associate Professor, Applied Psychology,
Antioch University New England

"Packed with useful information and wisdom for professionals and families, this book is all that the title implies and more. Jerry Bigner's edited work delivers a solid introduction to this recently acknowledged field.

This is a treasure trove of sound information, practical observations, and suggestions for clinicians and other service providers, teachers, researchers, families, and GLBT people. It is the best practical source I have seen. It should be required reading for professionals and students, and available for families and GLBT people struggling with the complicated questions of coming out and working out relationships with partners, siblings, parents, and children."

William C. Nichols, EdD, ABPP
Editor, *Contemporary Family Therapy*
and *Family Therapy Around the World: A Festschrift for Florence Kaslow*

NOTES FOR PROFESSIONAL LIBRARIANS AND LIBRARY USERS

This is an original book title published by The Haworth Press, Inc. Unless otherwise noted in specific chapters with attribution, materials in this book have not been previously published elsewhere in any format or language.

CONSERVATION AND PRESERVATION NOTES

All books published by The Haworth Press, Inc., and its imprints are printed on certified pH neutral, acid-free book grade paper. This paper meets the minimum requirements of American National Standard for Information Sciences-Permanence of Paper for Printed Material, ANSI Z39.48-1984.

DIGITAL OBJECT IDENTIFIER (DOI) LINKING

The Haworth Press is participating in reference linking for elements of our original books. (For more information on reference linking initiatives, please consult the CrossRef Web site at www.crossref.org.) When citing an element of this book such as a chapter, include the element's Digital Object Identifier (DOI) as the last item of the reference. A Digital Object Identifier is a persistent, authoritative, and unique identifier that a publisher assigns to each element of a book. Because of its persistence, DOIs will enable The Haworth Press and other publishers to link to the element referenced, and the link will not break over time. This will be a great resource in scholarly research.

An Introduction to GLBT Family Studies

THE HAWORTH PRESS
Haworth Series in GLBT Family Studies (GLBTFS)
Jerry Bigner, PhD
Editor

A Gay Couple's Journey Through Surrogacy: Intended Fathers by Michael Menichiello

An Introduction to GLBT Family Studies edited by Jerry J. Bigner

Titles of Related Interest:

Fatherhood for Gay Men: An Emotional and Practical Guide to Becoming a Gay Dad by Kevin McGarry

Queer Families, Common Agendas: Gay People, Lesbians, and Family Values edited by T. Richard Sullivan

An Introduction to GLBT Family Studies

Jerry J. Bigner, PhD
Editor

The Haworth Press
New York • London • Oxford

For more information on this book or to order, visit
http://www.haworthpress.com/store/product.asp?sku=5792

or call 1-800-HAWORTH (800-429-6784) in the United States and Canada
or (607) 722-5857 outside the United States and Canada

or contact orders@HaworthPress.com

The Haworth Press, Inc., 10 Alice Street, Binghamton, NY 13904-1580.

This book is a compilation of articles previously published in the *Journal of GLBT Family Studies*, 1(1)(2) (2005), published by The Haworth Press, Inc.

Cover design by Lora Wiggins.

Library of Congress Cataloging-in-Publication Data

An introduction to GLBT family studies / Jerry J. Bigner, editor.
p. cm.
A compilation of articles previously published in the Journal of GLBT Family Studies.
Includes bibliographical references and index.
ISBN-13: 978-0-7890-2496-1 (hard : alk. paper)
ISBN-10: 0-7890-2496-9 (hard : alk. paper)
ISBN-13: 978-0-7890-2497-8 (soft : alk. paper)
ISBN-10: 0-7890-2497-7 (soft : alk. paper)
1. Gays—Family relationships. 2. Lesbians—Family relationships. 3. Bisexuals—Family relationships. 4. Transsexuals—Family relationships. I. Bigner, Jerry J.

HQ76.25.I59 2006
306.85086'64—dc22

2005027805

CONTENTS

ABOUT THE EDITOR

Jerry J. Bigner, PhD, is Professor Emeritus in the Department of Human Development and Family Studies at Colorado State University in Fort Collins. Dr. Bigner is the editor of the *Journal of GLBT Family Studies* and the Haworth Text Series in GLBT Studies. He is a member of the Editorial Board of the *Journal of Couple and Family Therapy* and is a reviewer for *Family Relations.* His principal research focus is on parent-child relations with an emphasis on GLBT parents and their children. Dr. Bigner is the author of *Parent-Child Relations,* now in its seventh edition, and two life-span development texts. He has over fifty research publications and twenty chapters in texts relating to parent-child relations, therapeutic issues, and gay and lesbian issues. Dr. Bigner is a research member of the American Family Therapy Academy and the National Council on Family Relations. Dr. Bigner has provided expert witness testimony on behalf of gay and lesbian parents and for the Canadian same-sex marriage litigation.

doi:10.1300/5792_a

Contributors

Eric Aoki, PhD, is an associate professor of intercultural communication, interpersonal communication, and ethnography of communication, Department of Speech Communication, Colorado State University (Eric.Aoki@colostate.edu). His research specialization includes diversity studies with a critical eye toward ethnicity, gender, media, and queer communication. In addition to teaching and academic writing, Eric enjoys writing poetry, reading books, watching films, and traveling the globe. He has painted with oils and acrylics since the age of four. His art typically addresses the politics of identity with regards to being an ethnic minority and a gay male in the United States.

Kimberly F. Balsam, PhD, is a postdoctoral research fellow, Department of Psychology, University of Washington, Seattle, Washington.

Michael Bettinger, PhD, MFT, is retired from private practice in San Francisco, California (mcpsycle@well.com). For thirty years he provided counseling services to gay men, gay male couples, and families and others in relationships involving gay men. He has additional therapeutic expertise in polyamorous and nonmainstream relationships and sexualities. He uses a theoretically based growth model and the intergenerational (or transgenerational) family systems approach in his clinical practice.

Amity P. Buxton, PhD, is the executive director of the Straight Spouse Network (dir@ssnetwk.org). She is an author/researcher on spouses in mixed-orientation marriages (gay/lesbian-heterosexual, bisexual-heterosexual, and transgender-heterosexual), postdivorce coparenting of mixed-orientation couples, and concerns of children after the disclosure of one of their parents in a heterosexual relationship.

doi:10.1300/5792_b

Jacky Coates, MA, is currently enrolled in the MSW program at the School of Social Work & Family Studies at the University of British Columbia, Vancouver, British Columbia. She also works as a counselor at the Domestic Violence Unit of the Vancouver, British Columbia, Police Department where, in partnership with a specialized police officer, she provides follow-up support to victims of intimate-relationship violence. She can be contacted at jacky.coates@vancouver.ca.

Bertram J. Cohler, PhD, is William Rainey Harper Professor of Social Sciences, The University of Chicago (bert@midway.uchicago.edu). His research work includes the study of intergenerational relations in American families, presently focusing on ambivalence and the management of offspring disclosure to other family members of identity as a sexual minority.

Colleen M. Connolly, PhD, is an associate professor at Texas State University-San Marcos (cconnolly@txstate.edu). She is a counselor-educator teaching within the emphasis of family therapy and past president of the Association for Gay, Lesbian, and Bisexual Issues in Counseling, a division of the American Counseling Association.

Anthony R. D'Augelli, PhD, is a professor in the Department of Human Development and Family Studies, Pennsylvania State University (ard@psu.edu). He is a community psychology specialist with a research focus on sexual orientation development over the lifespan.

Rhonda J. Factor, BA, is a doctoral candidate in clinical psychology at the University of Vermont. She is currently a research associate at Cornell Weill Medical College and holds a clinical post-doctoral fellowship at the University of Stony Brook's Wo/Men's Center. She may be contacted via e-mail: RFactor@together.net.

David E. Greenan, PhD, is a psychologist and family therapist in private practice in New York City. He is an adjunct professor at Teachers College, Columbia University, and a consultant through the Minuchin Center to hospitals that serve inner-city poor families. Together with Gil Tunnell, he is the co-author of the highly acclaimed book *Couple Therapy with Gay Men* (Guilford, 2003).

Gianna E. Israel is a current HBIGDA member and former founding AEGIS board member. She has provided nationwide telephone consultation, individual and relationship counseling, and gender-specializing evaluations and recommendations since 1988. She is principal author of the book *Transgender Care,* with Donald Tarver, MD (Temple University Press, 1997).

Esther D. Rothblum, PhD, is a professor of women's studies at San Diego State University. Her research and writing have focused on lesbian relationships and lesbian mental health, and she is editor of the *Journal of Lesbian Studies.*

Vincent J. Samar, JD, is an adjunct professor of philosophy at Loyola University and Oakton Community College and an adjunct professor of law at the Illinois Institute of Technology, Chicago-Kent College of Law. He is the author of *Justifying Judgment: Practicing Law and Philosophy; The Right to Privacy;* and *The Right to Privacy: Gays, Lesbians, and the Constitution,* as well as numerous articles relating to gay rights and legal philosophy. He is also the editor of *New York Times, 20th Century in Review: Gay Rights Movement.*

Mary Kay Sicola, JD, MA, is an assistant professor (part-time) of communication studies at Southwestern University, Austin, Texas. She is also an attorney/mediator in private practice and founder of The Family Law Project, an organization dedicated to providing affordable access to the legal system and emphasizing nonadversarial means of dispute resolution.

Sondra E. Solomon, PhD, is an assistant professor of psychology in the Department of Psychology at the University of Vermont. She is also an assistant clinical professor of psychiatry in the College of Medicine at the University of Vermont. Her research interests include adults living with HIV in rural communities, discrimination and prejudice about chronic illness, and cross-cultural curriculum transformation.

Richard Sullivan, DSW, is an associate professor, School of Social Work & Family Studies, University of British Columbia. He has worked in the practice and study of child welfare and family policy for thirty years. His recent research has focused on adoptions, both domestic and intercountry. He teaches child development, child welfare practice, and family policy and has served on the boards of several child and family advocacy organizations.

Mary Swainson, MSc, is affiliated with the Child & Family Consultation Service, York House, Newham Primary Care Trust, London

National Health Service, United Kingdom (mary.swainson@newhampct.nhs.uk). Her area of clinical and research expertise is systemic psychotherapy.

Fiona Tasker, PhD, is a professor at Birkbeck College, University of London, United Kingdom (f.tasker@bbk.ac.uk). Her areas of research expertise include lesbian parenting, gay parenting, and lesbian and gay affirmative systemic psychotherapy.

Gil Tunnell, PhD, is an adjunct assistant professor of psychology and education, Teachers College, Columbia University. He also has a private practice in New York City.

Foreword

This volume marks the coming of age of the study of gay, lesbian, bisexual, and transgender (GLBT) families. Not many years ago, most family scholars and practitioners viewed homosexuality mainly as an individual characteristic and not as a way of being in relationships. It was a big step to begin paying attention to gay and lesbian *couples,* a step that placed sexual orientation in a relational context. However, the field still tended to define GLBT people only in terms of their erotic lives. Once attention expanded to include GLBT *families* (a term that embraces couples, parents, children, and youth, as well as intentional communities), a new harvest of teachings emerged for the field of family studies. As a recipient of this bounty, I am honored to write the Foreword for this book. I first discuss how the field of family studies can benefit from the systematic study of GLBT families, and then I offer recommendations, some of them challenging, for this exciting area of research.

GLBT family studies can help to unravel the Gordian knot of gender in family research. In the past, we had no way to tease out the extent to which important aspects of marriage and other heterosexual relationships stem from the fact that they involve men and women, as opposed to emerging from dynamics inherent in modern intimate relationships. For example, we knew that a decline in frequency of sexual relations occurs over time in heterosexual couples, but is this cooling off a function of men and women living together over time or is it a more general function of intimate relationships over time? From studies looking at both straight and same-sex couples, we now know that it is the latter.

Or take demand-withdrawal patterns in a couple relationship, in which one partner wants more time/attention/communication and the

doi:10.1300/5792_c

other feels put upon and backs away. For years, scholars and therapists attributed this common dynamic only to gender socialization: in simple form, women want more connection and men want more autonomy. However, because of research and therapy with same-sex couples, we now know that demand-withdrawal (or pursuer/distancing) patterns are common in intimate relationships no matter what the gender of the partners. On a less benign level, when we learned from research and clinical observation that domestic violence may be as common in same-sex couples as in straight couples, we had to rethink our understanding of the dark side of intimate relationships. Not that gender is irrelevant as an explanation for this and other aspects of couple relationships (for example, male-female couples tend to have less equitable divisions of household labor) but it is not as big a player in many areas as we had imagined before GLBT family studies arrived on the scene. This dethronement of gender has important real-world policy implications for parenting, both biological and adoptive, as the research continues to indicate that it is the quality of parenting in two-parent families and not the gender of the parents that accounts for children's well-being.

An area where GLBT family studies may lead to future breakthroughs in the field of family studies is the influence of ecological factors on couple and family relations. Broader community and cultural forces affect all families, but these influences can be difficult to detect and measure in mainstream family forms, which receive widespread cultural support. GLBT families face an array of cultural influences (documented extensively in this book), many of them toxic but some more mixed or even supportive in certain local communities. These forces operate at multiple levels, from individual internalization of homophobia to the attitudes and behavior of extended family members, to levels of support or undermining in local communities, to the work environment, and to larger city, state, and national policies, laws, and practices that affect GLBT families. What is more, many of these ecological influences are themselves changing—some for better and some for worse. If family scholars using human ecology and related theories in family studies take up the challenge of conceptualizing and measuring the complex interactions between GLBT families and their environmental contexts, it will give us tools to better understand all families in their environments.

A third important contribution of GLBT family studies is research on the social construction of norms for family living. Many chapters in this book explore how GLBT people are creating their family lives almost from scratch.

> How do gay or lesbian partners coparent when the prevailing social norms apply to coparenting by a mother and a father?
> How do they work out division of household labor when this has been viewed as gender specific for millennia?
> How do GLBT couples develop ways of relating in their own versions of biological, adoptive, and stepfamilies?
> What relationships do they choose to have with sperm donors and surrogate mothers?
> How do they work out patterns of relationship with grandparents of children from previous heterosexual marriages and first-time same-sex marriages?
> Does legal recognition of their unions change how same-sex couples plan their lives together?
> GLBT families are pioneers in forging intentional families with members not connected by traditional ties. How do they work out norms of support and reciprocity?

We are witnessing the rapid evolution of the bottom-up construction of new ways to conceive family life, with GLBT people borrowing selectively from tradition and making up the rest on their own. For scholars interested in the social construction of family norms and practices, could there be any richer gold mine?

A final contribution lies in the intersection between values and social science. The authors in this book are not disinterested scholars studying GLBT families from a distance. They are social activists and change agents. In my view, family scholars and practitioners have always been thus, but we have blinded ourselves to the impact of our work on the larger culture. What we define as family, what we say is important about family life, how we do our research and practice, and how we talk about the fruits of our research and practice—all of these reflect our values and have real-world effects. We are not neutral and never have been. GLBT scholars and practitioners, like feminist and ethnic minority professionals before them, are embracing a stance of the publicly engaged scholar and practitioner. I hope they provide the final nail in the coffin of value-free, politically neutral family studies, which never existed in the first place.

I now offer some recommendations and challenges for the specialty of GLBT family studies. My remarks come from three decades of studying and sometimes participating in the work of feminist family studies and ethnic minority family studies. In creating a new area of study for a marginalized group, it is tempting to overturn a deficit model by creating an idealized model of family life for the population being studied. Perhaps this in an inevitable step in the evolution of an area of study associated with a social movement. In family studies and family therapy, we went through a period in which women in relationships were written about as inherently relational, collaborative, nonhierarchical, and nonexploitative, as distinguished from men and their relational styles. The same occurred for African-American family studies: for a couple of decades acceptable scholarly discourse focused on areas such as strong multigenerational black family bonds, the strengths of black single mothers, and the role flexibility of black couples, but it was difficult to discuss issues such as the steep decline of married, two-parent households and the growing evidence that multigenerational social support was eroding. We are largely past the idealization phase of these two movements in the field and now can address women's roles and African-American families with the greater complexity they deserve.

GLBT family studies may be going through the same historical evolution; at this stage, it's challenging to describe problems in GLBT families when you know that enemies (and I use the term literally) may pounce. In the 1980s, one of my family therapy students wrote a superb class paper with case studies of lesbian couples who had experienced violence in their relationships. When I urged the student to submit the paper for publication she demurred, saying that she did not want to contribute to negative images of lesbian couples. This kind of self-censorship, while understandable, diminishes the prospects for understanding and helping GLBT families.

When scholars and practitioners do write about problems in GLBT families, it is tempting for them to explain these problems as stemming exclusively from homophobia, just as early feminist and African-American writers sometimes used sexism and racism as universal explanatory categories. In my mind, the real challenge is to sort out the relative influences of human frailty (of whatever gender or sexual orientation), the challenges of being a family of any form, the unique challenges of specific family forms, and ecological factors such as homophobia, racism, sexism, and poverty. Human behavior is the product of many interacting forces.

More specifically, I encourage scholars of GLBT families to consider several recommendations. First, conceptualize and measure homophobia as a variable and not just as a global social construct. (Here I extend the idea of feminist sociologist Janet Chafetz, who encourages feminist researchers to nuance the concept of patriarchy; not all companies, countries, and family forms are equally patriarchal.) To be useful in research, a concept must vary across individuals, groups, and time. GLBT families and their members no doubt experience different degrees and kinds of homophobia, and they live in environments with different degrees and manifestations of homophobia. Before assuming that, say, domestic violence in GLBT couples stems from internalized homophobia, researchers should try to measure homophobia (as best they can) and see if it varies along with levels of domestic violence in GLBT couples. However, they should not stop with correlations between internalized homophobia and domestic violence. They should also measure other predictors of domestic violence, such as partners' interpersonal skills in conflict management, as well as factors such as psychological adjustment and life stress. From this larger picture might emerge a complex view of the role of homophobia and other risk factors for domestic violence in GLBT couples. I do not underestimate the challenge of this kind of work, but I believe it is what the field needs.

Here is another example of a challenging research agenda framed as a research question. What are the distinctive advantages and disadvantages (or strengths and weaknesses) of same-sex parenting and opposite-sex parenting for the well-being of children? This question moves past the question of whether being raised in same-sex households harms children, but it does assume that trade-offs and weaknesses may be inherent in both family forms which might be worth knowing about and trying to offset. Would GLBT family researchers self-censor if they found, for example, that children from same-sex households enter adulthood with internal conflict related to the "missing" parent of the other sex? I hope these researchers would publish the findings, just as I hope that researchers who study dynamics of opposite-sex families would not shrink from reporting how male-female gender roles create challenges for young adults who grow up with mothers and fathers in the home. Maybe I am being too idealistic here because enemies of same-sex families would no doubt use these findings for their own purposes. However, in the long run I believe that brave, balanced scholarship will win over most of our fellow citizens—if not in this generation, then in a future one. If those of us who value GLBT families are not willing to ask difficult questions and follow the evidence where it leads us, you can be sure that others will do so, draw their own conclusions, and dominate the public conversation about GLBT families.

The field of GLBT family studies will need an infusion of research funds to achieve its promise. An inherent limitation in current research is the difficulty in obtaining representative samples of a relatively small percentage of the larger population whose members have reason not to disclose their identity. GLBT families who volunteer to be studied may not represent the diversity of GLBT families in the nation and, certainly, GLBT families who present for therapy are not representative. Thus, we risk drawing inflated or deflated conclusions about GLBT families. With the U.S. Defense of Marriage Act in place for the foreseeable future, no major federal grants will be provided for the broad sampling of communities needed to recruit representative GLBT families. GLBT family scholars will need to court progressive foundations and private donors to conduct this kind of expensive research.

Finally, I encourage researchers in GLBT family studies to consider the emerging research paradigm of participatory action research or community-based action research (Mendenhall & Doherty, 2005). This work involves community members as active cocreators of research projects that aim to generate knowledge relevant to a community for the purpose of bringing about social change. Participatory action research seems ideally suited to be part of the repertoire of GLBT family studies, since research participants are already stakeholders in the studies and have a vested interest in bringing about social change. As the newest kid on the block in family studies, GLBT family studies can take advantage of all the research models available to family scholars, including quantitative, qualitative, and action research, in order to grow the field beyond the productive and inspiring start represented in this breakthrough book.

REFERENCE

Mendenhall, T. J., & Doherty, W. J. (2005). Action and participatory research methods in family therapy. In F. Piercy (Ed.), *Research methods in family therapy* (2nd ed., pp. 100-118). New York: Guilford Press.

William J. Doherty, PhD
Department of Family Social Science
University of Minnesota
St. Paul, Minnesota

Acknowledgments

I would like to acknowledge the generosity and foresight of Mr. Bill Cohen, publisher of The Haworth Press, Inc., and the willingness of others (too numerous to mention here) at the company who have provided the opportunity for the development of the *Journal of GLBT Family Studies,* the first two issues of which are the basis of this text. They have all been extremely supportive and helpful. I also wish to express my deep appreciation to the authors of the chapters appearing here, especially to those members of the editorial board who have given so freely of their time and expertise in providing the material for these issues of the new journal and this text.

doi:10.1300/5792_d

Introduction

Jerry J. Bigner

This text is drawn from the first two issues of a brand-new publication, the *Journal of GLBT Family Studies,* of which I am honored to serve as the first editor. The nature of this new periodical and why it has come about may not be clear to many. It essentially formalizes a new branch of the field of family studies by focusing exclusively on GLBT (gay, lesbian, bisexual, transgender) issues. Although researchers have been publishing material of this nature for some time, no single publication until now has provided a home solely for the scholarly examination of these topics.

The field of family studies emerged from a long association and involvement with family sociology. It has become recognized as a distinct interdisciplinary field of inquiry into the development and behavior of the diverse family structures that are found in contemporary societies around the world. This field seeks to provide information and education about family structures as social systems, discovering how developmental changes among members affect the entire system and vice versa, and applying findings to improve the quality of life for individuals and their families.

As societies have changed, so have attitudes about the diverse segments that compose them. GLBT individuals have become more visible at every level of society within recent years, in tandem with changing attitudes. Until recently, the notion that GLBT families exist within the fabric of society has hardly been recognized. As visibility has mounted, so have the controversies that have become associated with heightened interest among GLBT individuals in what could be perceived as traditional heterosexual family interests.

Although the various GLBT communities have perhaps always had their own unique brand of family life, little has been known until recently about such issues, and even more needs to be known now. Research into GLBT family issues has increased considerably within

doi:10.1300/5792_01

the past two decades as investigators have begun to address a number of issues particular to this population, such as parent-child relations, relationship issues, disclosure of sexual-orientation issues, functioning of alternative family structures, the lack of traditional gender influences, and so on. Researchers and scholars interested in GLBT family issues provide valuable information as society grapples with emerging issues and implications affecting GLBT individuals and families, as well as other families. For example, since heterosexual families are likely to be producing the majority of GLBT individuals, family-of-origin issues remain an area of interest, as well as questions that arise when GLBT individuals form families of choice, stepfamilies, and other types of family structures. Likewise, the field of couple and relationship therapy plays an important role in assisting all families in making healthy adjustments to challenges and crises they encounter in their life spans. This field is just beginning to address GLBT family and relationship therapeutic issues and needs as researchers have increasingly recognized this neglected segment of American society in their investigations.

The chapters of this text, based on the charter issues of the new *Journal of GLBT Family Studies,* feature the thoughts and visions of their authors, who are the recognized experts in this new academic field. Most of these authors are members of the journal's editorial board who have expertise in particular areas of GLBT family studies. Their chapters illustrate their particular expertise, suggest future trends in these areas, and provide examples of the topics, research questions, and methods of inquiry that typify what GLBT family studies are all about and how this knowledge may be applied to problems confronting society regarding homosexuality and family relationships.

PART I: GLBT FAMILY ISSUES

Chapter 1

A Process of Change: The Intersection of the GLBT Individual and His or Her Family of Origin

Colleen M. Connolly

Strong and pervasive familial and societal stressors impact the living and loving of a gay, lesbian, bisexual, or transgender (GLBT) individual, couple, or family. These issues affect not only GLBT individuals but also their families of origin and extended families, resonating across the larger cultural and social terrain.

Experiences of sexual discovery and integration are as varied as the members of the GLBT communities. One way to better understand this process is to track the life-stage events that occur as the GLBT person experiences coming out of the closet.

Many GLBT clients discover their sexual orientation and gender identity later in the life span; others remember an awareness from the beginning. That which is known to self is not always known to others, and vice versa. Thus, the question of disclosure—who, when, what, where, and why—is an important process across contexts and the life span.

Looking through various lenses—individual, couple, family, and societal—helps clinicians facilitate the GLBT person and/or family of origin as they adapt, transition, and transform through the inevitable changes that occur during this process. We will attend to the clinical implications and future research trends in this intersection of GLBT identities and the family of origin; however, let us begin by reflecting upon those constraints that are so prevalent and pervasive in our society and can so heavily influence family dynamics.

doi:10.1300/5792_02

SOCIETAL AND FAMILIAL CONSTRAINTS

Oppressive beliefs, attitudes, and behaviors against the GLBT populations abound. The triad of cultural oppression—homophobia, heterosexism, and the internalization of both—significantly impact the culture (Brown, 1995). These stressors affect the GLBT individual, couple, and family profoundly and overtly; they also affect the populations in insidious ways.

Lives are complicated by homophobia and stigma as a heterocentric social and extended family network surrounds the GLBT person and her or his family of origin (Brown, 1988). Discrimination, such as in employment, health care, legal systems, and social services (Granvold & Martin, 1999), can occur in abstract or more concrete ways. Homophobia and heterosexism marginalize the GLBT population, legitimizing discrimination and denying basic human and civil rights (Bigner, 2000).

Heteronormativity, "the systemic privileging of the heterosexual couple as the social and sexual ideal" (Fields, 2001, p. 2), perpetuates the stigma against this population. Regrettably, this type of system places those who are GLBT in a constant state of living within a hostile environment, whether they are fully aware of or automatically responding to those societal stressors. Adapting to a hostile environment can produce feelings of chronic unrest and disequilibrium (Mallon, 1999).

This hostile environment can translate into prejudice against all within the GLBT spectrum: homophobia, biphobia (Dworkin, 2000), and transphobia (Carroll & Gilroy, 2002; Carroll, Gilroy, & Ryan, 2002). It occurs in both externalized and internalized ways. The externalized, societal homoprejudice (Logan, 1996) and discrimination reinforce the internalized fear and anxiety over being different from the heterosexual norm. What then often occurs is a phobia or prejudice within the sexual-minority person, as societal stigma becomes internalized. Coping with this fear, anxiety, and vigilance within a dismissive and often hostile world translates into what are—or simply appear to be—mental health issues.

The homoprejudice and societal constraints also permeate the family of origin in overt and covert ways. The GLBT person typically grows up in a heterosexual family that maintains the unexamined expectation that all children also are heterosexual (Brown, 1988;

Savin-Williams, 1996), will marry different-sexed persons, and will begin a traditional family (Matthews & Lease, 2000). Because they are socialized to hide this differentness, those who are GLBT struggle to try to figure out how they fit into the family and into the world-at-large (Mallon, 1999).

Unlike most ethnic and cultural minorities, the GLBT person typically does not share the same minority identification with parents (Brown, 1988; Green & Mitchell, 2002). As a result, they do not get to observe parents dealing with the prejudice and discrimination—along with the pride in traditions and connection—that a minority family experiences (Green & Mitchell, 2002).

In addition to the lack of preparation against the impending discrimination, GLBT disclosure is often met with family hostility (Mallon, 1999). Instead of taking sides against the oppressor, parents and family sometimes become the main oppressors (Green, 2002; Green & Mitchell, 2002), and the family environment can become like "living with the enemy" (Green, 2002, p. 277; Green & Mitchell, 2002, p. 557) instead of a place of refuge.

Self-esteem issues are common and constant as individuals learn they are not loved for who they are "even in (or especially in)" the family (Brown, 1988, p. 69). Moreover, those who are GLBT face the real possibility of being cut off or disowned by their family of origin as members react—not to something done but to an identity that is fundamental to the GLBT person's sense of self (Green, 2002; Green & Mitchell, 2002).

Continued relations are voluntary (Green, 2000; Green & Mitchell, 2002), and rejection remains an ever-present possibility (Green, 2000). As a result, many GLBT people live double lives, which has been de rigueur for most of these individuals throughout history and geography (Green, 2002). A tremendous amount of energy is expended in maintaining these multiple identities and being vigilant against disclosure that could harm social standing or instigate prejudicial and even life-threatening actions from others (Davison, 2001).

Juggling multiple parts of life can result in external inauthenticity (Mallon, 1999), internal incongruence, confusion, and conflict. The GLBT identity is often pushed down and away due to fear of consequences—some imagined, but many times real.

Family reactions are rarely neutral and typically have a wide range: positive and negative, static and erratic, with overt and covert communication. It is within this context of constraint that the GLBT person becomes aware of and/or discovers her or his sexual orientation and negotiates personal identity.

GLBT AWARENESS AND DISCOVERY

Multiple factors affect awareness of sexual orientation and gender identity. It is often helpful to conceptualize in levels of the GLBT discovery process. For example, Ben-Ari (1995) noted three stages in the coming-out process: (1) prediscovery experiences, thoughts, and feelings; (2) the actual act of discovery; and (3) postdiscovery experiences, thoughts, and feelings.

Considering the life-cycle stage in which the discovery and postdiscovery experiences occur is pivotal in the therapeutic process. In addition, some questions one might ponder include: Was discovery experienced as a result of self-awareness in the GLBT individual, being informed by a member of the family of origin, or as a result of a relationship outside the family? Does the discovery provide some relief in making sense of the past (Herdt & Beeler, 1998), or does it produce confusion and turmoil?

The GLBT person often experiences more difficult transitions through stages of life than heterosexuals because of negative cultural biases (Brown, 1988). Certain developmental processes occur during adolescence, adulthood, and later adulthood. Awareness and discovery—or lack thereof—at particular junctures influence the normative developmental flow.

Some people are aware of their sexual orientation very early in life (Sanders & Kroll, 2000) or have always known to some degree. However, many become aware of a GLBT sexual orientation or gender identity at puberty. This period involves an inherent struggle with gender socialization, sexual yearnings, and identity.

For some youths, it is as if puberty stamps in the GLBT orientation and identity and provides both clarity and a label for feelings that previously were poorly understood (Savin-Williams, 1996). However, actual coming out may be delayed if the individual's family of origin is sufficiently conservative or constraining (Harry, 1993).

Parents and youths often experience a wide emotional chasm and lack of mutuality at the time of puberty, and a threat of the youth's sexual orientation creating intergenerational discontinuity can intensify an existing rift (Savin-Williams, 1996). Any deviance from the heterosexual prescription can separate youths psychologically from their family of origin, whether in an explicit or implicit manner (Savin-Williams, 1996). The family of origin may fear that this orientation/identity discovery will be prominent in "shaping the future" of the youth (Herdt & Beeler, 1998, p. 186) in a way that is not congruent with the family's hopes and dreams (Matthews & Lease, 2000; Savin-Williams, 1996).

The transition to adulthood typically includes a shift from an "ascribed set of audiences . . . to an achieved or self-chosen set" (Harry, 1993, p. 38), bringing with it expanded choices. Yet one who becomes aware of a GLBT identity when already an adult often does so while negotiating and maintaining a career and deciding whether to couple or to have children. The question of how orientation and identity will be viewed by society is not a quandary faced by most heterosexuals at this same life-cycle stage. Facing the societal and familial constraints can greatly impact life choices.

If one does not come out early in life, it is not uncommon to find identity issues reemerging in the thirties, forties (Mallon, 1999), and beyond. It can be likened to a "reliving of adolescence, suppressed and hidden during the chronological years" (Mallon, 1999, p. 76).

Becoming aware of being GLBT as an older adult may be very different from earlier in life. Herdt and Beeler (1998) note some differences with the typical older adult, who is more inclined to have greater stability and resources than during prior years. Nurturing friendships, in addition to possible partnership, often are more important at this life stage (Blando, 2001) than previously. Older adults typically experience more stability and financial, emotional, and social resources (Herdt & Beeler, 1998), which reduces dependency on family of origin. Coming out later in life even may involve some relief in explaining the past, as the GLBT person reflects and reviews life experiences (Herdt & Beeler, 1998).

Many view sexual orientation as fluid and dynamic across the life cycle with self-identification being primary (Golden, 1994). One person may self-identify as GLBT when in the teens; another person may stay in a prediscovery stage well into later adulthood.

In sum, social and family context and stage of the life span for both the GLBT person and his or her family members all have important clinical implications. Taking these processes into account helps in identifying, integrating, and finding congruence/comfort in sexual orientation and gender identity. Yet once someone becomes GLBT-aware, a question follows: to disclose or not to disclose.

THE QUESTION OF DISCLOSURE

Those who are GLBT have difficult decisions to make regarding disclosing sexual orientation and identity, to whom, and under what circumstances (Savin-Williams, 1996). Sometimes there is a coming-out process; at other times, it involves being found out (Mallon, 1999). Coming out may be beneficial or problematic (Bepko & Johnson, 2000). Therefore, no hard-and-fast rule exists about disclosing one's sexual orientation or gender identity to the family of origin (Bepko & Johnson, 2000).

Both disclosure and secret-keeping can be stressful and provoke intense anxiety (Merighi & Grimes, 2000). Family reactions can alleviate stress or exacerbate it (Goldfried, 2001). Herdt and Beeler (1998) note that most literature addresses the basic question: "Why disclose?" rather than "whether to disclose or *not* to disclose" (p. 180). These authors question outcome and ask, "coming out *but going where?*" (Herdt & Beeler, 1998, p. 193).

We can view openness about these matters with the family of origin as an ideal (Bepko & Johnson, 2000) or we can view this as a potentially life-threatening situation. Coming out may provide the GLBT person a "goodness of fit with [her or his] environment . . . a rebalancing process" (Mallon, 1999, p. 76). However, it remains essential to assess the importance and impact of the family on the individual (Bepko & Johnson, 2000). Things to keep in mind include the level of dependence or independence from a physical, emotional, financial, or social stance (Herdt & Beeler, 1998) and whether the GLBT individual is vulnerable to financial or emotional blackmail (Brown, 1988).

Green (2000, 2002) provides some useful guidelines in making a decision about disclosure and in assessing the impact on relational health. Green's points include an assessment of the GLBT person's experience with the family of origin in the following areas:

1. the preexisting levels of closeness, openness, and conflict;
2. the amount of shared time experienced;

3. the importance of the family as a source of social identity and economic support;
4. the availability of alternate forms of support; and
5. the cost/benefit appraisal of the anticipated responses of family members.

Disclosing or not disclosing may not indicate strength in mental health or demonstrate a differentiated self; it simply may reflect a realistic assessment of potential consequences (Green, 2000, 2002; Green & Mitchell, 2002). Green (2000) notes that not coming out may be the best position when the person has good reason to believe that intractable negative consequences will occur or that few, if any, positive outcome will result. Assessment of conflict, distance, support, and potential for violence are critical in maintaining safety.

Disclosure may occur across all contexts or in one or two areas of the GLBT person's life. Brown (1988) observed the complex strategies that sexual minorities often employ while trying to live a parallel lifestyle with their family of origin. Common patterns for juggling the closet include (1) maintaining rigid geographical and emotional distances to reduce the chance of exposure; (2) developing an "I-know-you-know (so let's not talk about it)" pattern of communication; and (3) accepting a "Don't tell your father" attitude as a means of maintaining secrecy with certain people. Some families adopt the stance, "Let's keep it in the family," and ask the GLBT member not to disclose to others outside the family (Mallon, 1999). This juggling of physical distance, collusion, and selectivity of knowing (Herdt & Beeler, 1998) can be short-term or last over a lifetime.

These methods necessitate categorizing people and contexts ("Who knows?"; "Who doesn't know?") and compartmentalizing areas of life ("Who knows whom?") to maintain privacy and safety. Harry (1993) suggests that the most normal scenario is where one lingers partly in and partly out of the closet and then adapts disclosures in the changing contexts.

The GLBT person may decide the risks are too great or the timing is not right to reveal his or her sexual orientation to others within the family of origin. If so, various approaches may take place. For instance, the individual may continue to assess and reassess disclosure possibilities over time, maintain multiple lives, deny living an authentic life, or create a new life and support system instead.

However, let us assume that disclosure is made to at least the family of origin. With that assumption in mind, let us now look at the process of change as family members adapt, transition, and possibly transform along the way.

THE PROCESS OF CHANGE

Once a GLBT identity is revealed, a process of *adaptation* to the new information typically follows. Because of societal homoprejudice, the stigma affects the GLBT person(s) and the family of origin (Fields, 2001). In other words, the family also experiences the dilemmas of coming out (Beeler & DiProva, 1999). Sanders and Kroll (2000) make an important point: "Often, when a young person comes 'out of the closet' of fear and shame, the family goes into that same closet" (p. 437). Parents frequently experience guilt and self-blame (Mallon, 1999), and the entire family often feels sadness, loss, and blame (Beeler & DiProva, 1999). The family's coming-out process and movement through levels of awareness and integration occur over time (Bepko & Johnson, 2000) and can become quite complex. Moving from initial disclosure to parental acceptance can be a long journey that one never fully completes (Green, 2002).

Families typically internalize the socialized, negative view of a GLBT identity and apply it to their child, (Mallon, 1999) sibling, or parent. Attitudes about gender and sexuality come into play, and the disclosure is filtered through the family's typical coping mechanisms (Green, 2002; Green & Mitchell, 2002).

Mallon (1999) provides some examples of family dynamics once disclosure is made. Some families move toward more closeness. The information can open up communication and intimacy within the family of origin. Families can become stronger, closer, and more honest as a result.

Other families get caught in conflict, which can erupt and disrupt the family system over time. The disclosure can "generate the sort of conflict that destroys the system and marks its members for the rest of their lives" (Mallon, 1999, p. 83). When homophobia becomes the normative factor for relating to or about the GLBT family member, dysfunction is much more likely to result (Brown, 1988).

The familial impact often pivots upon the point in the life span a GLBT-identified individual's orientation or identity emerges, the degree of openness involved, and the context. However, clinicians might explore what special stressors are present in the system at the time of disclosure. For example, are other family members concurrently experiencing a difficult life stage or stressors such as chronic illness or divorce? Just as the GLBT person learned resilience and adapted to the oppressive societal constraints over time (Mallon, 1999; Sanders & Kroll, 2000), families also need time to adapt, emerge, and transition.

In addition to adapting to the new information and circumstances, *transitions* often occur during this process. As a result of the disclosure, relational dynamics typically shift and new patterns are established. Ways that families experience intimacy, distancing, and boundaries may change. With a lack of cultural models guiding families when responding to disclosure, families are left to their own devices to re-create and redefine relationship dynamics (Beeler & DiProva, 1999).

Transitions can be made smoother for the GLBT person by expanding and solidifying additional or alternative sources of support and resources. Creating a family of choice (for example, see Sanders & Kroll, 2000, p. 441), expanding the friendship network, and connecting with co-workers can all be advantageous. Some note that created family, friends, and co-workers are viewed as stronger sources of GLBT support than the family of origin, although having both would undoubtedly be ideal (Green, 2002).

At times GLBT individuals decide to transition by removing family members from involvement in their lives. Sanders and Kroll (2000) note the concept of opening up space for substitute and more effective family figures by making decisions about a *parentectomy* or *siblingectomy* or *family-member-ectomy*. Decisions about the salience (Green, 2000; Green & Mitchell, 2002) and irreplaceability (Harry, 1993) of family members may inform the client's decision and help facilitate smoother transitions.

However, the disclosure also can create an opportunity for *transformation* within the family of origin. Mallon (1999) notes that many families experience a transformational process, but the author uses this term to refer to both helpful and harmful changes in the family. The word *transformation* is used here in the sense of experiencing grief and transforming it into healing.

Savin-Williams (1996) posits that once parents become comfortable with the issue of sexual orientation and gender identity, they can become "agents of social change" (p. 178). This position can be a way of indirectly helping to improve the life of their child and her or his loved ones. Fields (2001) explored parents' responses to their children coming out as lesbian or gay. Some parents considered it a stigma to be overcome, while others framed it as a mark of honor of which to be proud.

Families can seek out GLBT-positive information about the community (Beeler & DiProva, 1999), learn about orientation and identity, and apply it relationally and socially. Savin-Williams (1996) contends that youth feel affirmed when parents join with them in acts countering homophobia and become social activists in schools and communities.

We have explored change as an inevitable process that is complicated by society's homoprejudice, the family's internalization of stigma associated with the GLBT family member, levels of awareness, and decisions about disclosure. Families, at times, only accommodate and adapt to the change; some transform along the way.

CONCLUSION

Coping with societal constraints is a daunting task. These constraints permeate the family system and create seen and unseen challenges. Awareness can be impeded. Discovery can be feared. Those who are GLBT often live double lives and/or risk family reactions ranging from disappointment to hostility.

The literature is geared toward family nonacceptance or acceptance of a GLBT member; it is often implied that families remain somewhat static or move in a linear progression toward the more positive end of the change continuum. However, pockets of homoprejudice—or potential pitfalls—may still exist and emerge at unforeseen times.

Everyone within the system holds his or her own unique perspective based on family roles, gender socialization, and life experiences, to name a few. What may have once been a solid, affirming family that provided safety and security for the GLBT individual or couple may take an unexpected and unanticipated turn. New people entering into the system or life-altering experiences can change a member's philosophical stance or stir up long-held but hidden prejudicial beliefs.

It is important for all of us to expect the unexpected, sometimes even in the best of circumstances.

Coming out, whether in some contexts or all contexts, creates a different life than previously. However, disclosing to the family of origin is not required to live successfully in this world, and although coming out creates a different life, it does not necessarily create a better life (Herdt & Beeler, 1998).

The GLBT person and family members adapt and transition whether they stay connected, disconnect then reconnect, or separate from one another's lives. However, some families are able to use the awareness and disclosure to heal personal wounds and familial or cultural injuries.

Each person must make decisions based on her or his unique circumstances, needs, and desires. Clinicians facilitate decision making, help clients weigh possibilities and probabilities when looking toward the future, and support their changing life experiences.

The therapist integrates theory and practice, combines the personal and professional, and conceptualizes sexual orientation and gender identity by seeing its impact on the individual and family of origin. We will now explore some clinical implications when doing GLBT family-of-origin work and look at future research trends.

Clinical Implications

Some specific clinical points come to the forefront when approaching the intersection of family of origin and GLBT individuals, couples, or families. Naming the process, recognizing injuries and attending to grief, understanding the affiliative nature of GLBT relationships, and respecting the client's choice to disclose or not disclose are important considerations.

First, we do well to identify and name the process. Sanders and Kroll (2000) see problems as symptoms of oppression and believe in naming those processes that are restraining and demeaning to GLBT youths and their families. Disclosure can generate a family crisis (Mallon, 1999; Savin-Williams, 1996). Even if parents suspected their child was GLBT, they still often feel caught off-guard by the revelation (Savin-Williams, 1996). Identifying and naming events and processes can normalize the experience for them.

Clients often seek clinical intervention during this time in life, even if they do not declare it as the presenting problem. Because of the subtle nature of societal homoprejudice and the internalization of the fears and stigma, the issue often lies under the surface, waiting to be invited into conversation. Moreover, the ripple effect from the GLBT individual, couple, family of origin, society, and then back again results in many more people being affected by this issue than may at first be apparent.

Few, if any, roles or models exist to guide families through this process (Herdt & Beeler, 1998). Thus, families typically require encouraging support and accurate information during the period of crisis and beyond (Mallon, 1999).

Second, our clinical work involves recognizing the depth and pervasiveness of injuries and working with grief when needed. Clients need therapists to recognize that "violence to the soul can be as severe as violence to the body" (Sanders & Kroll, 2000, p. 437) and attend to the emotional and spiritual injuries in addition to the physical risk assessment.

Grief occupies a central place when working with GLBT clients (for example, see Matthews & Lease, 2000). Brown (1988) suggests that clients may expect a negative family response and subsequently experience an anticipatory grief reaction. For most sexual minority clients, the affective responses to grief may be more intense and longer lasting than for a heterosexual client because of the lack of cultural acknowledgement of losses.

However, it is important to be cognizant of other themes occurring alongside the grieving. Not only might it move toward productive areas of discussion that otherwise may be ignored, but it also may provide more concrete therapeutic intervention (Beeler & DiProva, 1999).

Third, clients need therapists to focus on the affiliative nature of GLBT relationships. Both different-sex and same-sex relationships are "affiliative investments in valued relationships over time" (Sanders & Kroll, 2000, p. 435). It is important to focus on an affectional (Scrivner & Eldridge, 1995) and affiliative understanding (Sanders & Kroll, 2000) of a GLBT person's life, yet some therapists fail to address the sexual side of a relationship when it is needed (Butler & Clarke, 1991), whether out of fear, lack of knowledge, or overcompensating. So, approach with an affiliative understanding of GLBT persons rather than a sexual conceptualization (Sanders & Kroll, 2000), but do not err by omitting the sexual assessment.

Fourth, clients deserve therapists who respect their right to make choices about disclosure and direction in their lives. Green (2002) stresses the importance for therapists to focus on a pro-choice approach to disclosure, paying particular attention to potential dangers for the client. Green (2000) argues the lack of legitimacy in family therapists' second-guessing clients' decisions about coming out to their families, especially given the current knowledge on the subject. This author suggests therapists explore advantages and disadvantages of coming out to family but that the best ethical course of action is not to generically presume what decision is best or coax the client in a certain direction. If a client weighs the options and decides not to come out to the family of origin, that decision "should be respected as a viable, psychologically healthy decision" (Green, 2000, p. 264).

In order to honor and fully attend to clients' experiences, therapists need to actively and continuously examine their unconscious biases and assumptions and guard against their own heterocentric bias (Green & Mitchell, 2002). Our own life experiences—positive or negative—can overshadow the clinical relationship if we do not stay steadfast.

In sum, it may benefit the clinician to conceptualize stages and understand typical individual and family dynamics in each. Moreover, it is important to have realistic expectations for the therapeutic work, taking into consideration the person's identity development, level of coping skills, and the current life-stages issues.

Future Trends

We have reviewed some clinical implications to our work with GLBT-connected families. We also need to be mindful of the depth, breadth, and impact of societal constraints. It may be tempting to forget the past community history and struggles, become complacent, and accept the present as good enough and not continue to push for sociopolitical change. However, some argue the impossibility of practicing positive, affirmative therapy with individual clients without attending to global injustices and oppression of those who are transgender (Carroll & Gilroy, 2002), bisexual, lesbian, and gay.

The quality of life for the GLBT client and community may continue to improve as a result of increased visibility and vocal support of professionals and a heightened understanding of multiple minority status. Visibility has increased tremendously, largely as a result of the community's tenaciousness and proactivity. Just as parents can help youth by becoming activists and agents of social change (Savin-Williams, 1996), clinicians and educators—whether they are GLBT or friends and allies of the community—can also use their professional power and personal voice to advocate for the rights of the GLBT and their families of origin.

Many therapists and educators are openly GLBT, but many more are not. The trend toward greater community visibility and stronger familial, social, and legal supports—while not without strife—may help more and more professionals come forward with pride in their sexual orientation and gender identity. This can have a tremendous social and familial impact.

Another area that could improve the quality of GLBT life is to increase recognition and understanding of the multiple minority status of our clients and families. Those who are GLBT may or may not regard their sexual orientation or gender identity as primary and often manage multiple loyalties among their cultural identities (Johnson & Colucci, 1999). It is important for clients' increased awareness and relational growth to provide room for the clients' and families' self-identification of those identities and areas of diversity; facilitate their discovery of primary and secondary loyalties, if they exist; and allow that an individual's GLBT identity need not be seen as primary.

In addition to factors that may improve the quality of life for those who are GLBT, two key areas of research are opening. First, the field has increased study on gay and lesbian issues in the family of origin and, although less frequently, the study of bisexuality (Dworkin, 2000). However, one particular area for future study is expanding our understanding of the experience of being transgender.

Carroll, Gilroy, & Ryan (2002) note the insufficient attention to transgender issues in research and clinical training. This is not only in family therapy: the larger multicultural movement has been remiss in their inclusion of transgender issues (Carroll & Gilroy, 2002). These authors recommend clinicians and researchers rethink their own assumptions regarding gender, sexuality, and sexual orientation and adopt a positive and affirmative disposition for those who are transgender (Carroll, Gilroy, & Ryan, 2002), bisexual, lesbian, and gay.

The family therapy field would do well to continue to expand the appreciation and celebration of those individuals with nontraditional gender identities (Carroll & Gilroy, 2002) and sexual orientation. Advocating for political, social, and economic rights and educating others about such issues becomes primary in expanding an affirmative and proactive approach (Carroll, Gilroy, & Ryan, 2002) for those within the community and their families.

In addition, many in the family therapy field have pointed out the need to approach and research sexual minorities from a perspective of strength and resilience (for example, see Laird, 1993). Steps have been taken (for example, see Connolly, 1998) and strides have been made. However, a focus on strength and resilience against adversity continues as a pivotal area of future research.

Societal and familial constraints permeate the history of GLBT communities. The present remains underscored with challenging decisions about degree of disclosure and context, yet the family therapy field, with its maturity, strength, and voice, has power and potential to continue to reform and transform the relational quality and dynamics of GLBT individuals and their families of origin.

REFERENCES

Beeler, J., & DiProva, V. (1999). Family adjustment following disclosure of homosexuality by a member: Themes discerned in narrative accounts. *Journal of Marital and Family Therapy, 25*(4), 443-459.

Ben-Ari, A. (1995). The discovery that an offspring is gay: Parents', gay men's, and lesbians' perspectives. *Journal of Homosexuality, 30*(1), 89-112.

Bepko, C., & Johnson, T. (2000). Gay and lesbian couples in therapy: Perspectives for the contemporary family therapist. *Journal of Marital and Family Therapy, 26*(4), 409-419.

Bigner, J. J. (2000). Gay and lesbian families. In W. C. Nichols, M. S. Pace-Nichols, D. S. Becvar, & A. Y. Napier (Eds.), *Handbook of family development and intervention* (pp. 279-298). New York: John Wiley & Sons.

Blando, J. A. (2001). Twice hidden: Older gay and lesbian couples, friends, and intimacy. *Generations, 25*(2), 87-89.

Brown, L. S. (1988). Lesbians, gay men and their families: Common clinical issues. *Journal of Gay & Lesbian Psychotherapy, 1*(1), 65-77.

Brown, L. S. (1995). Therapy with same-sex couples: An introduction. In N. S. Jacobson & A. S. Gurman (Eds.), *Clinical handbook of couple therapy* (pp. 274-291). New York: Guilford Press.

Butler, M., & Clarke, J. (1991). Couple therapy with homosexual men. In D. Hooper & W. Dryden (Eds.), *Couple therapy: A handbook* (pp. 196-206). Philadelphia: Open University Press.

Carroll, L., & Gilroy, P. J. (2002). Transgender issues in counselor preparation. *Counselor Education & Supervision, 41*(3), 233-242.
Carroll, L., Gilroy, P. J., & Ryan, J. (2002). Counseling transgendered, transsexual, and gender-variant clients. *Journal of Counseling & Development, 80*(2), 131-139.
Connolly, C. M. (1998). Lesbian couples: A qualitative study of strengths and resilient factors in long-term relationships. *Dissertation Abstracts International, 59,* 7A. (UMI No. 9838850).
Davison, G. C. (2001). Conceptual and ethical issues in therapy for the psychological problems of gay men, lesbians, and bisexuals. *Journal of Clinical Psychology, 57*(5), 695-704.
Dworkin, S. (2000). Individual therapy with lesbian, gay, and bisexual clients. In R. M. Perez, K. A. DeBord, & K. J. Bieschke (Eds.), *Handbook of counseling and psychotherapy with lesbian, gay, and bisexual clients* (pp. 157-181). Washington, DC: American Psychological Association.
Fields, J. (2001). Normal queers: Straight parents respond to their children's "coming out." *Symbolic Interaction, 24*(2), 165-187.
Golden, C. (1994). Our politics and choices. In B. Greene & G. M. Herek (Eds.), *Lesbian and gay psychology: Theory, research, and clinical applications* (pp. 54-70). Thousand Oaks, CA: Sage.
Goldfried, M. R. (2001). Integrating gay, lesbian, and bisexual issues into mainstream psychology. *American Psychologist, 56*(11), 977-988.
Granvold, D. K., & Martin, J. I. (1999). Family therapy with gay and lesbian clients. In C. Franklin & C. Jordan (Eds.), *Family practice: Brief systems methods for social work* (pp. 299-320). Pacific Grove, CA: Brooks/Cole.
Green, R.-J. (2000). "Lesbians, gay men, and their parents": A critique of LaSala and the prevailing clinical "wisdom." *Family Process, 39*(2), 257-266.
Green, R.-J. (2002). Coming out to family . . . in context. In E. Davis-Russell (Ed.), *The California School of Professional Psychology handbook of multicultural education, research, intervention, and training* (pp. 277-284). San Francisco: Jossey-Bass.
Green, R.-J., & Mitchell, V. (2002). Gay and lesbian couples in therapy: Homophobia, relational ambiguity, and social support. In A. S. Gurman & N. S. Jacobson (Eds.), *Clinical handbook of couple therapy* (pp. 536-568). New York: Guilford Press.
Harry, J. (1993). Being out: A general model. *Journal of Homosexuality, 26*(1), 25-39.
Herdt, G., & Beeler, J. (1998). Older gay men and lesbians in families. In C. J. Patterson & A. R. D'Augelli (Eds.), *Lesbian, gay, and bisexual identities with families: Psychological perspectives* (pp. 177-196). New York: Oxford University Press.
Johnson, T. W., & Colucci, P. (1999). Lesbians, gay men, and the family cycle. In B. Carter & M. McGoldrick (Eds.), *The expanded family life cycle: Individual, family, and social perspectives* (3rd ed., pp. 346-372). Boston: Allyn & Bacon.

Laird, J. (1993). Lesbian and gay families. In F. Walsh (Ed.), *Normal family processes* (2nd ed., pp. 282-328). New York: Guilford Press.

Logan, C. R. (1996). Homophobia? No, homoprejudice. *Journal of Homosexuality, 31*(3), 31-53.

Mallon, G. P. (1999). Gay and lesbian adolescents and their families. *Journal of Gay & Lesbian Social Services, 10*(2), 69-88.

Matthews, C. R., & Lease, S. H. (2000). Focus on lesbian, gay, and bisexual families. In R. M. Perez, K. A. DeBord, & K. J. Bieschke (Eds.), *Handbook of counseling and psychotherapy with lesbian, gay, and bisexual clients* (pp. 249-273). Washington, DC: American Psychological Association.

Merighi, J. R., & Grimes, M. D. (2000). Coming out to families in a multicultural context. *Families in Society, 81*(1), 32-41.

Sanders, G. L., & Kroll, I. T. (2000). Generating stories of resilience: Helping gay and lesbian youth and their families. *Journal of Marital and Family Therapy, 26*(4), 433-442.

Savin-Williams, R. C. (1996). Self-labeling and disclosure among gay, lesbian, and bisexual youths. In J. Laird & R.-J. Green (Eds.), *Lesbians and gays in couples and families: A handbook for therapists* (pp. 153-182). San Francisco: Jossey-Bass.

Scrivner, R., & Eldridge, N. S. (1995). Lesbian and gay family psychology. In R. H. Mikesell, D. Lusterman, & S. H. McDaniel (Eds.), *Integrating family therapy: Handbook of family psychology and systems theory* (pp. 327-344). Washington, DC: American Psychological Association.

Chapter 2

Life-Course Social Science Perspectives on the GLBT Family

Bertram J. Cohler

The smallest self-sufficient social unit (Parsons, 1955), the family, is responsible for continuing support and socialization across the course of life. Living within the multigeneration, modified extended family characteristic of contemporary urban society (Litwak, 1965; Sussman, 1965), older family members continue to induct younger members into new roles not only in childhood but across the course of life (Brim, 1966; Hagestad, 1974, 1981). However, it is less often recognized that younger family members, in close proximity to social and technological change, reciprocally induct older family members into new conceptions of such cardinal roles as parenthood and work. Particularly as a consequence of increased proximity to social change, including the technological and social innovations associated with postsecondary education, younger family members reciprocally induct parents and other relatives into new definitions of their roles within the family.

Nowhere is the challenge of social change for relations within the family more important than in the area of sexuality and sexual life-ways or culturally shaped ideas and emotions, roles, and rituals understood as the foundation for personhood through the life course (Herdt, 1997; Hostetler & Herdt, 1998). This clearly includes the situation when GLBT youth disclose their alternative sexual orientations to brothers and sisters, parents, and other relatives. These offspring then teach parents and other relatives new conceptions of their own roles in relation to GLBT youth (Dew, 1994; Fricke & Fricke, 1991). One gay young man, a business consultant, participating in a coming-out group described how he had used a PowerPoint demonstration in

doi:10.1300/5792_03

helping his parents to understand both what it meant to be gay and what changes this disclosure would have on their relationship and on their roles as parents of a gay son who is in a committed relationship with another man.

This discussion uses the life-course perspective in the social sciences (Elder, 1995) in order to understand the interplay between social change and family process within GLBT families. Sexual lifeways other than those normally presumed by the larger society have emerged over the past three decades from a largely secretive and subversive subculture to increased recognition and acceptance within heteronormative society. Although considerable cross-sectional study has been done of offspring disclosing their sexual orientations to parents and other relatives (Herdt & Koff, 2000; Savin-Williams, 2001), and also detailed study of the adjustment of offspring and the marital tie in families in which two parents identify as gay or lesbian (Patterson, 1995, 2000, 2002; Stacey & Biblarz, 2001), less study of these families has been done over time and across generation-cohorts of both GLBT offspring and GLBT parents.

We know little about the relationships between gay and lesbian offspring and their own parents through the adult years and into the family of the second half of life, or the manner in which continuing social change such as enhanced visibility of transgender family members affects relationships across generations. Also, little study has been done of middle-aged gay and lesbian parents and their young adult offspring. We know very little about the relationships between parents identifying with an alternative sexual lifeway or their relationships with both straight and gay offspring after childhood and adolescence.

In all this study of sexual-minority families exists the question of the relevance of comparisons with heteronormative family study. Although such comparative study might provide additional understanding of the significance of alternative sexuality for family life, it is possible that findings from such comparative study are not relevant for understanding the GLBT family over time, as offspring and parents move into the second half of life. Blumstein and Schwartz (1990) and Peplau and her colleagues (Peplau, 1991; Peplau & Cochran, 1990; Peplau, Venigas, & Campbell, 1996) have questioned the value of using heterosexual relationships as a model for understanding same-sex relationships. Peplau (1991) suggests studying same-sex relationships on their own terms, rather than in terms of deviance from heterosexual norms of marriage and family.

LIFE-COURSE PERSPECTIVES AND THE GLBT FAMILY

The present discussion is founded on the presumption that life courses are in large measure determined by shared conceptions among members of particular generations or cohorts of persons born in some range of adjacent birth years moving together through the course of life. These members of a generation-cohort share the common experience of particular sociohistorical changes which interplay with individual life circumstances and such intracohort variation as geography, social position, and sexual orientation in determining the meaning of these changes for particular lives (Elder, 1974/1998, 1995; Elder, Johnson, & Crosnoe, 2003; Settersten, 1999). This life-course perspective on families, aging, and social change suggests that it is difficult to generalize about the course of lives over time except within the context of the lived experience of men and women growing up and growing old within a distinctive social and historical context. This context provides the framework within which the course of particular lives is understood (Bertaux, 1981; Hardy & Waite, 1997), including the meaning of sexuality itself (Chauncey, 1994; Parks, 1999; Rosenfeld, 2003; Sadownick, 1997; Stein, 1997).

Sexual identity is among those aspects of social life that appear to be most influenced by this complex interrelationship of culture, history, and demography. The organization of same-gender sexuality in particular reflects the dramatic social transformations of the past several decades. Discussion of family and life course within families in which some members have an alternative sexual identity must begin with recognition of the importance of this social change for both sexual identity and family life. The organization of same-sex desire around a homosexual and then later a lesbian or gay identity became possible only during the course of the twentieth century (Chauncey, 1994). For example, the cohorts of gay men and women currently in later adulthood came of age during an era in which no visible gay role models or other cultural resources existed to support their early development. Older cohorts of gay men faced the kind of stigma and discrimination that is virtually unknown to the present generation of young adult gay men and women (Jacobson & Grossman, 1996; Vacha, 1985). Transgender men and women still largely lack such supports and may encounter considerable community stigma.

In addition to emphasizing historical or cohort analysis, the life-course perspective recognizes the extent to which lives are shaped by developmental continuities and discontinuities and expected and eruptive life changes. It is clear that cohort and social context both enter into awareness and expression of same-sex desires, and that social change and cohort play an important role in understanding the GLBT family in the contexts of time and place. It is often assumed, for example, that sexual orientation and identity are stable throughout adulthood. However, increasing anecdotal and empirical evidence suggests that sexual desires and identities can be fluid through the course of life (Dunne, 2001). For example, several participants in the Chicago Study of Lesbian and Gay Adult Development and Aging (Cohler, Hostetler, & Boxer, 1998; Herdt, Beeler & Rawls, 1997) claimed little awareness of same-sex desires until well into middle-age, before which time they felt very satisfied in their marital relationships and heterosexual lifeways. Bozett's (1993) review of research findings indicated that a third of divorced gay men and more than three-fourths of divorced lesbians were unaware of their homosexuality at the time of their marriages.

Much study to date concerning families with members identifying with alternative sexual lifeways has been primarily concerned with tracing the developmental processes involved in the disclosure to self and others of one's sexual orientation (coming out), typically in late adolescence or early adulthood (Harry & DuVall, 1978; Herdt & Boxer, 1996; Savin-Williams, 1990, 1997). Somewhat less study has been devoted to the relationships with parents and other relatives following consolidation of identity among gay men and lesbians across the years of stable adulthood (Cohler & Boxer, 1984) and into middleage, and to the GLBT family in the second half of life.

FROM LIFE-CYCLE TO LIFE-COURSE FAMILY STUDY

Normative family study has traditionally been focused on presumed stages in the life cycle of the family founded on an analogy with stages of individual development (Havighurst, 1948). Further, this family development model has presumed that stages of family life are necessarily defined in terms of the parent-offspring relationship. Earlier formulations such as the family development model posed by Reuben Hill and his colleagues (Duvall, 1951/1971; Mattessich & Hill, 1987; Rodgers & White, 1993) presumed that the study of the family began with courtship and proceeded through marriage, the preparental years, the advent of parenthood, the years of active parenting, and the death of one spouse and the transition to widowhood of the surviving spouse and ended with the death of the surviving spouse without consideration of the marital-parenthood tie within the context of the modified extended family of contemporary urban society. In addition to presuming an ideal type of postwar nuclear family including husband, wife, and children (ideally one of each gender), which is at odds with the reality of family households in contemporary society, this is a heteronormative model of family life stages founded on marriage and parenthood, and one which does not acknowledge change in the family as a consequence of social change.

Just as a life-cycle model of psychological development (Erikson, 1950/1983, 1982; Vaillant & Milofsky, 1980) founded on presumed stages of personality development largely fails to account for the impact of social change upon the course of individual lives over time, the life-course perspective on family structure and process focuses more explicitly both on the effect of generation-cohort upon individual careers and upon the effect of these changes upon interlinked family process over historical time—altering the careers or timing of role entrances and exits through the course of life or the effect of change in the careers of some family members upon other family members. For example, parents of gay and lesbian young-adult offspring often express regret that they might not become grandparents (although new possibilities for parenthood within the GLBT community have changed that stereotyped view) or feel the significance of being a grandparent for a child adopted by a gay offspring and his or her partner. The college-age son in Dew's (1994) memoir observes that his "coming out" meant that his family had to come out as well. Dew reports that when couples in her social circle gather at social occasions, discussion often turns to the lives of young adult sons and daughters, including their marital status. An awkward moment occurs when she tells the group that her son is gay.

Social Timing and Family Organization

Following Durkheim's (1912/1995) discussion of time and the ritual life of the community, studies of how people understand the course of life suggest that persons maintain an internal timetable for expectable role transitions (Neugarten, Moore, & Lowe, 1965; Neugarten & Hagestad, 1976; Roth, 1963; Sorokin & Merton, 1937). Families may also be portrayed as following an expectable course over time. This perspective on the course of life, viewed in terms of socially defined role transitions within the family, has replaced the more traditional concept of developmental task in individual and family study, as initially described by Havighurst (1948) and Duvall (1951/1971). A life-course rather than life-cycle view of the family admits both to the effect of continuing social historical change in the study of family life over time through dual focus on expectable transitions over the course of life of family members and recognition of the impact of such unexpected events as the Great Depression, the two world wars, and other major sociohistorical changes.

Family members continually compare the course of their own lives with a socially shared timetable. They determine whether they are on time, early, or late for such role transitions as first job, advent of parenthood, or retirement (Neugarten & Hagestad, 1976). Even unpredictable life circumstances—adverse or positive—occur in the context of these expectable life changes. Eruptive life events, such as widowhood in the fourth versus the eighth decade of a woman's life, pose particular problems because few consociates exist to provide support and assistance (Kahn & Antonucci, 1981; Plath, 1980). One of the functions served by Parents and Friends of Lesbians and gays (PFLAG) is provision of such a convoy of social support in which parents of newly out gay and lesbian offspring can learn what it is like to be the parent of an offspring adopting an alternative sexual lifeway.

Seltzer (1976) and Cohler and Boxer (1984) suggest that positive morale or life satisfaction is largely determined by the sense of being on time for expected role transitions. The sense that life changes occur in the expected order and on time, consistent with other members of a cohort or generation, enhances the sense of personal congruence and well-being. Being late seems to have certain advantages: men who make a late transition to parenthood are more settled in their careers and more comfortable with themselves than men who make this transition on time (Daniels & Weingarten, 1982; Nydegger, 1980, 1981). Little is known about issues of social time in families in which members have an alternative sexual lifeway, such as in the transition to parenthood, which may take place at somewhat later ages than is often reported among straight families.

Generation and Life Course

The concept of generation is central to the life-course perspective (Cain, 1964; Ryder, 1965). Following Mannheim (1928/1993), Troll (1971), Bengtson and Allen (1993), and Laufer and Bengtson (1974) have all defined generation with reference to three age-linked characteristics: position within a cluster of four or five groups alive contemporaneously; period or point in the course of life, such as youth or middle-age; and cohort or persons of a given birth year who have experienced similar social and historical events. The age distribution in a given society at any one time creates groups of individuals with particular understandings of self and others, determined in part by shared interpretations of historical events.

Elder and his colleagues (Elder, 1974/1998, 1995; Elder et al., 2003) have addressed the problem of integrating a life-course perspective with study of the family from the perspective of interdependent lives. Consistent with Troll's (1971) earlier discussion of the means of generation within the study of the family, they note that chronological age of family members serves a marker both for place within the course of life, from young to old, and as a marker of particular social-historical or period- and cohort-linked experiences of family members, as well as an indicator for the shape and scope of the present role portfolio of these family members.

It is particularly important in family study to focus on the distinction between period and cohort and to recognize the significance of social and historical change as factors largely governing the sequence of transitions into and out of major social roles throughout the course of adult life (Dannefer, 1984; George, 1993, 1996; Hogan & Astone, 1986; Marini, 1984). Elder (1995) has addressed the problem of integrating a life-course perspective with study of the family from the perspective of interdependent lives. A family life-course perspective relies upon the dual concepts of generation as a shorthand position marker for families within the historical context experienced by each family member and place in the expectable course of life.

Cohort and linked social-historical events shape all aspects of lives, including the health of family members (for example, the present generation of young adults uses fewer cigarettes than previous generations and is more health conscious, a phenomenon which may result in later mortality and increased physical well-being later in life). However, as Settersten (1999) has noted, considerable intracohort variation exists, including that within GLBT members of the same subcohort of self-identifying gay men and women, such as in differences in geography (McCarthy, 2000; Sears, 1991, 1997; Smith & Manciske, 1997), social class (Appleby, 2001), ethnicity (Espin, 1993; Savin-Williams, 1996), and gender itself.

However, recognizing the reality of continuing historical and social change, at least to some extent, members of adjacent birth years, roughly over a decade, do share some common perspective on social life and across subcohorts, which is distinctive from that of earlier or later cohorts (Cohler, in preparation; Davis, 1979; Ryder, 1965; Schuman & Scott, 1989). This focus on the issue of timing of expectable and eruptive life changes in terms of those more generally expectable across the course of life differentiates the emerging field of life-course social science from the more traditional perspective represented in psychology by the work of Robert Havighurst (1948) and Erik Erikson (1950/1983), which emphasize a sequence of developmental tasks tied to particular ages and dependent upon each other.

LIFE-COURSE PERSPECTIVES ON SEXUAL-MINORITY FAMILIES

Little study has been done of the GLBT family from this life-course perspective (Cohler & Galatzer-Levy, 2000). Just as more generally in the community, GLBT persons realize role entrances and exits, such as those connected to relations with an intimate life partner and the unfolding of parenthood across a lifetime. Persons come to self-identify with alterative sexual lifeways at various points in a lifetime; the timing of this realization, itself affected by larger social changes, has an impact upon role transitions or careers of other family members in the modified extended family of contemporary society. Self-identification as gay or lesbian and determination to affirm this identity in the workplace may alter timing of entry into the labor market. The meaning of intimacy may be somewhat different among same- rather than opposite-gendered couples, and such differences may shape entrance into an enduring intimate relationship.

Differences in both timing of entry into such permanent relationships is further affected by the state. Current resistance to same-sex unions reflected in legislation has an effect upon the manner in which gay men and women both negotiate the relationship and the course of this relationship throughout adulthood. All too often discussion of the gay family fails to account for the effect of the state upon life within this sexual-minority family. For example, as a result of the lack of legal support, either for recognition of gay unions or for parenthood among gay couples, gay men may become parents somewhat later in life than their heterosexual counterparts. Efforts on the part of gay men to adopt or of lesbian couples to take advantage of donor insemination suggest that the transition to parenthood may differ both in timing and pathways into the parental role among gay as contrasted with straight couples.

Further, the still-prohibitive costs so often associated with donor insemination (DI) and adoption may mean that the couple must postpone the advent of parenthood until career advancement makes possible the income necessary for realizing the parental role in these ways. The death of a partner may be at ages comparable to those within the straight community, but particularly among men may be less a problem than for straight counterparts. Used to carrying out the basic household tasks, the gay widow may grieve this loss in ways similar to straight counterparts but may be better able to provide for his own self-care and may survive longer after widowhood than his heterosexual counterpart who may not have much experience providing such self-care.

Using a life-course rather than family-development perspective raises important questions for study. In the first place, much of the study of sexual-minority families to the present time has been based on cross-sectional study. For example, most studies of youth disclosing a gay or lesbian sexual orientation report on the process of disclosure through the time when the young person has made this disclosure to brothers, sisters, and parents and within the context of the present cohort of young adults, in a group which presumes both the legitimacy of the gay lifeway and in which the scourge of AIDS is being controlled through antiviral medication. Study of successive cohorts of young adults coming out to their families may understand their own sexuality and the course of their own lives in somewhat different terms. Indeed, the increasing visibility of parenthood among gay and lesbian couples may have already changed the terms of this discussion regarding the offspring's assumption of a gay identity.

Little information has been recorded on the family with a gay or lesbian offspring in the time following disclosure. With the son's or daughter's decision for commitment or marriage, this offspring role transition has an impact on parents as well. In this, as in other adult role transitions, GLBT offspring socialize their parents into a new understanding of their roles as parents. This has been particularly well portrayed in the co-authored account by a gay man, his partner, and his partner's parents, following the gay couple's decision to have a traditional Jewish wedding in the rather conservative Canadian community in which his partner had grown up (Wythe, Merling, Merling, & Merling, 2000). First the gay couple had to induct the partner's parents into a new conception of enduring intimacy between a same-gendered couple through backward socialization, which the younger generation sought to exert influence over the views of the older generation within the family (Brim, 1966; Hagestad, 1986), then to support the parents as they came out to their own parents and to the community in sending the wedding announcements, making arrangements with the rabbi, and planning the details of the ceremony, such as explaining to the hotel that the ceremony would be one involving two men.

Although his partner's parents had long known of their son's gay identity, residual sense of shame and stigma made it difficult for the parents first to accept the idea of a wedding, pleading instead for a quiet ceremony in the rabbi's study, and then struggling with the revelation that after the rabbi gave her blessing, the newly united couple would exchange a serious kiss! Other issues were explored as well, such as developing relations with their son-in-law's relatives (Serovich, Skeen, Walters, & Robinson, 1993). It is important to follow these gay couples into the adult years, as they decide whether to become parents, and to study the relationship between these two younger generations and their parents and grandparents.

The Transition to Parenthood

The life-course perspective on the study of the GLBT families through the adult years poses such questions as the relationship between single and partnered gay men and lesbians and their own older parents, the extent to which the partners of gay men or lesbians assume caregiving responsibilities for their own or their partner's parents, and the relationships between adult offspring of gay and lesbian parents and their grandparents and other relatives. Particular issues may be present in the transition to parenthood among gay and lesbian prospective parents that may differ from issues faced by their heterosexual counterparts. As in the case of same-gender partnership, gay and lesbian parenthood should not be understood merely by reference to normative models, although the normative study of parenthood provides a necessary point of departure and comparison. The study of gay and lesbian parenthood must begin with the recognition of the following two points: first, the rapid social transformations of the past three decades have led to dramatic changes in every aspect of gay and lesbian life, including family formation, which is no longer open only to those gay men and lesbians who have been in a heterosexual marriage.

As with most transitions in the course of life, parenthood fits into a larger social timetable. Although both marriage and parenthood are being delayed among younger cohorts, by the late twenties and early thirties individuals feel increasing social pressure to marry and start a family (Hogan, 1987; Sweet, 1977). For women, the biological clock continues to set an upper limit for the realization of motherhood, an issue relevant both for heterosexual women and women in a lesbian union. Within these rather broad biological and social limits, however, a great deal of individual variation exists in the timing of parenthood, and this timing—whether on time, early, time, or late—has important implications for the experience of parenting. Although no research has been done on the impact of social timing on the parental transition among gays and lesbians, such effects are undoubtedly mediated by the specific pathway followed, whether prior heterosexual marriage, DI, or adoption.

Irrespective of the timing of parenthood, parents almost inevitably experience role strain and overload for at least a year following the birth of their first child (Demick, 2002; Demo & Cox, 2001;

McLanahan & Adams, 1987). Survey findings show that more than one-third of women with young children report marked loss of morale (Campbell, Converse, & Rodgers, 1976; Weissman, Myers, & Thompson, 1981). Among gay and lesbian parents, such problems may be amplified by isolation from supportive kin networks, although extended "families of choice" (Oswald, 2002; Weston, 1997) may be a more important source of emotional and material support than among heterosexual families. Gay and lesbian parents may be better able than their heterosexual counterparts to take advantage of community resources and informal support systems in the absence of emotional support when tension exists between parents and their relatives resulting from their disclosure of their gay sexual identity and alternative lifestyle.

Parenthood and the Couple's Intimate Tie

Although the increased role strain associated with the transition to parenthood is largely confined to the parent-child tie, marital relationships are obviously also affected. In general, husbands and wives show little enduring change in the nature of their relationship following the transition to parenthood (Demick, 2002; Demo & Cox, 2001). However, most studies do report a modest, temporary decline in reported marital satisfaction among both husbands and wives after the first child's birth and, at least to some extent, after each successive birth (Belsky, Spanier, & Rovine, 1983; Cowan & Cowan, 1992; Demo & Cox, 2001). Companionate marriages, characterized by strong complementarity of interests and intimacy, are particularly adversely affected by the transition to parenthood (Feldman, 1971; Shereshefsky & Yarrow, 1973).

Successful political and legal challenges of the hegemonic view that parental homosexuality is detrimental to children's adjustment and well-being have led to award of custody based on factors other than sexual orientation. Further, in many states, sexual orientation is becoming increasingly irrelevant to foster care placement and adoption. Moreover, as Patterson (1995, 2000, 2002) and Stacey and Biblarz (2001) have emphasized and as we have here observed, there are many routes into parenthood among gays and lesbians, and gay parenthood can begin at different points in the life course.

Adjustment to the Parental Role

Extensive literature exists on the transition to parenthood within heterosexual couples (Demick, 2002), although little study has been done on the issue of adjustment to becoming parents among gay and lesbian couples. Among heterosexual couples, in contrast with work and marriage, individuals receive relatively little preparation for the reality of providing complete care for another person. It is difficult for prospective parents to imagine the time and effort required for child care or the extent of its effects on work and leisure. Gutmann (1975) and Chodorow (1978) have both argued that becoming a parent produces a sense of crisis and imperative unlike any other adult role transition, although they disagree about the consequences.

Although some research has questioned the assumption that the transition to parenthood is an inevitable source of challenge (Rossi, 1968, 1972), the term *crisis* nevertheless seems to apply well to the transition and to be supported by empirical research. In general, although findings vary according to the group studied and the questions asked, most studies show that the transition to parenthood is a source of at least moderate personal crisis for both mothers and fathers. The nature and degree of the crisis is determined, at least in part, by the timing of parenthood. It is widely believed that since gay and lesbian couples must work so hard at becoming parents, and with such extensive planning, that they must be particularly motivated for parenthood and will feel less strain accompanying the transition to parenthood than heterosexual counterparts. To date, little comparative study has been done of the psychological impact of the transition to parenthood among heterosexual and both gay and lesbian couples.

Social Timing and Parental Morale

Those who become parents late, particularly fathers, generally can tend better to the role demands of parenthood than their younger, on-time counterparts, having established more stable personal and work identities. Due to the relatively greater amount of preparation and planning involved (Falk, 1989; Moses & Hawkins, 1982), openly gay men and women who opt to become parents may also be older and more secure in their work and personal lives at the time of the parental transition, and thus may have much in common with their late heterosexual counterparts.

Academic interest in the effect of child care on parents has increased over the course of the past three decades, a shift largely motivated by a reconsideration of women's roles. Although men may have become somewhat more involved with their young children little change has occurred in the child care expectations placed on women, who are still overwhelmingly the primary caretakers (Rebelsky & Hanks, 1971). Hence, despite the many gains of the feminist movement, the transition to parenthood remains, in actuality, the transition to motherhood (Chodorow, 1978; Rossi, 1972). The challenges of this transition are intensified for the growing number of women who work outside the home, even during the preschool years. Although there is some evidence of a more equitable division of household labor and child care among gay and lesbian couples (Kurdek, 1995; Patterson, 1995, 2002), the biological parent—in the case of non-adoption—often shoulders the primary burdens of child care. Single gay adoptive parents may also experience a particularly difficult transition.

As this review has suggested, despite a large body of research on the transition into normative parenthood, we still know relatively little about the impact of this transition to parenthood on gay and lesbian parents. For instance, we lack a good comparative study of the motivation for parenthood among lesbians with children from a prior heterosexual marriage, gay and lesbian couples adopting, and lesbian couples choosing DI for one or both members of the couple. In a comparison of divorced gay fathers and divorced and married heterosexual fathers, Bigner and Jacobsen (1989) found few differences in motivation for becoming parents, although gay fathers experience particular adverse expectations and pressures to assume this quintessential adult role and may be less likely than straight fathers to be allowed to have their children live with them following a divorce (Bigner & Bozett, 1990). This constraint based on stigma within the judicial system has, in turn, made realization of the parental role even more significant for them than among heterosexual counterparts, who did not have to overcome social barriers in caring for their children. These authors report that gay fathers were more committed than straight paternal counterparts to providing ongoing care and more motivated to maintain close ties with children. Ricketts and Achtenberg (1990) have suggested, for instance, that the decision-making process leading to adoption may be very similar among gay, lesbian, and heterosexual couples, but much more research is needed. In general, we need good comparative research of the different pathways into parenthood, both normative and nonnormative, and on the effect of the pathway chosen on this important developmental transition (Kirkpatrick, 1996).

The GLBT Family of the Second Half of Life

Beyond focus on the pathways into parenthood among gay and lesbian couples and the adjustment of offspring through the school years, little information can be found regarding the gay and lesbian family, either with or without children, through the adult years. Some detailed study has been done of gay men through the years of middle and later adulthood (Adelman, 1991; Jacobson & Grossman, 1996; Kimmel, 1978; Minnigerode & Adelman, 1978; Reid, 1995; Vacha, 1985), although little of this discussion has focused on gay men in the context of the intergenerational family of contemporary society. Hostetler (2001) has studied a group of middle-aged gay men focusing on the decision to remain single or to have a life partner. About half of the men in his study reported an enduring intimate relationship with another man, while the other half of these men had decided to remain single and reported enjoying their own privacy. Few differences in morale or life satisfaction differentiated these two groups. However, it is important to recognize that categories of *single* and *partnered* are not static, and movement back and forth occurs as previously single individuals enter coupled relationships and as formerly partnered individuals become single, either through the dissolution of their relationship or the death of a partner.

For many older homosexual men, sexual orientation as such plays little role in their lives (Cohler et al., 1998). Just as among their heterosexual counterparts, these men have partners of many years, lead lives in which sexual orientation plays little role at the workplace, and engage in social activities in the evenings and on the weekend with other couples. Issues of stigma have played little role in their lives since they have kept their sexual orientation apart from their work life and take part in few community activities in which their sexual orientation would pose a challenge to others. They find appropriate religious congregations, often of other older gay and lesbian couples. Often reporting little contact with relatives, these older men and women depend on the families of choice they have created (Oswald, 2002). Men and women within this older cohort expected little from society in terms of understanding or accommodation to their sexual orientation and are not distressed by such social indifference. With a few notable exceptions, these men do not believe that sexual identity has played a central role in their lives.

These findings, from study of the family ties of this cohort of older gay men and women well into middle age at the time of the gay rights revolution, may not be replicated across subsequent cohorts of older gay men. Perhaps early pioneers of the next generation of middle-aged men moved into the "third age" (Laslett, 1996) of the young old, several recently retired men in coming-out groups and social groups run by a community service agency for the GLBT community have reported having children and grandchildren. These men come into the retirement years from diverse pathways.

One man, aware since childhood that he was sexually attracted to other men, had nevertheless married and had two children. At midlife, he had met a single, gay work associate with whom he began a furtive sexual affair. His wife ultimately discovered this relationship and asked for a divorce. At first his now-adult offspring were resentful that he had destroyed his marriage and disrupted the family and they refused to have anything to do with him. Subsequently father and offspring reconciled and now spend alternate holidays together. His former wife has since remarried and is no longer resentful. The former couple are on speaking terms and together attend celebrations for their children and grandchildren. It is not clear how his partner feels about the family; he is said to be polite but not engaged with his partner's family.

Another man had been married for nearly fifty years and had three children and five grandchildren. After his wife's death several years ago, he had traveled to Florida for a winter holiday, where he met another retired man who self-identified as gay. As a close friendship developed, his friend introduced him to gay sex, which he found immensely pleasurable. Now self-defining as gay, he lives with his friend in an intimate partnership in a house they bought together and enjoys a circle of older gay friends. His children and grandchildren are comfortable with his newfound sexual identity (and perhaps relieved that their father will not be socially isolated in later life), are frequent Florida visitors, and during the hot summer months he travels back to a Midwestern city, where he enjoys visiting with his family and playing tennis and golf with his children and grandchildren.

These vignettes reflect a shift in gay and lesbian families across the retirement years and into later life as a consequence of larger social changes which also affect the course of particular lives as older adults begin to move out of the labor market and into retirement. The present generation of much older gay men who were already in midlife at the time of the gay rights movement report being largely unaware of or indifferent to the events surrounding early gay liberation. Although they were not as hostile toward the gay rights movement as the older men described by Lee's (1987) study, these men chose to lead their lives quietly and apart from the social turmoil of the time.

These older men eschew terms such as *gay* and *queer* for their sexual identity and are critical of moves by younger cohorts to demand recognition of their same-gender sexual orientation within workplace and community. At the same time, they acknowledge that social and political change have made life easier for gay people. Two exceptions to this general lack of political involvement are a hairdresser who was an active participant in early homophile organizations and a veteran of the Korean War who, after a lifetime of accommodation, became an outspoken leader in the local chapter of a national gay veterans organization in the wake of Clinton's infamous "don't ask, don't tell" military policy. As the middle-age cohort moves into the retirement years it is likely to be a more activist generation, as indeed "baby boomers" more generally are, than the present generation of homosexual elders, and one which will expect medical and social services recognizing the needs of gay elders.

Although many of the older men in our study reported being in good health, they expressed a great deal of concern about the possibility of needing the services of a nursing home or other long-term care facility. While sharing the same concerns about such facilities as their heterosexual counterparts (Kelly, 1977; Lieberman & Tobin, 1983), they also fear discrimination or at least a lack of sensitivity regarding their sexual orientation, including the fear that they will be separated from their partners. Berger (1996) and Kehoe (1989) both note similar concerns among the gay and lesbian elders they studied. However, although both men and women in these studies feared declining health, other studies suggest that gay people's concerns about health are similar to those reported by older adults in general (Quam & Whitford, 1992; Tobin, 1996).

Taken together, existing research indicates that gays and lesbians experience similar levels of adjustment and morale in later life when contrasted with their heterosexual counterparts (Allen, Blieszner, & Roberto, 2001; Minnigerode & Adelman, 1978). Lee (1987) concluded that the present generation of gay men does not differ from their straight counterparts in terms of life satisfaction. In addition, although the older men in his study were often alone, they did not report greater loneliness than the elder population at large. Summarizing his own research, Kimmel (1979-1980) has commented: "homosexuality per se did not appear to have a negative effect on the respondents' adjustment to aging or satisfaction with life (p. 245)." However, extant research has concentrated primarily on convenience samples of white, middle-class, urban-dwelling men and women, as others have noted. The voices of nonwhite, working-class, and rural-dwelling gays and lesbians have rarely been heard (Abbleby, 2001; Oswald & Culton, 2003; McCarthy, 2000; Smith & Manciste, 1997). As one exception, Kehoe (1989) found that many older lesbians living in rural areas, lacking transportation, feel isolated and lonely. Future research will undoubtedly unearth other important differences in the experiences of "invisible" populations of gay men and women.

CONCLUSION

This discussion has posed an alternative framework to the traditional family development model for understanding the family life of persons self-identifying as gay or lesbian. Starting from the assumptions that social life is marked by historical and social change, which leads to generation-cohort groups sharing some commonality of outlook based on such shared experiences (such as the Great Depression or World War II) and recognizing that marked intracohort variability exists in the manner in which these events are experienced, the course of life for any cohort is marked by linked transitions into and out of socially defined, highly valued roles. The timing of these role entrances and exits may be viewed within a shared timetable as early, on time, and late. This life-course perspective provides a means for understanding the course of life among sexual minorities, who have selected alternative lifeways to those presumptively assumed in contemporary society. At the same time, it is important to recognize that persons adopting these alternative sexual lifeways may view such roles as spouse or life partner in ways that are different from heterosexual counterparts.

Study of alternative sexual lifeways and the family has generally provided in-depth, cross-sectional understanding of such discrete family transitions as open disclosure of alternative sexuality, formation of companionate ties, or realization of parenthood. Viewed from a life-course perspective, it is important to understand these role transitions in terms of larger social and historical changes, which provide the context for any particular role transition, the timing of this transition in terms of the course of life as a whole, and the manner in which a transition such as becoming a parent at a particular point in the course of adult life is linked to previous transitions such as time and social circumstances surrounding adoption of a gay identity. Adoption of the role of parent then is linked to other roles such as grandparent, as well as to timing and support during retirement. Further, the diversity of means leading to such role transitions as that of parenthood itself has implications for the subsequent course of life. The course of parenthood as offspring grow to adulthood and become parents themselves may be quite different depending on whether children are from a previous heterosexual marriage of one or both partners, the result of DI in the case of lesbian parents, surrogate mother in the situation of a gay couple, or adopted (with the time of adopting in the child's life and the circumstances of adoption—issues which must be recognized).

Finally, it should be noted that this discussion has focused primarily on the life course of those men and women who self-identify as gay (lesbians and gay men). Very little study has been done of men and women who self-define as bisexual in a continuing preference through the course of life for intimate relationships with both men and women. Questions abound: What does disclosure of bisexuality mean to the several generations within the family, and in what ways does the life course of bisexual men and women differ from that of straight counterparts? To what extent is bisexuality similarly understood among men who more often identify with a master narrative of always having been gay (Plummer, 1995) and women who may move more freely between intimate relationships with men and with other women without defining themselves as bisexual (Zinik, 2000)?

These issues assume equal salience in the lives of transgender men and women. To date very little study has been done of the life course of men and women who are successful in realizing surgical reassignment and of variation in the life course among those transgender men and women who seek same- and opposite-sex relationships. Clearly, both the timing of the surgical reassignment in the course of life and postsurgical sexual orientation is linked to the timing and understanding of such subsequent role transitions as marriage or partnership, decisions regarding parenthood, and the negotiation of role entrances and exits through the second half of life. Indeed, very little study has been done of the family in the second half of life or of the transition to middle and later life among transgender men and women. The life-course perspective provides the intellectual framework for such study as well as for study of the interplay between historical and social change and the relationship dynamics of members across generations within the modified intergenerational family in contemporary society.

REFERENCES

Adelman, M. (1991). Stigma, gay lifestyles, and adjustment to aging: A study of later-life gay men and lesbians. *The Journal of Homosexuality, 20,* 7-32.

Allen, K., Blieszner, R., & Roberto, K. A. (2001). Families in the middle and later years: A critique of research in the 1990s. In R. M. Milardo (Ed.), *Understanding families into the new millennium: A decade in review* (pp. 130-145). Minneapolis, MN: National Council on Family Relations.

Appleby, G. A. (Ed). (2001). *Working-class gay and bisexual men.* Binghamton, NY: Harrington Park Press.

Belsky, J., Spanier, G., & Rovine, M. (1983). Stability and change in marriage across the transition to parenthood. *Journal of Marriage and the Family, 45,* 567-577.

Bengtson, V. L., & Allen, K. R. (1993). The life course perspective applied to families over time. In P. G. Boss, W. J. Doherty, R. LaRossa, W. R. Schumm, & S. K. Steinmetz (Eds.), *Sourcebook of family theories and methods: A contextual approach* (pp. 469-499). New York: Plenum Press.

Berger, R. (1996). *Gay and gray: The older homosexual man* (2nd ed.). New York: Harrington Park Press.

Bertaux, D. (1981). From the life-history approach to the transformation of sociological practice. In D. Bertaux (Ed.), *Biography and society: The life history approach in the social sciences* (pp. 28-46). Newbury Park, CA: Sage Publications.

Bigner, J., & Bozett, F. (1990). Parenting by gay fathers. In F. W. Bozett & M. Sussman (Eds.), *Homosexuality and family relations* (pp. 155-176). Binghamton, NY: Harrington Park Press.

Bigner, J., & Jacobsen, R. (1989). The value of children to gay and heterosexual fathers. In F. W. Bozett (Ed.), *Homosexuality and the family* (pp. 163-172). Binghamton, NY: Harrington Park Press.

Blumstein, P., & Schwartz, P. (1990). Intimate relationships and the creation of sexuality. In D. P. McWhirter, S. A. Sanders, & J. M. Reinisch (Eds.), *Homosexuality/heterosexuality: Concepts of sexual orientation* (pp. 307-320). New York: Oxford University Press.

Bozett, F. W. (1993). Gay fathers: A review of the literature. In L. D. Garnets & D. C. Kimmel (eds.), *Psychological perspetives on lesbian and gay male experiences* (pp. 437-457). New York: Columbia University Press.

Brim, O. G., Jr. (1966). Socialization through the life cycle. In O. G. Brim Jr. & S. Wheeler (Eds.), *Socialization after childhood: Two essays* (pp. 1-49). Cambridge, MA: Harvard University Press.

Cain, L. (1964). Life course and social structure. In R. Faris (Ed.), *Handbook of modern sociology* (pp. 272-309). Chicago: Rand-McNally.

Campbell, A., Converse, P., & Rodgers, W. (1976). *The quality of American life: Perceptions, evaluations and satisfactions.* New York: Russell Sage.

Chauncey, G. (1994). *Gay New York: Gender, urban culture and the making of the gay male world, 1890-1940.* New York: Basic Books.

Chodorow, N. (1978). *The reproduction of mothering.* Berkeley: University of California Press.

Cohler, B. (In preparation). *Writing desire: Generation and life-story among men who have sex with other men.*

Cohler, B., & Boxer, A. (1984). Middle adulthood: Settling into the world-person, time, and context. In D. Offer & M. Sabshin (Eds.), *Normality and the life cycle* (pp. 145-204). New York: Basic Books.

Cohler, B., & Galatzer-Levy, R. (2000). *The course of gay and lesbian lives: Social and psychoanalytic perspectives.* Chicago: The University of Chicago Press.

Cohler, B., Hostetler, A., & Boxer, A. (1998). Generativity, social context and lived experience: Narratives of gay men in middle adulthood. In D. McAdams & E. de St. Aubin (Eds.), *Generativity and adult experience: Psychosocial perspectives on caring and contributing to the next generation* (pp. 265-309). Washington, DC: American Psychological Association.

Cowan, C., & Cowan, P. (1992). *When partners become parents: The big life change for couples.* New York: Basic Books.

Daniels, P., & Weingarten, K. (1982). *Sooner or later: The timing of parenthood in adult lives.* New York: Norton.

Dannefer, D. (1984). Adult development and social theory: A paradigmatic reappraisal. *American Sociological Review, 49,* 100-116.

Davis, F. (1979). *Yearning for yesteryear: A sociology of nostalgia.* New York: The Free Press/Macmillan.

Demick, J. (2002). Stages of parental development. In M. H. Bornstein (Ed.), *Handbook of parenting* (Rev. ed., Vol. 3, pp. 389-413). Mahwah, NJ: Lawrence Erlbaum.

Demo, D. H., & Cox, M. J. (2001). Families with young children: A review of research in the 1990s. In R. M. Milardo (Ed.), *Understanding families into the new millennium: A decade in review* (pp. 95-129). Minneapolis, MN: National Council on Family Relations.

Dew, R. F. (1994). *The family heart: A memoir of when our son came out.* New York: Ballentine Books.

Dunne, G. A. (2001). The lady vanishes? Reflections on the experience of married and divorced non-heterosexual dyads. *Journal of Sexualities, 4,* 20-30.

Durkheim, E. (1912/1995). *Elementary forms of the religious life* (Trans. by Karen E. Fields). New York: Basic Books.

Duvall, E. (1951/1971). *Family development.* Philadelphia, PA: Lippincott.

Elder, G. H., Jr. (1974/1998). *Children of the Great Depression: Social change in life experience.* Boulder, CO: Westview Press/Harper Collins.

Elder, G. H., Jr. (1995). The life course paradigm: Social change and individual development. In P. Moen, G. H. Elder Jr., & K. Lüscher (Eds.), *Examining lives in context: Perspectives on the ecology of human development* (pp. 101-139). Washington, DC: American Psychological Association.

Elder, G. H., Jr., Johnson, M. K., & Crosnoe, R. (2003). The emergence and development of life course theory. In. J. T. Mortimer & M. J. Shanahan (Eds.), *Handbook of the life course* (pp. 3-19). New York: Kluwer Academic Press.

Erikson, E. H. (1950/1983). *Childhood and society* (Rev. ed.). New York: Norton.

Erikson, E. H. (1982). *The life cycle completed.* New York: Norton.

Espin, O. M. (1993). Issues of identity in the psychology of Latina lesbians. In L. Garnets & D. Kimmel (Eds.), *Psychological perspectives on lesbian and gay male experiences* (pp. 348-363). New York: Columbia University Press.

Falk, P. (1989). Lesbian mothers: Psychosocial assumptions in family law. *American Psychologist, 44,* 941-947.

Feldman, L. (1971). Depression and marital interaction. *Family Process, 20,* 389-395.

Fricke, A., & Fricke, W. (1991). *Sudden strangers: The story of a gay son and his father.* New York: St. Martin's Press.

George, L. (1993). Sociological perspectives on life transitions. *Annual Review of Sociology, 19,* 353-373.

George, L. (1996). Missing links: The case for a social psychology of the life course. *Gerontologist, 36,* 248-255.

Gutmann, D. (1975). Parenthood: Key to the comparative study of the life cycle. In N. Datan & L. Ginsberg (Eds.), *Life-span developmental psychology: Normative life crises* (pp. 167-184). New York: Academic Press.

Hagestad, G. (1974). Middle-aged women and their children: Exploring changes in a role relationship. Unpublished doctoral dissertation, University of Minnesota.

Hagestad, G. (1981). Problems and promises in the social psychology of intergenerational relations. In. R. W. Fogel, E. Hatfield, S. B. Kiesler, & E. Shanas (Eds.), *Aging: Stability and change in the family* (pp. 11-46). New York: Academic Press.

Hagestad, G. (1986). Dimensions of time and the family. *American Behavioral Scientist, 29,* 679-694.

Hardy, M. A., & Waite, L. (1997). Doing time: Reconciling biography with history in the study of social change. In M. A. Hardy (Ed.), *Studying aging and social change: Conceptual and methodological issues* (pp. 1-21). Thousand Oaks, CA: Sage Publications.

Harry, J., & DuVall, W. (1978). *The social organization of gay males.* New York: Praeger.

Havighurst, R. J. (1948). *Developmental tasks and education.* New York: David McKay.

Herdt, G. (1997). *Same sex different cultures.* Boulder, CO: Westview Press.

Herdt, G., Beeler, J., & Rawls, T. (1997). Life course diversity among older lesbians and gay men. *Journal of Lesbian, Gay, and Bisexual Identity, 2,* 231-247.

Herdt, G., & Boxer, A. (1996). *Children of horizons* (2nd ed.). Boston: Beacon Press.

Herdt, G., & Koff, B. (2000). *Something to tell you: The road families travel when a child is gay.* New York: Columbia University Press.

Hogan, D. (1987). Demographic trends in human fertility, and parenting across the life span. In J. Lancaster, J. Altman, A. Rossi, & L. Sherrod (Eds.), *Parenting across the life-span: Biosocial dimensions* (pp. 315-349). New York: Aldine de Gruyter.

Hogan, D., & Astone, N. (1986). The transition to adulthood. *Annual Review of Sociology, 12,* 101-130.

Hostetler, A. (2001). Single gay men: Psychological well being, cultural models of adult development, and the meaning of being single by choice. Doctoral dissertation, Committee on Human Development, The University of Chicago.

Hostetler, A., & Herdt, G. (1998). Culture, sexual lifeways, and developmental subjectivities: Rethinking sexual taxonomies. *Social Research, 65,* 249-290.

Jacobson, S., & Grossman, A. H. (1996). Older lesbians and gay men: Old myths, new images, and future directions. In R. C. Savin-Williams & K. M. Cohen (Eds.), *The lives of lesbians, gays, and bisexuals* (pp. 345-374). Fort Worth, TX: Harcourt Brace College Publishers.

Kahn, R., & Antonucci, T. (1981). Convoys of social support: A life course approach. In S. Kiesler, J. Morgan, & V. Oppenheimer (Eds.), *Aging: Social change* (pp. 383-405). New York: Academic Press.

Kehoe, M. (1989). *Lesbians over 60 speak for themselves.* Binghamton, NY: Harrington Park Press.

Kelly, J. (1977). The aging male homosexual: Myth and reality. *Gerontologist, 17,* 328-332.

Kimmel, D. (1978). Adult development and aging: A gay perspective. *Journal of Social Issues, 34,* 113-130.

Kimmel, D. (1979-1980). Life-history interviews of gay men. *International Journal of Aging and Human Development, 10,* 239-248.

Kirkpatrick, M. (1996). Lesbians as parents. In R. Cabaj & T. S. Stein (Eds.), *Textbook of homosexuality and mental health* (pp. 353-370). Washington, DC: American Psychiatric Association.

Kurdek, L. (1995). Lesbian and gay couples. In A. D'Augelli & C. Patterson (Eds.), *Lesbian, gay, and bisexual identities over the life span* (pp. 243-261). New York: Oxford University Press.

Laslett, P. (1996). *A fresh map of life: The emergence of the third age* (2nd ed.). Houndmills, Basingstoke, Hampshire, UK: George Weidenfeld and Nicholson Ltd./Macmillan.

Laufer, R., & Bengtson, V. (1974). Generation, aging and social stratification: On the development of generational units. *Journal of Social Issues, 30,* 181-206.

Lee, J. A. (1987). What can homosexual aging studies contribute to theories of aging? *Journal of Homosexuality, 13,* 43-71.

Lieberman, M., & Tobin, S. (1983). *The experience of old age: Stress, coping and survival.* New York: Basic Books.

Litwak, E. (1965). Extended kin relations in an industrial society. In E. Shanas & G. Streib (Eds.), *Social structure and the family: Generational relations* (pp. 290-323). Englewood Cliffs, NJ: Prentice-Hall.

Mannheim, K. (1928/1993). The problem of generations. In K. H. Wolff (Ed.), *From Karl Mannheim* (2nd exp. ed., pp. 351-398). New Brunswick, NJ: Transactions Books.

Marini, M. (1984). Age and sequencing norms in the transition to adulthood. *Social Forces, 63,* 229-244.

Mattessich, P., & Hill, R. (1987). Life cycle and family development. In M. B. Sussman & S. Steinmetz (Eds.), *Handbook of marriage and the family* (pp. 437-469). New York: Plenum.

McCarthy, L. (2000). Poppies in a wheat field: Exploring the lives of rural lesbians. *Journal of Homosexuality, 39,* 75-94.

McLanahan, S., & Adams, J. (1987). Parenthood and psychological well-being. *Annual Review of Sociology, 5,* 237-257.

Minnigerode, F. A., & Adelman, M. R. (1978). Elderly homosexual women and men: Report on a pilot study. *Family Coordinator, 27,* 451-456.

Moses, A., & Hawkins, R. (1982). *Counseling lesbian women and gay men: A life-issues approach.* St. Louis: C. V. Mosby.

Neugarten, B., & Hagestad, G. (1976). Age and the life course. In R. Binstock & E. Shanas (Eds.), *Handbook of aging and the social sciences* (pp. 35-55). New York: Van Nostrand-Reinhold.

Neugarten, B., Moore, J., & Lowe, J. (1965). Age norms, age constraints, and adult socialization. *American Journal of Sociology, 70,* 710-717.

Nydegger, C. (1980). Role and age transitions: A potpourri of issues. In C. Fry & J. Keith (Eds.), *New methods of old age research: Anthropological alternatives* (pp. 127-145). Chicago: University of Chicago Press.
Nydegger, C. (1981). On being caught up in time. *Human Development, 24,* 1-12.
Oswald, R. F. (2002). Resilience with the family networks of lesbians and gay men: Intentionality and redefinition. *Journal of Marriage and Family, 64,* 374-383.
Oswald, R. F., & Culton, L. S. (2003). Under the rainbow: Rural gay life and its relevance for family providers. *Family Relations, 52,* 72-81.
Parks, C. (1999). Lesbian identity development: An examination of differences across generations. *American Journal of Orthopsychiatry, 69,* 347-361.
Parsons, T. (1955). Family structure and the socialization of the child. In T. Parsons & R. Bales, *Family, socialization and interaction process* (pp. 35-131). New York: Free Press.
Patterson, C. J. (1995). Lesbian mothers, gay fathers, and their children. In A. D'Augelli & C. Patterson (Eds.), *Lesbian, gay, and bisexual identities over the life span* (pp. 262-292). New York: Oxford University Press.
Patterson, C. J. (2000). Family relationships of lesbians and gay men. *Journal of Marriage and the Family, 62,* 1052-1069.
Patterson, C. J. (2002). Lesbian and gay parenthood. In M. H. Bornstein (Ed.), *Handbook of parenting* (Rev. ed., Vol. 3, pp. 317-338). Mahwah, NJ: Lawrence Erlbaum.
Peplau, L. A. (1991). Lesbian and gay relationships. In J. C. Gonsiorek & J. D. Weinrich (Eds.), *Homosexuality: Research implications for public policy* (pp. 177-196). Thousand Oaks, CA: Sage Publications.
Peplau, L. A., & Cochran, S. (1990). A relationship perspective on homosexuality. In D. P. McWhirter, S. A. Sanders, & J. M. Reinisch (Eds.), *Homosexuality/heterosexuality: Concepts of sexual orientation* (pp. 321-349). New York: Oxford University Press.
Peplau, L. A., Venigas, R. C., & Campbell, S. M. (1996). Gay and lesbian relationships. In R. C. Savin-Williams & K. M. Cohen (Eds.), *The lives of lesbians, gays, and bisexuals* (pp. 250-273). Fort Worth, TX: Harcourt Brace.
Plath, D. (1980). Contours of consociation: Lessons from a Japanese narrative. In P. B. Baltes & O. G. Brim Jr. (Eds.), *Life-span development and behavior* (Vol. 3, pp. 287-305). New York: Academic Press.
Plummer, K. (1995). *Telling sexual stories: Power, change, and social worlds.* New York: Routledge.
Quam, J., & Whitford, G. (1992). Adaptation and age-related expectations of older gay and lesbian adults. *Gerontologist, 32,* 367-374.
Rebelsky, F., & Hanks, C. (1971). Fathers' verbal interaction with infants in the first three months of life. *Child Development, 42,* 63-68.
Reid, J. (1995). Development in late life: Older lesbian and gay lives. In A. D'Augelli & C. Patterson (Eds.), *Lesbian, gay, and bisexual identities over the life span* (pp. 215-242). New York: Oxford University Press.

Ricketts, W., & Achtenberg, R. (1990). Adoption and foster parenting for lesbians and gay men: Creating new traditions in family. In F. W. Bozett & M. B. Sussman (Eds.), *Homosexuality and family relations* (pp. 83-118). Binghamton, NY: The Haworth Press.

Rodgers, R. H., & White, J. M. (1993). Family development theory. In. P. G. Boss, W. J. Doherty, R. LaRossa, W. R. Schumm & S. K. Steinmetz (Eds.), *Sourcebook of family theories and methods* (pp. 225-254). New York: Plenum Press.

Rosenfeld, D. (2003). *The changing of the guard: Lesbian and gay elders, identity, and social change.* Philadelphia: Temple University Press.

Rossi, A. (1968). Transition to parenthood. *Journal of Marriage and the Family, 30,* 26-39.

Rossi, A. (1972). Family development in a changing world. *American Journal of Psychiatry, 128,* 1057-1066.

Roth, J. (1963). *Timetables: Structuring the passage of time in hospital treatment and other careers.* Indianapolis: Bobbs-Merrill.

Ryder, N. B. (1965). The cohort as a concept in the study of social change. *American Sociological Review, 30,* 843-861.

Sadownick, D. (1997). *Sex between men: An intimate history of the sex lives of gay men postwar to the present.* San Francisco: Harper.

Savin-Williams, R. (1990). *Gay and lesbian youth: Expression of identity.* Washington, DC: Hemisphere Publications.

Savin-Williams, R. (1996). Ethnic- and sexual-minority youth. In R. C. Savin-Williams & K. M. Cohen (Eds.), *The lives of lesbians, gays, and bisexuals: Children to adults* (pp. 152-165). Fort Worth, TX: Harcourt Brace.

Savin-Williams, R. (1997). *And then I became gay: Young men's stories.* New York: Routledge.

Savin-Williams, R. (2001). *Mom, Dad, I'm gay.* Washington, DC: American Psychological Association.

Schuman, H., & Scott, J. (1989). Generations and collective memory. *American Sociological Review, 54,* 359-381.

Sears, J. (1991). *Growing up gay in the South: Race, gender, and journeys of the spirit.* Binghamton, NY: Harrington Park Press.

Sears, J. (1997). *Lonely hunters: An oral history of lesbian and gay southern life, 1948-1968.* Boulder, CO: Westview Press/Harper-Collins.

Seltzer, M. (1976). Suggestions for examination of time-disordered relationships. In J. Gubrium (Ed.), *Time, roles and self in old age* (pp. 111-125). New York: Human Sciences Press.

Serovich, J. M., Skeen, P., Walters, L. H., & Robinson, B. E. (1993). In-law relationships when a child is homosexual. *Journal of Homosexuality, 26,* 57-76.

Settersten, R. A., Jr. (1999). *Lives in time and place: The problems and promises of developmental science.* Amityville, NY: Baywood Publishing.

Shereshefsky, P., & Yarrow, L. (Eds.) (1973). *Psychological aspects of a first pregnancy and early postnatal adaptation.* New York: Raven Press.

Smith, J. D., & Manciske, R. J. (Eds.). (1997). *Rural gays and lesbians: Building on the strengths of communities.* Binghamton, NY: Harrington Park Press.

Sorokin, P., & Merton, R. (1937). Social time: A methodological and functional analysis. *The American Journal of Sociology, 42,* 615-629.

Stacey, J., & Biblarz, T. J. (2001). (How) does the sexual orientation of parents matter? *American Sociological Review, 66,* 159-183.

Stein, A. (1997). *Sex and sensibility: Stories of a lesbian generation.* Berkeley: University of California Press.

Sussman, M. (1965). Relationships of adult children with their parents in the United States. In E. Shanas and G. Streib (Eds.), *Social structure and the family: Generational relations* (pp. 62-92). Englewood Cliffs, NJ: Prentice-Hall.

Sweet, J. (1977). Demography and the family. *Annual Review of Sociology, 3,* 363-405.

Tobin, S. (1996). *Preservation of the self in the oldest years: With implications for practice.* New York: Springer Publications.

Troll, L. (1971). Issues in the study of generations. *International Journal of Aging and Human Development, 9,* 199-218.

Vacha, K. (1985). *A quiet fire: Memoirs of older gay men.* Trumansburg, NY: Crossing Press.

Vaillant, G., & Milofsky, E. (1980). Natural history of the male psychological life cycle: IX. Empirical evidence for Erikson's model of the life cycle. *American Journal of Psychiatry, 137,* 1348-1358.

Weissman, M., Myers, J., & Thompson, D. (1981). Depression and its treatment in a U.S. urban community, 1975-1976. *Archives of General Psychiatry, 38,* 417-421.

Weston, K. (1997). *Families we choose: Lesbians, gays, kinship.* New York: Columbia University Press.

Wythe, D., Merling, A., Merling, R., & Merling, S. (2000). *The wedding: A family's coming out story.* New York: Avon Books.

Zinik, G. (2000). Identity conflict or adaptive flexibility? Bisexuality reconsidered. In P. C. R. Rust (Ed.), *Bisexuality in the United States: A social science reader* (pp. 55-60). New York: Columbia University Press.

Chapter 3

Translove: Transgender Persons and Their Families

Gianna E. Israel

When I was invited to author for the premier issue of the *Journal of GLBT Family Studies* I found myself falling back on the old adage: "Write about what you know." After twenty years of being disowned by my biological family because I am transgender, I find myself keenly aware just how hard transgender men and women, like others in the GLBT community, must struggle to take their place at the family table and drink from the community well.

Transsexuals and cross-dressers, as well as drag queens and kings, comprise some of the individuals who fall under the transgender umbrella. Their needs start with basic acceptance of having a self-determined gender identity. This is similar to gays and lesbians wishing that their sexual orientation be respected (Brown & Rounsley, 1996). Other needs span a broad range of critical concerns. These include but are not limited to finding voice, gaining access to medical care, establishing fundamental civil protections, and maintaining and building families (Israel & Tarver, 1997).

GENERAL ISSUES

As a community counselor specializing in gender identity during the past sixteen years, I have identified those dynamics that are integral to understanding gender-identity issues and transgender persons. This chapter will focus primarily on transsexuals because it is those persons whose needs are the most likely to be misunderstood, who are repeatedly referred elsewhere or virtually ignored! Other transgender

doi:10.1300/5792_04

persons are important, too; however, they are more likely to find a niche where their differences are more readily accepted.

Understanding how people differ in their needs, experiences, beliefs, and identities speaks to the core of family members being able to get along, support each other, and even relate. When I started transgender transition as a young adult, at that time I was told that what I proposed was both "entirely unacceptable" and "unfathomable." Years later I have come to recognize the distinct weight and confusion the transgender person's loved ones bear when told of a contemplated or an impending transition.

For people who have an inkling of what gender issues are, a common sentiment expressed is, "Why can't you just be gay?" often followed by the sentiment, "It would be so much easier for everyone to accept and understand." For parties with no knowledge whatsoever of gender issues, disclosure for the new transman or transwoman becomes one of primarily adopting a caretaker role—usually to contain the family members' shock and distress—just at a time when the transgender person may need a great deal of support (Brown & Rounsley, 1996).

Subsequently, it is usually in everyone's best interests that disclosures to family be contained by speaking in very basic terms while at the same time emphasizing that the transgender person is in an exploration mode. Patience is needed because typically the person who is in the process of coming out as transgender does not have all the answers. He or she likely would not have many answers until an adequate knowledge base and set of transgender-related experiences have been established.

Because a dramatic disclosure may place the transgender person at risk, such as being thrown out of his or her home by other family members, it is best to gradually reveal information. This allows others to adjust to the situation, possibly affording the transperson time to make alternate arrangements in the event others do not come around.

Frequently, the first question a non-GLBT person asks of a transgender person is, "Does being transgender mean you are gay?" Here, at the onset of questioning, is where it is vital that correct, easy-to-understand information be relayed (Sullivan, 1990).

Sexual orientation indicates to whom a person is attracted. That can be to the same, opposite, both, or neither sexes. In other words, a person's sexual orientation can be gay, lesbian, bisexual, asexual, or heterosexual. This is true for transgender person, including those that transition, just as it is so for nontransgender persons.

Although this is an easy-to-understand concept for many GLBT readers, unfortunately it is not so easily understood by the general population. Also, stereotypes often inform people's assumptions. For example, a person's sexual orientation is not necessarily outwardly apparent. Often there is no reason for it to become a matter of public knowledge. For example, it is quite possible for straight-acting gay men to keep their sexual orientation to themselves. The same is true for transgender persons. In other words, unless a person is asked and chooses to disclose, his or her sexual orientation may be different from what others assume it to be (Cromwell, 1999).

Gender identity is defined and functions differently than sexual orientation. By definition it is comprised of (a) the maleness and femaleness a person feels on the inside; (b) how that gender identity is projected to the world; and (c) how others mirror that identity back to the individual.

For the sake of simplicity, let us create an imaginary character named Robert. If Robert feels like a guy on the inside, feels comfortable projecting his masculinity to others, and he then loves it when others respect these things about him—then it is reasonable to say Robert has a firmly rooted male gender identity. Each of the components constituting gender identity are inherently dynamic, yet they also work together. In Robert's situation these are consistent and feel comfortable to him.

Where the conundrum begins, however, is when these dynamics clash or are conflicted. Maybe Robert does not feel like a man or hates having a male body. Perhaps when he projects masculinity this does not feel like who he is or how he should act. What if Robert cringes whenever anyone acknowledges his masculinity? If these conflicts become persistent, then that, in sum, best describes *gender dysphoria* or *gender identity disorder* (Israel & Tarver, 1997).

Since the vast majority of people are perfectly comfortable with their gender identity, it becomes very difficult for others to relate to or understand what the transsexual person is experiencing. As humans we associate a person's identity with a fairly predictable set of criteria—sex, race, age, social status, character. This is especially so when we first meet someone.

In a general sense when a person is unfamiliar with transgender persons and does not know what name or gender pronoun to use, tactful questions can help dispel uncertainties. This is especially pertinent for persons who are in the process of or who have made permanent gender transitions. The more consistent a person appears and acts in the new gender, typically the less difficulty they are going to have in general social settings.

Matters become more complicated when the person is already known to others in one gender and announces his or her transition to people who have built a mental profile of who that person is. A few transgender persons find that family members are able to recognize that circumstances have been difficult or different for their loved one, and news received during disclosure is assimilated rapidly. For most family members, however, a concerted effort must be engaged to change preconceived profiles to meet or match those of the transperson (Boenke, 2003).

Gender identity is a matter of self-determination. This can be respected by observing a person's efforts at developing a consistent gender presentation and demeanor. If a male-born person consistently dresses as a woman and that person identifies as female, chances are that person wishes to be regarded as a woman. If she is permanently transitioning, she is considered male-to-female (MTF). Conversely, if a female-born person is apparently being all the man he can be, he generally will respond well to male affirmations. If he is permanently transitioning, he is considered female-to-male (FTM). Transgender persons need the same dignity and respect you would hope for if you looked in the mirror and did not see a familiar self looking back and thus were making extraordinary efforts to regain that sense of comfort and self-balance.

Later in this chapter case scenarios will help illustrate the preceding. Further, before we abandon defining sexual orientation, it is worth mentioning that I have observed in clinical practice that approximately three-fourths of transitioning persons will reexamine and explore their sexual orientation during transition. Of those who do this, approximately one-half will redefine their sexual orientation within the first few years of transitioning (Miller, 1996).

Although defining an outward gender identity becomes a fairly predictable process after a person's transition is established, actually recognizing impending change to sexual orientation is frequently much more surprising to transpeople and their loved ones. If this all seems amazing and confusing, initially it can be. I call this process of redefining sexual orientation the wild card of transition. A seasoned gender specialist can predict with reasonable accuracy where the cards may fall, but doing so may be counterproductive or fall on deaf ears.

Like young people going through puberty and exploring first-time intimate relationships, transitioning persons have to mature on their own terms (Cromwell, 1999)—and what a mystifying experience this exploration can be. How does a new woman (MTF) with an attraction to women express these unexpected feelings that conflict with an assumed or forced attraction to men to fulfill cultural (homophobic) biases that are expected of women?

Another example of this occurs when a new man (FTM) or transman finds himself sexually attracted to men. Most readers who can relate to sexual-orientation questions should be able to understand the following concept. Intrinsic differences exist between the way a woman feels toward men when she is attracted to them versus how a man might feel toward other men whom he finds sexually attractive and lovable. "I am attracted to men and want men to be attracted to my masculinity" is what gay FTM men are thinking. Transgender persons express a wealth of human diversity, and as with any population should be encouraged to safely explore these issues so that individuals can get their intimacy needs met.

FAMILY-OF-ORIGIN ISSUES

Returning to the primary theme of this chapter, we are left to ponder families who have a transgender member as well as the relationships transpeople choose. So much can be said about family of origin and how these persons look at a loved one's gender issues. Also, primary family issues are critical, such as when a transitioning person has a spouse or children or has been abandoned by these important persons. Finally, families of choice step beyond traditional roles but are no less important to the transman or woman, particularly when he or she has been disowned.

We know families of origin are changing beyond the stereotype of a father, mother, and any combination of older and younger siblings. However, other people also participate in raising a person. These can include second-degree relatives, such as aunts, uncles, and grandparents. However, as it was recently expressed to me by a client: "Any person who came through our door without knocking or using a key was considered family, and these adults were considered vital sources of guidance and comfort." Although this chapter will not further explore those relationships, it is worth recognizing that the family concept can be applied in a variety of meaningful ways for people.

Some families, parents in particular, are but a dream for many GLBT persons. These are comprised of those mothers and fathers who love unconditionally from the onset of a son or daughter's coming out. Like any parent, they are concerned and often have more questions than their offspring can answer right away, but they are supportive. They find nontoxic counseling, therapy, and support groups for their offspring and themselves. They support and aid disclosure to other family members. These are the parents who make all the difference in the world, and sometimes it just takes one to keep a transitioning person on a successful course.

I have noticed within my counseling practice that those individuals who have at least one parent or a close family member on their side often find just enough love and support to make it through unimaginable hardships associated with a harsh, transphobic society. Those who do not receive this support generally have a much harder time adjusting to society, employment, and relationship situations (Israel & Tarver, 1997).

For the remainder of transgender persons, including myself, being part of a family that does not care to understand about gender issues becomes a protracted process of trying to be heard and respected. Sometimes it happens partially; other times this just does not occur. The price GLBT persons pay for this ostracism is extremely high (Mottet & Ohle, 2003). Not only must a person spend more time adjusting to survive life, but he or she also invests enormous resources adjusting to and improving broken family dynamics. At worst, the parents fail to teach their offspring the basic social and relationship knowledge that most men and women know. The effect is best described as hobbling, and this often becomes the case for life.

Sibling relationships can be varied for each transgender person. Was it possible for the brothers and sisters to learn through their parents or on their own that gender or sexual differences are okay? If so, sometimes these persons turn out to become the new transperson's biggest cheerleader. Clients have reported to me that a brother or sister went out of his or her way to help the transgender person adjust to the new gender role. Guys will talk to their new brother about those things that men need to know and enjoy. Clothing, makeovers, and other subjects of concern to women become the focus within new sister relationships (Boenke, 2003).

The preceding all occurs when families talk. If a person's family does not, I strongly encourage new men and women to build on their relationships with other transgender friends or self-adopted family members so that these important functions occur (Brown & Rounsley, 1996). When sibling relationships fail, it is usually because these individuals adopted bigoted ideas from the parents or on their own. A simple example of this can be drawn from my own family. Since thrown out of the family home as a minor, even though twenty years have passed, I have heard from none of my siblings, and I am told that they are not interested in hearing from me. This is a significant loss of my familial community and the benefits that arise from those relationships. In the absence of biological family, as adults we will often cycle through adopted family as circumstances change. I can confidently say I would never have accomplished so much or had love in this lifetime without my adopted brothers and sisters.

CASE STUDY: A TRANSWOMAN (MTF)

Candy did not like riding the train to and from work each day. Men occasionally brushed up against her, and not having grown up as a woman sometimes it is difficult to know how to react. She decided that when she got home from work that she would call her mother. The attractive, blonde transgender woman looked at and appreciated her own reflection in the window. Very few people would ever guess her past as a tall, lanky male, climbing telephone poles as a line repairman. Now in her mid-twenties and fully transitioned, Candy was certain to attract other beautiful women. She felt some conflict with identifying herself as a lesbian. Not just yet, at least. After all, her mother was entirely supportive of her building a new life, but her father was not. How much more news could they possibly bear?

"It's unnatural, against God, and you'll bring a curse on the family," her father had said when she announced her transition plans several years ago, yet he allowed her to live at home. Since her mother and father divorced, Candy took turns staying with one or the other parent. This time around she stayed with her father. It was a bizarre relationship. This young new woman had spent hours on her appearance and undergoing painful electrolysis for facial hair removal. Then she spent several weeks recovering from genital reassignment surgery, yet her father still insisted on referring to her as "he." Even worse, when her father had company over, typically a woman from his own generation, he would introduce Candy as his son, usually with the forewarning, "Don't be scared by his appearance; he dresses like that to get attention."

On this particular evening Candy's telephone call with her mother went well. She was told to ignore light physical contact if it seemed accidental or not worth addressing, otherwise she needed to firmly but politely tell the man to give her space. What she heard made sense. Candy was grateful that her mother was available for these types of questions. She decided to tell her mother about her experiences dating women the next time they got together in person. As the call ended Candy's attention turned to thoughts of her father. What could be done?

The preceding scenario illustrates what often is the long-term result of disclosure to parents. Often one will be more understanding than the other to the point of being fully supportive. The other parent may adjust to the adult child's transition in order to avoid social embarrassment. In other words, some come around to a limited, partial acceptance. It is just enough to avoid major conflicts, but there may be no genuine effort to empathize.

Candy's situation is interesting because her father cares enough about his adult child to not throw her out on the street but has not yet learned to respect his new daughter's experiences. This young woman might consider confronting her father and saying how hurtful his behavior is, but the chance exists he may not care. If over time Candy finds that to be the case, it is in her best interests to limit contact with him since after a point trying to prove herself would be redundant and denigrating. Further, in order to engender empathy for her sexual-orientation issues, those people around her need to have a basic respect for others. Candy's mother has that, and there should not be a long-term problem with disclosing sexual orientation to her.

COUPLES' ISSUES

The child-parent case scenario in the preceding section illustrates dynamics that are similar to relationship issues that also can arise between the transgender person and his or her spouse and children. One prominent dynamic, which has been previously mentioned, is that most people find it challenging to set aside their preconceived ideas of who a loved one is and embrace the transperson's autonomy in self-determining his or her gender identity (Brown & Rounsley, 1996). Imagine the wide range of questions that may arise for a partner of a transgender person after a relationship of many years:

> "Is my husband a homosexual?" (MTF)
> "Is my partner straight or are we no longer lesbians?" (FTM)
> "Does my partner's being transgender suddenly invalidate the experiences we have shared?"
> "Why didn't my partner disclose gender issues sooner?"
> "Was he or she lying to me all of these years?"
> "Did I cause my partner to become transgender by not being man or woman enough?"
> "Is there something else wrong with me?"
> "Does still loving my partner after transition mean either of our sexual orientations have changed?"

As a reader, try and allow your mind to understand the implications of asking these questions. Couples may need to explore countless variations to these issues. Making sense of this new phenomenon in their lives is hard work. Those who are willing to communicate search for answers together, and redefine their relationship are the ones who benefit. They may forge a new partnership within their preexisting marriage or they may choose to be lovers or friends. After taking on responsibility to ensure that both parties will be okay, they may also choose to go separate ways. Those individuals willing to invest in each other despite the outcome are the real winners, and doing so takes extraordinary effort.

One dynamic which can inevitably become a hindrance to a couple's coming to terms with a partner's gender issues is when very rigid gender boundaries were the substance and norm of the relationship. People see their partners not only for how the loved one expresses himself or herself but also by formulating what characteristics an optimal mate should have. Breakups under these circumstances tend to become intolerant, and the transpartner may be told to move out of the family home quickly. When this occurs, transgender parents are then frequently denied access to children, and matters deteriorate rapidly from there (Miller, 1996).

Rather than focusing on the high drama of negative breakups, I encourage couples, if possible, to treat each other with the same basic dignity and respect that they had for each other during other difficult times during the relationship. Going back to the roots of the friendship allows the couple to plan a parting process. The couple needs to be mindful of how their behavior affects each other and their children, if they have any.

I have observed in counseling practice that a transsexual person can do a great deal of preparation for transition and can explore cross-gender roles to some extent while in a marital relationship. However, the end of the relationship is signaled when the transitioning person begins hormone treatments. Even when a couple plans on living together as friends, both parties should begin having their affairs in order at this critical stage. They need to define what alternatives exist so that each person can have his or her intimacy needs met, whether that be as a couple or as two independent persons.

Because individuals may transition gender at any time from late puberty to early old age, a variety of relationship situations may arise (Israel & Tarver, 1997). From observing trends among my clinical clients I have seen two peaks in age when transitioning is most likely to occur. The first peak arises when young persons grasp the mantle of adulthood. For some this will occur near high school graduation or during college. For those young people able to locate resources, it is a marvelously energetic time to learn survival both as an adult and transgender man or woman. Most fare very well if they can avoid parental conflicts and learn how to ward off peer harassment. In addition, if discretion is used in disclosing to romantic interests, most young adults are capable of forming long-term, meaningful relationships.

Some young persons who are thrown out or run away to escape an abusive home situation find at best their circumstances can be described as hellish—but not necessarily impossible. In my own experience I fell into this latter group. This occurred during the late 1970s and early 1980s when there was no room at the inn for transgender kids. The most common words I heard from almost all helping organizations was that my lifestyle did not fit into their religious beliefs. Countless homeless shelters turned away *sissy* and *sinful* minors like myself (Mottet & Ohle, 2003). This still occurs today, which explains why I am an advocate of secular-based, not faith-based, helping organizations. Today, with resources and educational programs opening to all, I have seen transgender youths move from being homeless to becoming new community leaders, lawyers, and doctors. Because this is a new evolution, the sense of gratitude I feel when I hear of this positive news can be compared to what GLBT persons often feel on the first occasion they see a male couple or female couple holding hands and walking down the street without harassment. Hope and freedom really is possible, for some.

The second peak of transitioning occurs in adults in the early forties group. Clinically, these are referred to as late-stage transsexuals (Miller, 1996). I do not endorse that term, however, because it places an unnecessary focus on age-based stereotypes and totally disregards the pretransitional aspects of a person's life. Individuals who transition later in life carry an amazing wealth of experiences and skills into transitioning and their new lives and, no different from other persons, the outcomes of these individuals' success at transitioning depends on their ability to surround themselves with transpositive resources and people.

CASE STUDY: A TRANSMAN (FTM)

Something was just nice about being a man. Jake could feel it every time a woman walked by, or for that matter sometimes a cute sissy guy. He would never say so out loud because saying such things could get him in trouble, but those sweethearts were put here to keep him happy. Now, if he could just find the right one to do so every day!

Eleven years of testosterone treatments had changed things. Jake's voice could never be mistaken for a woman's. He sure did not look like girl. With some serious weight lifting his body was muscular and hard. He had to be careful with his anger. Arms like his could swing out and hurt a softer person. Jake liked the feeling of having raw power. Yes, there was something nice about manhood and motherhood.

Well, imagine that! Some years back before transition Jake was involved with a woman. Then, Jake was a very butch woman. She and Valerie did not care what anyone said. They were the first lesbian couple in their city that they knew of who had a stand-in guy do the deed. Then came that little bundle of joy, so that's what they named their daughter. Joy still called him Mom, and that was fine, though Jake felt more like a father.

Ring! Ring! Tonight was the night. Jake rang the doorbell. He was going to get some. Well, get some of something, he just didn't quite know what. Tonight he was visiting an all-night sex party dubbed "Transmen, Drag Kings, Butches, and Their Honeys." What a sight to be seen! With dykes at every table Jake swore he must be the only man in the club. "Hey, I'm here, bring out the sweet honeys!" he felt like shouting.

At the bar our nice guy was in for a shock. "You can stay if you're trans-friendly, however this is a safe space for us . . . men really aren't allowed here," said a gal with a paste-on moustache. Jake reeled in shock but kept his mouth shut. This kind of party was the new trans, where being a man did not count for much and being a transsexual was like screaming, "Medical freak!" on a crowded bus.

If the preceding case scenario sounds odd, it should—because definitions of transgender and transsexual are changing. When I started my counseling practice in 1988, matters were slightly less complicated. Transsexuals wanted genital reassignment, and transgender was an umbrella term socially constructed to be inclusive of everyone (Israel & Tarver, 1997). In 2005, those differences which seemed to bring people together are, in some respects, driving transpersons apart.

Our nice guy Jake is basically a transman. He is a FTM transsexual. He has gone through transition and is well adjusted. Yet, after all this effort, he is encountering FTM transgender persons whose ideas are deconstructionist in nature. Any woman with masculine feelings can state that she "is now a new man" and demand to use the men's room—all of this without putting an effort into a masculine appearance or transition. These types of social changes are very confusing to the average transperson. Imagine if you can how dealing with a transgender mother or father must be for children. Again, here is another example of where keeping matters simplified is a good plan.

ISSUES AFFECTING CHILDREN

Looking at issues pertaining to children of transgender parents will be the last focus in this chapter. It is uplifting to learn that early in his life (as a woman) Jake strove for that sense of normalcy and family we all as GLBT persons seek (Boenke, 2003). He has been able to give his love to a daughter. Other GLBT people form many types of nontraditional relationships in order to get their relationship needs met. For many of us, children carry forward our hopes and dreams. If you have any doubt about this consider how much love and effort parents will put into their children so their offspring may have a better life than they did as children. Or contemplate the hurtful fact that many GLBT adults who may want children may never have them.

Unlike the adult loved ones of a transgender person, children are wholly dependent on their parents, transgender and nontransgender alike. When a transgender parent comes out, the probability is high that the subject of separation and divorce will arise. In those circumstances the couple must remember that children are supposed to be a product of two adults' love for each other. They should always be treated as such. Children are also their own unique young persons, and both parents must resolve to not make the parent's transgender issues about the children (Brown & Rounsley, 1996).

Just as with gay parenting, with transgender parents, there is the misconception that telling one's children at a young age causes harm. The common fear is that they will not understand or will develop confused ideas about sex and gender. It has been my experience in clinical practice that younger children actually adjust better than older children such as teenagers. After approximately age five, a child's gender and sexual orientation is generally intact (Israel, 1997). They may spend another decade or so adjusting to that and learning about the world and themselves. Children primarily look to their parents for love, comfort, and guidance.

Interestingly, the process of disclosing to children is fairly straightforward. Children want to know and should be reminded that they are loved unconditionally. They want to know things are going to be okay. One of the problems to arise for children of any age is that of peer harassment. Children need to be taught to articulate that their mom or dad being different is about the parent, not the child. Moreover, children need to be taught to stand up to bullies, and when that does not succeed parents and teachers are responsible for intervening (Brown & Rounsley, 1996).

Earlier in this chapter I stated that the brothers and sisters of a transgender adult often will react to gender issues, depending upon what lessons they learned in life about people who are different. The same is true for every child of a transgender parent. Younger children are still dependent on their parents for guidance; however, older ones—particularly teens—may have begun adopting their own ideas and plans for life. Who they identify as may not include having a transgender parent, and in some instances teens and adult children reject the situation entirely.

Does the preceding mean that older children would not come around? Not necessarily. However, the onus is on the transgender parent to relay lessons about *differences* with the hope that the children eventually do (Boenke, 2003).

CONCLUSION

In conclusion I have good news to report. The vast majority of transgender men and women lead positive, fulfilled, family-focused lives. Even as walking targets of hatred and prejudice, these courageous persons find ways to keep hope alive. As a reader, you can contribute to that process by taking the time to learn about your transgender brothers and sisters. Ask questions, socialize, and give others the same opportunities in life that you hope for yourself. It is equally important that you share of yourself—we want and need to know about your ideas and experiences. This is what being family is all about.

REFERENCES

Boenke, M. (2003). *Transforming families: Real stories about transgendered loved ones.* Hardy, VA: Oak Knoll Press.

Brown, M., & Rounsley, C. (1996). *True selves: Understanding transsexualism.* San Francisco: Jossey-Bass.

Cromwell, J. (1999). *Transmen and FTM's: Identities, bodies, genders and sexualities.* Chicago: University of Illinois Press.

Israel, G. (1997). Impact on children. Retrieved December 17, 2005 from http://www.firelily.com/gender/gianna/impact.children.html.

Israel, G., & Tarver, D. (1997). *Transgender care: Recommended guidelines, practical information, and personal accounts.* Philadelphia: Temple University Press.

Miller, N. (1996). *Counseling in genderland: A guide for you and your transgendered client.* Boston: A Different Path Press.

Mottet, L., & Ohle, J. (2003). *Transitioning our shelters: A guide to making homeless shelters safe for transgender people.* New York: The National Coalition for the Homeless and the National Gay and Lesbian Task Force Policy.

Sullivan, L. (1990). *Information for the female-to-male cross-dresser and transsexual.* Seattle, WA: Ingersoll Gender Center.

INTRODUCTORY TRANSGENDER RESOURCES

Literature

Brown, M., & Rounsley, C. (1996). *True selves—Understanding transsexualism.* San Francisco: Jossey-Bass.

Devor, H. (1997). *FTM: Female-to-male transsexuals in society*. Bloomington: Indiana University Press.
Halbertstam, J. (1998). *Female masculinity*. Durham, NC: Duke University Press.
Israel, G., & Tarver, D. (1997). *Transgender care: Recommended guidelines, practical information, and personal accounts*. Philadelphia: Temple University Press.
Prieur, A. (1998). *Mexico City: On transvestites, queens, and machos*. Chicago: University of Chicago Press.

National Organizations

Transgender Forum
http://www.tgforum.com/
Transgender Aging Network
c/o Loree Cook Daniels, 6990 N. Rockledge Avenue, Glendale, WI 53209
E-mail: LoreeCD@aol.com
http://www.forge-forward.org/
Transgender aging and social support

Chapter 4

A Family Matter: When a Spouse Comes Out As Gay, Lesbian, or Bisexual

Amity P. Buxton

Spring 2003: A United States congresswoman proposes an amendment to the Constitution limiting marriage to a man and a woman.

November 2003: The Massachusetts supreme court affirms the constitutionality of civil marriage between two adults of the same gender in that state.

January 2004: The president of the United States announces a billion-and-a-half-dollar initiative to promote marriage, shortly after proclaiming Marriage Protection Week.

February 2004: The new mayor of San Francisco issues marriage licenses to same-gender couples, including two lesbians who had been together for fifty-one years. Nine days later, the governor orders the attorney general to stop further issuance of licenses.

Though from opposite ideological poles and on a collision course, these escalating actions that affected the state and national political campaigns that autumn were all taken in support of the institution of marriage. At one pole, conservative politicians, organizations, and religious denominations decried the erosion of marriage, citing biblical passages, cultural history, and sociological studies about the effects of broken homes and single parents and predicted that same-gender marriages will increase that erosion. At the other extreme, progressive politicians, advocacy groups, and some faith communities sought legal sanction of same-gender marriages, citing research data and

doi:10.1300/5792_05

examples of long-term relationships, responsible partnering, and robust family units.

The Massachusetts court decision was the tipping point for these escalating actions and also the apex of years of work by same-gender couples to gain the legitimacy of a civil marriage. In contrast to these lengthy efforts was the ease by which starlet Britney Spears married a friend in Las Vegas on a whim just before President George W. Bush announced his marriage initiative. Impetuous as these young people were, the marriage was so legal that only a civil annulment could undo it. Contrasting with the long-term commitment of many same-gender couples is the 50 percent of legally married couples who divorce.

In between these contrasts is a little-known cadre that belongs to both sides of the current marriage debate: mixed-sexual-orientation couples in which one spouse is heterosexual and the other is gay, lesbian, or bisexual. Among the bisexuals, many suspected or knew they were attracted to persons of the same gender and wanted a long-term relationship. They also knew they could not achieve that goal in a same-gender marriage.

The lack of legally recognized same-gender marriage and societal expectations to marry someone of the opposite gender drew them away from admitting or acting on their same-gender attraction and toward marrying in the traditional mode. Denying, hiding, or repressing their same-sex desires, they decided to marry. Most loved their fiancée (Ross, 1983). Those who knew they were homosexual were not sexually attracted to their fiancés. A few told their fiancés, vowing to make the marriage work and believing that marrying was the right thing to do or that it would stop them from having same-gender feelings.

Once married, many had children. Those who knew or suspected their same-gender attractions repressed them or acted on them secretly. Those who were unaware of these feelings discovered them. Denial and suppression gnawed at their self-esteem and hope for a happy marriage and often made them become less present to their straight spouses. In the end, no longer able to deny or repress their same-gender desires, many acknowledged them and came out to their spouses. Some did so early in the marriage, others after ten or fifteen years, and still others after twenty-five to forty years.

Unlike coming out as a single person, the disclosure was a family matter, profoundly affecting their spouses and children. No matter how much either spouse wanted to preserve the marriage or how much they loved each other, the revealed gap of their sexual orientation made it difficult to attain that goal. Ultimately, the majority divorced, separated for periods from their children, and often lived as single parents.

The persons whom this divorce statistic represents differ from typical couples. Both spouses become prey to antigay attitudes or actions in their community, workplace, or faith community. The heterosexual spouses struggle for many years to resolve concerns about sexual rejection and deception, traditional concepts of marriage and gender, and, as did their disclosing spouses, long-held attitudes about homosexuality. Their minor children, as with most children of divorce, suffer abandonment issues and a division of loyalties, and having a gay, lesbian, or bisexual parent exacerbates these concerns. Playmates or schoolmates tease them for having such parents or hurt them indirectly by making antigay remarks. The disclosure confuses teenagers as they develop their own identities, sexualities, and value systems. Many children get caught in the middle of adult debates about gay and lesbian families.

The minority of couples who stay married struggle privately to integrate the disclosed circumstances into their lives and still appear to outsiders as opposite-gender couples. As they work to maintain their marriages, they stay closeted to avoid antigay attacks and being found out at work, in social circles, or within their faith community.

Therein lies the tragedy that this chapter addresses. Both spouses in a mixed-orientation marriage value the institution of marriage, but the difference of sexual orientations compromises their ability to realize their hopes within the form of marriage espoused for centuries. Ironically, until the disclosure, many of them and their children were seen as model families, and a number exemplified the church-going, nuclear-family ideal. Had the heterosexual spouse married a heterosexual partner and the gay, lesbian, or bisexual spouse who was more strongly drawn to same-gender persons married a homosexual partner, both spouses would more likely have achieved the values of marriage and family that contribute to the stability of our society.

Instead, husbands and wives are coming out and families are breaking up in growing numbers since such events first came to public notice in the 1980s (Auerback & Moser, 1989; Buxton, 2001). The increase of gay, lesbian, and bisexual persons in public positions and multiplication of support organizations and Internet venues for homosexual and bisexual persons have encouraged those who are married to validate their same-gender attractions and come out. In my role as executive director of the Straight Spouse Network (SSN), an organization of straight spouses and mixed-orientation couples, I hear from four to five new individuals daily. SSN support groups and Internet lists draw about 7,000 spouses at any one period—doubling in two years.

It is estimated that up to 2 million gay, lesbian, or bisexual adults in the United States have been or are married (Buxton, 2001), yet mixed-orientation couples are overlooked in the current gay marriage arguments, barely touched upon in the literature, and often inappropriately counseled by therapists with little knowledge about such marriages. Thus, we lack key information that might help us better examine family issues implied by both sides of the marriage debate, expand our understanding of core ingredients of a healthy relationship regardless of the gender of the partners, and provide more effective help for families of mixed-sexual-orientation couples. To remedy that lack, this chapter presents what is known about spouses in postdisclosure, mixed-orientation marriages and their children. It concludes with a sketch of possible trends for families in which one or both partners are gay, lesbian, or bisexual and how we might bring about a more promising future for them and increase the number of lasting marriages and strong families.

WHERE WE ARE

The following description of mixed-orientation marriages is based on my continuing review of the literature and self-reports from over 8,000 gay, lesbian, bisexual, transgender, and heterosexual spouses in such marriages gathered over eighteen years in my research and as executive director of SSN. The network's seventies support groups in the United States and six in the European Union, South Africa, Australia, and Switzerland; Internet e-mailing lists; and contacts in every U.S. state and eleven other countries have put me in touch with spouses representing a cross-section of location, ethnicity, race, socioeconomic class, educational level, age, religion, and political party. Because much has been written about coming-out experiences of gay, lesbian, and bisexual persons (see References), the emphasis here is on the heterosexual spouses, the couples, and their children.

After summarizing the coming-out process of married gay, lesbian, or bisexual spouses, I describe common issues of heterosexual spouses and stages through which they typically progress. Next is an analysis of the stages through which mixed-orientation couples move. Finally, I summarize children's concerns and parenting behaviors that help them cope. Two caveats: the description covers known spouses only (though many describe their experiences when "unknown") and common, typical experiences—not the multiplicity of individual stories.

GAY, LESBIAN, AND BISEXUAL SPOUSES

By the time gay, lesbian, or bisexual spouses come out to their spouses, they have worked at least partially through a web of deterrents such as, social expectations, long-held religious and moral values, and antigay societal attitudes. Whether they knew, denied, or were unaware of their same-gender attractions before marrying, their reactions and behaviors as they discovered or rediscovered them in the marriage included most of the following:

1. surprise that their same-gender feelings are still there or confusion at discovering them;
2. guilt and self-hate for having those feelings when married;
3. questioning feelings, searching for information and validation, and experimenting with homosexual behaviors;
4. therapy to accept their orientation or to attempt to change their attractions and behavior; and
5. inadvertent infatuation or falling in love—reliving their adolescence, now with same-gender attractions.

Internal conflict predominated. As they felt more like themselves, many felt more restricted by their marriage. Responsibilities, the structure of married life, and, often, parenthood intensified their turmoil and guilt more than if they were single—a struggle documented in autobiographical accounts (Abbott & Farmer, 1995; Bauman, 1986; Norman, 1998; White, 1994; Whitehead, 1997). Although a few tell their wives or husbands early on, most spend months and some spend years before disclosing. Some never come out. Others deny it even to husbands or wives who discover clues, such as stained underwear, condoms in a gym bag, gay porn on the Internet, phone numbers on matchbooks, phone or restaurant bills, or e-mails and notes expressing love to someone of the same gender.

Disclosure starts the second wave of coming out in a family. Issues of their spouses and children and how they typically resolve them are detailed elsewhere (Buxton, 1994, 1999). Here, their experience is painted with a broad brush.

HETEROSEXUAL SPOUSES

Whether their partners disclosed or the heterosexual spouses discovered evidence of same-sex attraction or activity, heterosexual spouses' concerns revolve initially around sexuality, marriage, and children and then address identity, integrity, and their belief systems. Their husbands or wives tussled with concerns in these same areas, but the heterosexual spouses' concerns are different. Resolving them is not a linear process, as the following analysis suggests. The issues overlap and recur, yet certain concerns seem to dominate the spouse's struggle in the order presented.

Initial concerns relate to aspects of their immediate, everyday lives. Sexual rejection as a man or a woman is one of the first of which they are aware, making many feel sexually inadequate or undesirable. This self-image is often reinforced by their partners' former or current criticism or lack of sexual interest. Spouses of bisexual mates think they were not sexual enough to keep the partners' same-gender attraction from becoming active. Other spouses feel they were sexually shortchanged, that their years in the marriage were wasted, and that their damaged sexuality may never heal. Those who had satisfying marital sex or continue lovemaking after disclosure become confused. Wives whose husbands acted outside the marriage fear exposure to a sexually transmitted disease (STD), especially AIDS, and often get tested. Pregnant wives fear for their fetuses. The coming out also makes the spouses' heterosexuality an issue. Some question their orientation for a while.

Regarding the marriage, most spouses continue to love their partners and wonder whether the marriage will continue. Some deny that it might not. Others, hoping their marriage will last, question what form it might take. Could they handle nonmonogamy? Would their partners agree to be monogamous? Some worry that their partners might leave or question whether they themselves should leave. A number become aware of marital difficulties previously ignored, becoming less certain about staying together or clear that this is a last straw. If the partners were active or have lovers, many want to end the marriage or fear that their partners will leave. Those who discovered clues that their partners deny as proof wonder if they can live with "an elephant in the living room."

Spouses worry how children will be affected by having a gay, lesbian, or bisexual parent and will want to protect them from any hurt. Major questions are how and what to tell them, what friends and schoolmates will say, and whether they might turn out to be gay or bisexual, too. Most spouses worry about how a possible family break will affect the children.

This cluster of problems revolves around the disclosure and stays center stage for about a year. Often empathetic with their partners' struggle, most spouses cannot focus, sleep, or eat. Some become suicidal. Gradually, they become aware of their own issues regarding identity, integrity, and belief system. A common trigger for this shift is asking, "What about me?" In answer, many discover low self-worth. Some had self-esteem issues before marrying, but many lost self-confidence as their partners blamed them for this or that. Many assumed the criticized behavior explained why their partners did not find them desirable or complained that they were uncommunicative or not a good wife or husband. Hoping to kindle sexual interest, quell criticism, or please their partners, spouses accommodated their wishes until little of their own identity remained.

Heterosexual spouses also feel deceived, no matter how little time elapsed between the disclosing partners' self-admission that they were gay, lesbian, or bisexual and their disclosure or their spouses' discovery. If their partners are active or have a lover, the deception is devastating. Feeling duped by the person with whom they were most intimate and whom they trusted the most provokes a deep sense of betrayal. They lose trust in their partner and in their own judgment and perception. Those who grew up believing that homosexuality is morally wrong are stricken to discover they are married to someone whom their church or temple condemns and who is the parent of their children. In one fell swoop, their moral compass is shattered, leaving them no measure of what is true or false, right or wrong. Their integrity is at stake.

Like their partners, many spouses feel stigmatized by and powerless in the face of social attitudes against homosexuality or same-sex behavior. As one husband and father of two teenagers said, "We will never receive a reasonable forum to make society understand that making it difficult to be gay impacts the lives of more than just the gay person." Many spouses keep the disclosure secret, fearing that their partners might lose their jobs or positions in their church, temple, or community. Others, told by their partners not to tell, make up stories to explain their partners' whereabouts to family and friends. Unused to lying, they are disturbed by covering for their partners. If the spouse does share the secret with a trusted family member or friend, he or she is often uncomfortable with homosexuality and reacts negatively or urges the spouse to leave the marriage quickly. Such pressure increases a spouse's guilt.

Spouses in faith communities that condemn homosexuality face intense challenges. Some, after reflection, condemn the sin but continue to love the sinner. Others reconcile what their doctrine says with their own positive experience of being married to such an "evil" person. Still others discard dogmatic beliefs and work out their own moral position. These stay quietly in their church or temple, choose another denomination, or lose their faith entirely.

The disclosure or discovery also shatters spouses' concepts of marriage, gender, sexuality, and life's meaning. Marriage is not forever. Men and women are not always attracted to the opposite gender. For spouses of bisexual partners—attracted to both men and women—the either-gay-or-straight binary view of sexuality no longer holds. Besides having to rethink their assumptions and expectations in these basic areas of their lives, they also feel bereft of long-held beliefs that formed their blueprint for living. Values that had given their life meaning are in shambles. The breakdown of belief systems, loss of integrity, and sexual rejection are the most disturbing issues and the ones that take the longest time to resolve.

Working through these and the more practical concerns proceeds in stages. The stages overlap, but most spouses seem to progress in a forward direction from shock to incorporating the new information into their lives. Their challenge differs from that of their partners in that the change to be incorporated is not theirs. Initial reactions are a mix of shock and disbelief, devastation and relief to know the truth, futility, and hope. Denial of the meaning and implication of the disclosure is common. As spouses handle daily family activities, they gradually become aware of new factors that stem from their husbands' or wives' new identity and/or gay-related activities. Partners may spend more time at the computer, more telephone calls may come from strangers, and outside activities may take partners away from the family circle. The partners' hairstyle, clothes, conversations, and interests often change so much that some spouses call them "pod people"—inhabited by aliens. Noticing such changes, spouses feel abandoned.

Within the first or second year, most spouses regain enough equilibrium to face the reality of such changes and their own pain. Many hesitate in examining the reality for fear of finding out what it portends. Once they look candidly at what is going on, they slowly realize the changes are there to stay. They cannot undo them. The partner is not going to stop being attracted to the same gender. Acknowledging that the disclosure was not a bad dream, spouses finally admit their pain—no more denial or cheerful pretence.

As spouses look objectively at their pain and postdisclosure lives, they begin to understand what the coming out actually implies about them, their marriage, and their children. Accepting these implications provokes perhaps the most intense outbursts of anger as they realize that they can never regain what they thought the marriage was. Decisions were made for them unilaterally; they lived someone else's lie; they must start a new life within or outside the marriage; and, if they divorce, their children will suffer.

Once spouses accept their current reality, they next let go of the past, including assumptions about their marriages, their partners, and their futures. No longer clinging to the marriage, partner, and themselves as they were, they grieve all their losses, leading to a long period of mourning. For spouses who separate or divorce, letting go includes learning to unlove the spouse romantically. A last step for some is forgiveness.

Spouses usually start to heal by the third year. This stage coincides with their dealing with identity issues and encompasses hands-on care of their physical, sexual, mental, emotional, and spiritual health.

Their gradual healing reinforces their forming a stronger sense of worth and confidence.

As healing proceeds, most spouses begin to reconfigure their lives. The partners' coming out changed so many parts of their lives and shattered so many assumptions about basic concepts that spouses cannot rebuild. Instead, they spread out their values on the table to decide which they want to preserve. Needs are examined and prioritized. Strengths are unearthed or discovered, and weaknesses admitted and strengthened. As they weed out superficial interests, cultivate neglected ones, and plant new ones, most find something of meaning beyond immediate problems, often in the arts, nature, sports, philosophy, or spirituality. About three years after disclosure, spouses begin to reconfigure all aspects of their being and create a new blueprint for living based on a realistic appraisal of their lives and framed with new purpose and hope.

Transformation is the last stage, when they act on their new belief systems and gain perspective—whether divorced or still married. They laugh again, hone parenting skills, find new jobs or avocations, start careers or resume ones left for marriage, finish college or seek an advanced degree, develop a wider social network, help other spouses in similar situations, date if they divorce or recommit to marriage, or become advocates for social justice.

Spouses' progress in dealing with these challenges is never smooth or evenly paced. Ultimately, each resolves issues by himself or herself. Obstacles unrelated to the disclosure often interfere, such as illness or death in the family, a child's accident, or a job loss. More important, what seems like a volcano of emotions makes it harder to clarify concerns and compromises their ability to resolve them constructively (Buxton, 2004a).

Emotions surge in clusters, but one seems to predominate at each stage. Hurt experienced as fear, anger, and grief is the most intense and persistant, often erupting like land mines. Some spouses become stuck in one of these emotions and its explosive power turns back onto them. Feeling hurt colors the early months, when pain is most keen. When hurt feelings persist, spouses take on a victim self-image and blame disclosing spouses instead of taking responsibility for resolving their own problems. Anger arises in several stages, including rage at possible sexual damage and possible exposure to STDs, wrath over the deception, fury at the changes in their lives, frustration that their spouses are liberated from their closet while they are now in it, irritation that they are dealing with fallout on the family while their spouses are out and about and resentment that their dreams are destroyed as their spouses are realizing new ones. If spouses cannot resolve their anger, their health becomes at risk, and they become bitter and vindictive. Fear is felt most during the accep-tance stage. This can be generalized fear of the unknown, panic about the possible end of the marriage, anxiety about children, uneasiness about others' reactions, or terror about beginning a new life alone. Spouses who become obsessed with fears about what might or might not happen become paralyzed, taking no steps to deal with present reality. The last major emotion, grief, becomes strongest as spouses let go of the past. Unlike widows or widowers, they still encounter their partners' physical presence. Although bereaved persons find sympathy from friends and family, mixed-orientation spouses find few who understand their loss. Persisting grief leads to clinical depression, despair, and suicidal thoughts or attempts.

Working through feelings and issues typically lasts at least three years and often six or more. Most spouses feel that they are battling on their own against something they do not understand and over which they have no control. Compounding this sense of powerlessness is exhaustion from working on the marriage, parenting, taking care of home and family, and often working at a job, where they tell no one what is going on. Isolation magnifies their view of problems and intensifies emotions.

Isolated, spouses feel more and more helpless until they find others fighting the same issues. Finding peers, most explode in gratitude—"I am not alone; I am not crazy." Peers in face-to-face or Internet groups know immediately what spouses are talking about, validate their feelings, nurture their self-confidence, explain that they were not the cause of their spouses' turning gay, lesbian, or bisexual, and reassure them that they will get through the crisis and achieve strength and understanding. As real-life examples of alternate ways of handling issues, pointing out problem areas and constructive strategies, and offering reality checks for feelings, peers are the spouses' most helpful resources.

If a spouse stays angry, fearful, hurt, and grieving for a prolonged period, most peers advise him or her to seek therapy. Therapists who understand the impact of disclosure provide the most effective help.

In some cases, however, therapists' assumptions that mixed-orientation marriages never last, lack of knowledge about homosexuality or bisexuality, or negative judgments about same-sex behavior interfere with their grasping the source of a spouse's bitterness, victimization, despair, or panic. In other cases, therapists offer suggestions that are irrelevant to disclosure issues or advise spouses to divorce and move on. Not finding therapeutic help increases spouses' pain.

With peer support and relevant therapeutic help, most spouses keep moving forward. Progress is slow and cannot be hurried. Sometimes, spouses pause to view how far they have come and to sight paths ahead. Those who rush find themselves in a few years facing all the unresolved issues and accumulated feelings that lay churning inside.

MIXED-ORIENTATION COUPLES

The spouses' journey proceeds side by side with that of their gay, lesbian, or bisexual partners. Yet, the latter are way ahead of the heterosexual spouses in resolving issues. Most have somewhat accepted their sexual orientation, though some may still be trying to reconcile conflicting identities and integrate their orientation with societal or religious values. Most have begun to heal and are starting to reconfigure themselves as married or soon-to-be formerly married persons. As they step forward with new personae and behaviors developed to at least the toddler stage, the heterosexual spouses are just being born into the disclosure world. The two spouses usually stay out of step for up to three years.

How they deal with their relationship issues varies from couple to couple. A couple's decisions depend on their age, length of marriage, geographic location, faith community, work situation, and their children's needs. However, there is no single route that couples in any one demographic group take, and all do not reach the same outcome. Despite such differences, couples report a common pattern of strategies and stages of decision making (Buxton, 2001; 2004a,b).

About a third of known mixed-orientation marriages break up shortly after the disclosure or discovery. The disclosing partners leave to be with their lovers or to live in the gay culture, or the heterosexual spouses ask their partners to leave because of the betrayal or their own moral judgment against homosexual behavior. The remaining two-thirds of couples stay together to examine, try out, clarify, and prioritize individual and relational needs, wants, values, and goals.

Immediately after the disclosure, couples who stay together often become closer. They now share the partners' secret, and the disclosing partners are gratified if not astounded that they were not rejected. Some call it the honeymoon period. Lovemaking is often more frequent, and both want to explore all possibilities to stay married. As they work on their relationship, most couples do not tell outsiders except perhaps a trusted family member or friend, a counselor, or a clergyperson. They read about and discuss issues, and some find a face-to-face or Internet support group of peers.

Integrating the partner's new identity and life into family activities usually preoccupies a couple. For a time, children's needs may get less attention as disclosure concerns mount or gay-related events compete with family activities such as the children's school plays or soccer games. At the same time, financial difficulties, family illness, sick relatives, or family events often interfere with their postdisclosure work.

As couples try to figure out ways to stay married, a major question is what form their marriage might take. Spouses weigh alternatives in the light of beliefs about marriage and homosexuality. The most common choices are monogamy, open marriage for one or both, or a closed loop (the spouse has one committed lover, often also married). Among couples who choose monogamy, some, believing that homosexual behavior is wrong and marriage is forever, create a celibate monogamous marriage. Others embrace homosexuality or bisexuality but decide to be monogamous because they both believe that monogamy is the proper form of marriage. The disclosing partners love and feel so committed to their spouses that they want to express their love sexually only to them, or the heterosexual spouses do not want their partners to be intimate with anyone else.

Couples who choose an open or closed-loop marriage value the quality of their relationship as more important than its structure and ignore societal or religious proscriptions against extramarital sex or homosexual behavior. Their rationale is that the heterosexual spouse cannot satisfy the gay or lesbian partner's sexual needs or the same-gender needs of the bisexual spouse. As long as both spouses freely agree to an extramarital relationship, it is not infidelity. In most cases, the outside relationship is secondary to the marriage. Protected sex is required and the arrangement is usually kept secret from anyone outside the arrangements. Fewer heterosexual spouses seek lovers than their partners; many fear their partners may fall in love and leave.

The different stages at which the individual spouses are involved (in processing the disclosed orientation) often interfere with couple communication and problem solving, especially early on. Heterosexual spouses' pain, anger, fear, and sadness may make it difficult to listen empathetically to their partners' problems or delight in their new interests. Meanwhile, as the disclosing spouses gain self-confidence and feel more at peace about their same-gender attraction, many find the marital arrangement confining. They become withdrawn and depressed, and their distress upsets or saddens their wives and husbands.

In other cases, the gay, lesbian, or bisexual partners become more absorbed in their coming-out activities and less involved in the marriage and family. When their spouses express jealousy, anger, or hurt about neglect, the partners often become defensive or accuse them of being homophobic. To avoid further pain, some heterosexual spouses suggest limits about what they want to know or not know about their partners' gay activities and/or suggest times for their spouses to go out and come home. The disclosing spouses often react by saying that their spouses are controlling. Arguments, blow-ups, and meltdowns follow, often to be later regretted or denied.

Diverging trajectories such as these reach a crisis point sometime in the second year or so after the disclosure. When one or both spouses sense such distancing, about half of the couples divorce—some to keep their friendship alive before they become enemies, others to end the struggle, and still others to free each other to live a more fulfilling life.

The remaining couples take a different route. One or the other calls a halt to the rising discord in order to take stock of common concerns relating to the overarching value of their relationship. Together, they decide to redefine the marriage and adjust their interaction so that it meets the needs and goals of each of them. Heterosexual spouses seek to understand their partners' needs and adapt their thinking and behavior accordingly. Lesbian, gay, or bisexual spouses temper their new pursuits to refocus on their spouses' needs. Together, they clarify values to embody in the marriage and family.

Honest communication, peer support, and taking time to redefine their marriage are strategies most often reported by couples who stay married for several years or more after the disclosure (Buxton, 2001; 2004a). They talk and listen to each other with candor and not defensiveness, explicitly commit to the marriage, and compromise to set mutually agreed-upon boundaries. Disclosing spouses reassure their spouses of their love, and many couples continue intimacy if not lovemaking. For bisexual-heterosexual couples, because of the bisexual spouses' dual attraction, marital sex is mutually pleasurable. Problems are spelled out and resolved with flexibility and resilience in a trial-and-error process. They show mutual respect and support, demonstrate love, and keep their friendship alive while respecting each other's space, interests, and autonomy. Some couples take time off from disclosure issues just to enjoy each other's company. Peer support provides the most help. Couples counseling helps some couples, especially when therapists guide them to develop effective communication strategies.

After two or three years, about half of these couples decide to divorce, believing that separation is the better way for each of them to grow, maintain their friendship, and give their children the attention they need. Through their joint work to stay married, many have a deeper bond than that of most heterosexual couples. Following their divorce, they provide their children with homes grounded in love, truth, and justice.

The remaining half of these couples (roughly a sixth of all postdisclosure couples) stay together for three or more years after the disclosure. Their decision is based on the belief that their marriage enables each of them to grow mentally, emotionally, and spiritually; to practice truth, love, and equality in their lives; and to provide a loving, caring, and secure home for their children.

CHILDREN OF MIXED-ORIENTATION COUPLES

For couples with children, informing them that a parent is gay, lesbian, or bisexual is of major concern. Most feel that the truth is important, more than the hurt it might cause, and that family secrets are toxic. The key question is when and how to tell.

Timing depends on many factors. Older children, looking back, say that it is best to disclose sooner rather than later so that the children do not feel that they were not trusted. If the disclosing parent is out publicly, parents want the children to know before hearing from outsiders, who may have antigay attitudes or inaccurate ideas about being gay. Many wait until the heterosexual parent is enough at ease with the disclosure that he or she can model acceptance rather than distress. In some cases, both parents tell the children. In other cases, the gay, lesbian, or bisexual parent alone tells them. If the disclosing parent does not want the children to know, the other parent sometimes tells them, thinking that it is important that they know, or to answer a child's question. Others refer children to the disclosing parent.

The gay or bisexual parent fears rejection, confusion, or anger when they tell their children. In fact, initial reactions vary. Some are shocked or confused, and some show no reaction but go about their business. Others fear it means divorce. If deception was involved, many become angry. Since children are keen observers and sensitive to what happens in a family, some suspected something serious was going on and are glad that it was not the worst news that they feared, such as a terminal disease.

In the children's eyes, their parent remains their parent regardless of sexual orientation. However, the parent's sexual orientation has an effect on them that varies depending on their age. Preschoolers do not understand sexual orientation but know about a parent's love and same-gender friendships. School-age children may know about gay characters on television and the pejorative use of *gay* or *dyke* in their school or neighborhood but now those topics and terms gain a personal meaning. Children fear friends' reactions and rejection. Middle school children, not wanting to appear different, try to hide their parent's orientation. Those whose parents have a same-gender partner may give the partner a false identity, such as "aunt." Those in conservative faith communities fear that their parent will go to hell. For teenagers, the disclosure intensifies developmental concerns about their own sexuality, identity, and future goals.

If the parents decide to divorce, the divorce is the more upsetting news. The two-parent unit appears to provide children with a safety net. Losing that raises fears of being permanently separated from the noncustodial parent or abandoned by the custodial parent. They feel conflicting loyalties and do not want to divide time between two homes. Having one of their parents be gay, lesbian, or bisexual exacerbates those feelings. Parents advise not telling children about the divorce and the partner's sexual orientation at the same time, lest the children blend the announcements and blame the disclosing parent for the divorce.

When told about the divorce, children want reassurance that their lives will not change too much, that both parents still love them, and that they will have a caring, safe home with both parents. Once the divorce occurs, gay-related issues mount for children when they spend time in their gay parents' homes, especially those with a same-gender partner. Many middle school children do not want their parents' lovers at events or evidence of their existence in the home when friends visit. Sometimes, playmates cannot play with them in that home. Some heterosexual parents become concerned about the children's exposure to same-gender hugging and kissing or sleeping arrangements. In most cases, the two parents negotiate what to do based on standards applicable to having any boyfriend, girlfriend, or stepparent in a divorced parent's home.

Whether their parents stay together or divorce, children crave good parenting. Sexual orientation has nothing to do with effective or ineffective parenting. Children want both parents to be there for them, caring for them, setting limits, and paying attention to them. They want them to listen to their fears, worries, and anger about their parent's being gay without getting mad. They do not want their parents fighting. They want the noncustodial parent to keep his or her word about visits, calls, or attendance at school events. If their noncustodial parent has a lover, they want their parent to spend time with them, not the lover, when they visit or travel together.

Because of typical divorce factors—not sexual orientation—effective parenting after divorce does not always occur. Either parent can disappoint a child. Some with unresolved issues say negative things about the other parent. Often the parents who came out become so absorbed in their new lives that they neglect the children. Others, due to psychological problems or antigay beliefs, engage in custody battles that hurt the children. In other cases, stepparents make antigay remarks, or same-gender partners disparage the straight parent. In time and with support, many parents become more cooperative (Buxton, 2000).

By the time they are young adults, most children have worked through their concerns. They no longer feel embarrassed or fear rejection, and many appreciate the courage of their gay, lesbian, or bisexual parents to come out and learn the importance of truth, equality, and integrity. They show greater tolerance and sensitivity, and many value their years living in a gay or gay-positive community, becoming, as one said, "bicultural." Their peers provide the most help in arriving at this point. A few stay confused, hurt, or angry, while a number become active in advocacy groups in their schools or colleges.

THE FUTURE AND HOW WE MIGHT GET THERE

The future holds promise for mixed-sexual-orientation couples and their children to the degree that family members, friends, and therapists become more knowledgeable about their needs and provide support and relevant therapy. Therapists can offer more relevant counseling as they became familiar with issues described here and in studies listed in the References. Family wounds could then heal more quickly. More couples could work out lasting marriages and, should they divorce, become more effective coparents. More children would grow up in nurturing climates. As such families increase, they would provide one another with more positive role models and peer support.

Looking further ahead at the future of all families with one or both parents being gay, lesbian, or bisexual, I foresee two scenarios emerging from the current same-sex marriage debate. One would be codifying marriage as an opposite-gender relationship and perpetuating nonacceptance of homosexuality and same-sex behavior. Were this to happen, we would most likely see an increase in closeted gay, lesbian, and bisexual persons in mixed-orientation marriages, leading to more divorces and single parents as well as pain for everyone.

The other scenario would be two-pronged: increased acceptance of gay, lesbian, and bisexual persons as normal human beings who do not choose their sexual orientation and wider understanding of marriage as a coupling and sometimes a parenting endeavor not defined by gender. This double shift in social thought would improve the quality of life for mixed-orientation and same-gender couples. With increased acceptance, fewer gay, lesbian, and bisexual persons would marry heterosexual spouses if they wanted a committed relationship and a family. Those who did so would be honest with their spouses-to-be. Such marriages, having full disclosure, would hold more promise for lasting and fewer risks of ending. Sexual-orientation differences would remain, but both spouses would know the challenges and strategies to create an enduring marriage. Meanwhile, more gay, lesbian, and bisexual persons who want a committed relationship and children would feel freer to bond with same-gender partners. Without conflicting orientations and prey to fewer negative social attitudes, they could focus on strengthening their relationships and families. Concurrently, a wider understanding of marriage as a coupling and parenting endeavor not defined by gender would lead to legitimatizing same-gender relationships as marriages. As more same-gender couples married and fewer mixed-orientation couples divorced, the institution of marriage itself would begin to heal.

This cataclysmic shift can be achieved despite the deepening chasm between the polarized views of homosexuality and marriage. An ideological divide can be breached by concrete examples of real-life persons. Putting a face on homosexual and bisexual persons has already broken down many social and political barriers. Similarly, more visibility of and interaction with same-gender couples and gay, lesbian, and bisexual parents can weaken abstract generalizations heard in current arguments. Person by person, attention now paid to the sexual orientation of same-gender couples and gay, lesbian, or bisexual parents could shift to their relationships and parenting. In turn, such couples and parents could seek to understand the moral and religious concerns of those favoring only opposite-gender marriages and respond to their arguments with their experiences that illustrate the family values assumed to be lacking. Through such dialogues, some members of conservative groups and orthodox denominations might change their thinking. Slowly, public support of same-gender couples and gay, lesbian, and bisexual families might reach the majority level, leading to the promise of legal marriages.

However, we are not there yet. In this transition period, professionals who work with such couples and families are in a unique position to accelerate change in that direction. To do so, they need more tools. Currently, when persons in same-gender or mixed-orientation relationships seek help from therapists, family lawyers, or medical practitioners their presenting relationship, parenting, or health-problem areas often are intertwined with issues about sexual orientation or societal negativity about which many therapists are unaware. If these concerns are not addressed, the clients' pain from them continues to interfere with resolving the presented problems. To serve them better, professionals need to know more about the singular issues that affect families with gay, lesbian, or bisexual parents—factors described in this chapter and in a growing body of literature. With this knowledge, they can distinguish between gay-related issues and relationship, parental, or health issues and help clients cope more effectively with each. Therapists, for example, could help couples develop more effective communication skills and ways to handle family dysfunctions. They could also help such clients become visible in their communities, and they could educate professional peers and the public through conferences or articles on such families and the social attitudes that affect them.

The experience of mixed-orientation couples plays a special role. Theirs is a cautionary tale about the domino effect of negative social attitudes on families in which one spouse is gay, lesbian, or bisexual and the irony of assuming that spouses in an opposite-gender marriage are heterosexual. At the same time, mixed-orientation couples who stay married are models of strategies to develop enduring marriages and strong families in the face of social negativity and profound differences between the spouses. Being aware of societal forces that brought about their marriages and plagued both spouses can spur us to work toward dissipating such forces and cultivating greater acceptance of gay, lesbian, and bisexual persons. Knowing how couples kept their relationships robust and their families intact, we can encourage such behaviors in all families: honesty, love, friendship, commitment, mutual respect and support, patience, flexibility, resilience, and compromise on the part of the partners, alongside parenting that is caring, responsible, attentive, and loving so that their children become responsible, contributing adult citizens. Are not these values that the national marriage debate is all about? My hope is that we can turn that debate into a conversation about these values and how all couples and families can be helped to *actualize* them.

REFERENCES

Abbott, D., & Farmer, E. (1995). *From wedded wife to lesbian life: Stories of transformation.* Santa Cruz, CA: Crossing Press.

Auerback, S., & Moser, C. (1989). Groups for the wives of gays and bisexual men. *Social Work, July-August,* 321-325.

Bauman, R. (1986). *Gentleman from Maryland: The conscience of a gay conservative.* New York: William Morrow and Company.

Buxton, A. P. (1994). *The other side of the closet: The coming-out crisis for straight spouses and families.* New York: John Wiley & Sons.

Buxton, A. P. (1999). The best interest of children of lesbian and gay parents. In R. Galatzer-Levy & L. Kraus (Eds.), *The scientific basis for custody decisions* (pp. 319-346). New York: John Wiley & Sons.

Buxton, A. P. (2000). From hostile to helpful: Parallel parenting after a mixed-orientation couple divorce. In J. Wells (Ed.), *Home fronts: Controversies in nontraditional parenting* (pp. 201-213). New York: Alyson Press.

Buxton, A. P. (2001). Writing our own script: How bisexual men and their heterosexual wives maintain their marriages after disclosure. In B. Beemyn & B. Steinman, (Eds.), *Bisexuality in the lives of men: Facts and fiction* (pp. 157-189). Binghamton, NY: Harrington Park Press.

Buxton, A. P. (2004a). Paths and pitfalls: How heterosexual spouses cope when their husbands or wives come out. *Journal of Couple & Relationship Therapy, 3*(2/3), 95-109.

Buxton, A. P. (2004b). Works in progress: How mixed-orientation couples maintain their marriages after the wives come out. *Journal of Bisexuality, 4*(1/2), 58-82.

Norman, T. (1998). *Just tell the truth: Questions families ask when gay married men come out.* Kansas City, MO: Prehension Publications.

Ross, M. W. (1983). *The married homosexual male: A psychological study.* Boston: Routledge & Kegan Paul.

White, M. (1994). *Stranger at the gate: To be gay and Christian in America.* New York: Simon-Schuster.

Whitehead, S. L. (1997). *The truth shall set you free: A memoir.* San Francisco: HarperSanFranciso.

Chapter 5

Genograms Redrawn: Lesbian Couples Define Their Families

Mary Swainson
Fiona Tasker

Lesbians and gay men have historically been seen as a threat to family values and have been excluded from ideas about the family. Simon (1998) points out that the association of the term *family* with the rearing of children as well as biologically and legally defined relationships excludes many systems of significant others. Gay men and lesbians are unable to form relationships legitimized by law in most countries, and in the face of inequality they have broadened and reworked the very concept of family (Slater, 1995), often including friends and ex-partners as family members. This chapter considers how to assist lesbians in representing family relationships and appraises the use of genograms (family trees), which are often used in family therapy to depict family relationships.

LESBIAN FAMILY RELATIONSHIPS

Family can be seen as a social construct that has changed over time and differs across cultures. It is constrained by heterosexism and traditional concepts of gender roles (Weeks, 1990, 2000). For example, ideas about the family within family therapy theory have moved from a universal idea of the family based on the white Western model of the nuclear family (e.g., Minuchin, 1977) to encompass a wider range of different family forms and cultures (Falicov, 1995). However, lesbian

doi:10.1300/5792_06

and gay families are often still excluded from consideration (Healey, 1999).

Much of the existing literature on the families of lesbians and gay men focuses on the relationships of lesbian or gay youth to their families of origin, in particular considering the impact of homophobia on family relationships (Tasker & McCann, 1999). Less attention has been given to how lesbian or gay couples relate to both their own and each other's family of origin. In this chapter, we use *family of origin* to mean both partners' biological or legally defined extended-family relationships. Laird (1996) suggests multiple factors for the dearth of research on lesbians in the context of their families of origin, including a preoccupation with traditional ideas of the family and the political history of the lesbian community, where radical lesbian feminists themselves have rejected family as a patriarchal institution. She reviews studies that show that most lesbians, although having differing degrees of problems with their families of origin, were not rejected by them and that these relationships often improved over time.

Race and culture affect beliefs, expectations, and openness about sexual identity in relation to family of origin (Savin-Williams, 1996). In some cultures, the importance of maintaining family ties can outweigh disapproval of sexual orientation (Liu & Chan, 1996). Greene (1994) states that family ties are even more important for lesbians and gay men in the face of rejection and hostility from the outside world. Relationships with family of origin members may also change over time. Having a child can significantly alter the attitudes of the family of origin toward their lesbian members (Muzio, 1999).

Most of the literature on lesbian and gay couples and family emphasizes the importance of friendships and networks of support—largely, though not exclusively, from within the gay community (Basham, 1999; Laird, 1996; Siegal & Walker, 1996; Slater, 1995). Close friends form familial relationships that change and endure over time but these are often marginalized by the wider society and ignored in family therapy (Green, Bettinger, & Zack, 1996). The term *family of choice* has been used to designate these socially formed networks of emotional, practical, and financial support (Weston, 1991), and this convention is followed in this chapter.

Part of the difficulty that lesbian families confront in being given recognition seems to be that key relationships lack language to describe them. This has been highlighted in relation to the nonbiological coparent role in planned lesbian families. Muzio (1999) remarks on the unique stresses of a lesbian coparent's position "in a legal as well as social and emotional netherworld" (p. 207) with no language to describe her relationships and often no legal protection should her couple relationship end. Lacking any legal or biological status, she can be excluded from playing a full parental role, regardless of her child care responsibilities or her bond with the child (Lott-Whitehead & Tully, 1999; Morningstar, 1999). Therapists, like others outside the family, may presume the biological mother is the primary caregiver and reinforce feelings of illegitimacy (Mitchell, 1996).

Whether and how to confront marginalization and invisibility is an issue that lesbian families must confront. If couples are out they are open to hostility and challenge; if not, their relationship is ignored (Greene, 1994). They may be out within their immediate families of origin, but the relationship may not be acknowledged to wider family or family friends. The relationship may be named or left unsaid, and this will be partly influenced by the relational style of the particular family as well as by culture, ethnicity, class, and other social factors (Laird, 1996). One study found that more open families suffer less stress (Lott-Whitehead & Tully, 1999), but others show that homophobic attack is a reality (Cogan, 1996; Greene, 1994). Slater (1995) rates social oppression linked to homophobia and heterosexism as the main stressor in lesbian family life.

FAMILY LIFE-CYCLE THEORY AND GENOGRAMS

Family life-cycle theory is an important concept for thinking about families in family therapy practice (Carter & McGoldrick, 1980). It looks at family development over time and focuses on transitional stages and intergenerational patterns. Slater (1995) has developed a model of the lesbian family life cycle that considers the different developmental stages that affect lesbian families. Although she notes the diverse backgrounds of lesbian families and cautions against overgeneralization, Slater believes her model provides markers for crucial milestones for lesbians, who have to continually invent family forms, in contrast to heterosexual couples, who are constantly provided with guidelines from society. Carter and McGoldrick's (1999) updated family life-cycle framework now includes a chapter that adapts the model to include gay and lesbian perspectives (Johnson & Colucci, 1999). However, the family life-cycle approach has received criticism. For example, Gorell-Barnes (1998) acknowledges the limitations of this approach as being "constrained by cultural and social norms" (p. 46), and this is particularly so in relation to considering lesbian and gay families (Malley & Tasker, 1999).

The genogram is a therapeutic technique closely associated with the family life-cycle model. Burnham (1988) gives a useful summary of the symbols used, the information gathered, and the potential therapeutic value of the genogram, linking it to various models of family therapy. No suggestion is made that the family should construct their own genogram, and the emphasis is on its use by therapists as a family assessment tool. Burnham suggests starting with the nuclear family. He does say that significant friends, neighbors, or professional helpers can be included, but he does not give examples of where they could fit in. More recently, genograms have not only been used for family assessment but also have been developed as a therapeutic technique. For instance, Byng-Hall (1995) describes how he redraws genograms during sessions to help rewrite family scripts. Gorell-Barnes (1998) adapts Byng-Hall's ideas by asking families to construct their own genograms, sometimes outside the session, and expands their use to include looking at family stories from different viewpoints or to consider a specific issue in therapy such as gender roles across generations.

Genograms have been used with lesbian families. For example, in a case study of therapy with a lesbian couple Basham (1999) shows a five-generational genogram of the couple's families of origin using traditional symbols. It includes one previous partner but no family of choice. However, no discussion has been undertaken with lesbian couples about the process of drawing a genogram or consideration of how useful it might be in representing lesbian family relationships—the topics explored in the present chapter.

The purpose of the current study was to generate ideas about family, incorporating the lived experience of lesbian couples, and to develop theory about the usefulness and appropriateness of using the genogram with lesbian families. This chapter uses the term *family* to mean the lesbian couple, with or without children, except where a couple rejects this definition. It was undertaken with awareness of the context of negative definitions within the wider community, for example, the effect of Section 28 of the Local Government Act 1988 in the United Kingdom which refers to homosexuals having "pretended family relationships" (see Richardson [1996] for a discussion of the negative effects arising from this legislation). The research questions addressed were: (1) How do lesbian couples define their families? (2) Is the genogram a useful tool for depicting those definitions? (3) Does the presence of children in the relationship make a difference to defining family?

METHOD

Grounded Theory

A qualitative Grounded Theory approach was chosen for this study as being the most appropriate way of examining the experiences of the participants and the meanings they ascribed to those experiences. Qualitative research is concerned with understanding and describing causal processes in a limited number of particular cases rather than looking for representativeness, reproducibility, and more universal applicability (Starrin Dahlgren, Larsson, & Styrborn, 1997).

Grounded theory was originally proposed by Glaser and Strauss in the 1960s (Glaser & Strauss, 1967) and has subsequently developed in different ways (Glaser, 1992; Strauss & Corbin, 1998). A key feature of the method is constant comparison, which involves an ongoing interplay between data collection and analysis. These occur simultaneously, so that as themes emerge they are followed up by the researcher in the subsequent collection of data. Data most commonly gathered for Grounded Theory are the research interviews that are recorded and transcribed verbatim (Pidgeon & Henwood, 1996). An abbreviated version of Grounded Theory was followed in considering the data for this project in that no new categories arose from coding of the final interview but no further interviews were sought to validate and expand the grounded theory developed from these initial analyses (Willig, 2001).

Constructionist ideas have modified the Grounded Theory approach by emphasizing the active and reflexive role of the researcher. The final Grounded Theory model is more than a "strict redescription" of the data (Pidgeon & Henwood, 1996, p. 99). From this perspective, the interviewer's (first author) professional knowledge (as a trainee family therapist) and personal knowledge, experiences, and values as a lesbian, mother, daughter, sister, partner, grandmother, and friend no doubt influenced the interviews and became interwoven with the discourses of the participants.

Sample

To explore the usefulness of genograms in representing lesbian family relationships, the study needed to recruit couples who had been together for a relatively long period of time (over five years) and who were not currently in therapy. Couples also had to be prepared to be interviewed together in order to draw genograms and to explore joint conceptualizations of family. We therefore sought to interview couples whose relationship could be loosely described by Slater's (1995) fourth generative stage of the lesbian family life cycle as having made an enduring contribution to each other's lives, either through working on joint projects and/or sharing in parenthood.

A brief introductory letter was drawn up outlining the purpose, scope, and method of the research with details regarding confidentiality and the degree of commitment required. Contacts within the lesbian community were then asked to distribute this letter of invitation to couples known to them, and couples were invited to contact the first author to enquire about participation if they wished. It was not expected that this self-selected group of participants would represent the range of diversity in the lesbian community, for example, in terms of race, class, or disability, but that a degree of difference would be evident. Seven couples replied, and six couples were interviewed.

The key characteristics of each participating couple are shown in Table 5.1. The ages of participants ranged from the early thirties to the early fifties, and all were able-bodied. All the couples were cohabiting. All participants were in full-time employment except one, who was primarily caring for a young child. One couple live in Southeast England and the rest in London, although many of the participants have family connections in other countries. The sample is not representative of the diversity in the lesbian population, but considerable difference is found both between the couples and between individuals. The sample group contained sufficient social and life experience for a richness of data to be collected and analyzed.

TABLE 5.1. Information about participating couples.

Name	Children	Self-descriptions, ethnicity, and class	Genogram type	Couple as family
Julia and Rosie	2 (marriage)		separate but shared	family
Claire and Lin	2 (marriage)	French Chinese	separate	not family
Carol and Ann	1 (known donor)	Jewish	shared	family
Peggy and Mary	None		separate	not family
Vonnie and Pat	1 (prev. rel.) 1 (donor)	Jewish	shared	family
Kathy and Sam	None	Working-class Jewish, American	separate and shared	family

Note: Names have been changed to preserve confidentiality.

Procedure

A choice of venues was offered to participants, and all chose to be interviewed in their own homes. In order to conduct a systemic investigation, couples were interviewed together for approximately one hour and fifteen minutes. However, no children or other family members were included, as this would have meant different constellations of family members taking part at each interview. Written consent for participation was obtained prior to the interview, and it was made clear that this could be rescinded at any time. The interviews were tape recorded and transcribed by the interviewer.

The interview was semistructured to allow flexibility in following up emerging themes. Participating couples were initially asked, "When you think about family, what comes to mind?" They were then asked to draw a genogram themselves to generate discussion about the process and fit (for example, they were asked whether they had left people out of the family tree and why). If participants asked about ways of drawing a genogram, they were given basic information about symbols used in family therapy as outlined in Burnham (1988). Couples were then asked to consider whether any connections existed between who was depicted on the family tree and the extent to which the couple were out to that person and accepted. They were also asked to consider whether concepts of family and the genogram were the same for both of them or different. Toward the end of the interview they were asked whether they wanted to redraw their genogram to generate ways of depicting family relationships that might be more representative of their ideas about family. These genograms, together with the interview transcripts, formed the data for analysis.

RESULTS

Drawing Lesbian Genograms (Family Trees)

All participants were familiar with the idea of the family tree. None of the couples had attempted to draw one as a joint endeavor previously. A quote from Julia (one of the participants) indicates how surprised she was to be asked: "You know, people don't ask lesbians about their families. It's not a question I've ever been asked before, what do I feel is my family?"

A key distinguishing feature that emerged through the data was whether the couples defined themselves to be a family or not: Four of the couples did, and two did not. The two couples who did not describe their relationship as family produced separate genograms with little overlap. For example, Figure 5.1 shows Claire's individually drawn genogram showing her relationship with Lin, Claire's family of origin, and part of Lin's family of origin. Lin's individually drawn genogram showed only Lin's family of origin, including Lin's other siblings. No friends were included on either Claire's or Lin's genogram. Not defining themselves as family did not imply lack of commitment to the couple's relationship. The other couple who did not describe their relationship as family named individual friends on their own genograms but had no shared family of choice. Like Claire and Lin, they also had families of origin that were excluding of the lesbian partner.

Couples who saw themselves as family produced either a shared or separate genogram but with considerable shared content if separate (see Figure 5.2, Sam and Kathy's joint genogram, and Figure 5.3,

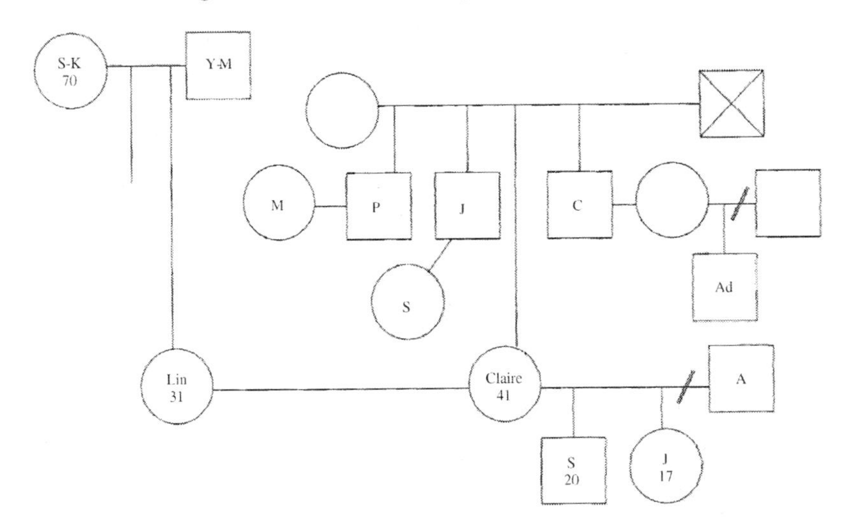

FIGURE 5.1. Claire's individually drawn genogram (Couple 2).

Rosie's individual genogram). This meant that their genogram included themselves; any children, whether of the relationship or from a previous relationship; members of both families of origin; and a shared family of choice. For example, in Figure 5.2, Sam and Kathy do not distinguish between family of origin and family of choice. The two couples who had children together produced the fully shared genograms. One of these couples had a known donor who was included in their genogram with his family of origin. The two other couples produced separate genograms for each individual participant, mainly distinguishing between each other's family of origin, although with considerable overlap and inclusion. Families of choice were similarly shared and depicted on each genogram.

In order to evaluate the usefulness of different genograms collected for portraying lesbian families, the transcriptions of each interview were analyzed using the process of open coding and constant comparison following Strauss and Corbin's (1998) Grounded Theory procedure. This resulted in four categories (summarizing twenty-six initial codes) directly related to the drawing of the genograms: (1) definitions of family; (2) tiers and circles; (3) family as process; and (4) heterosexism (see Table 5.2). These categories are considered in turn.

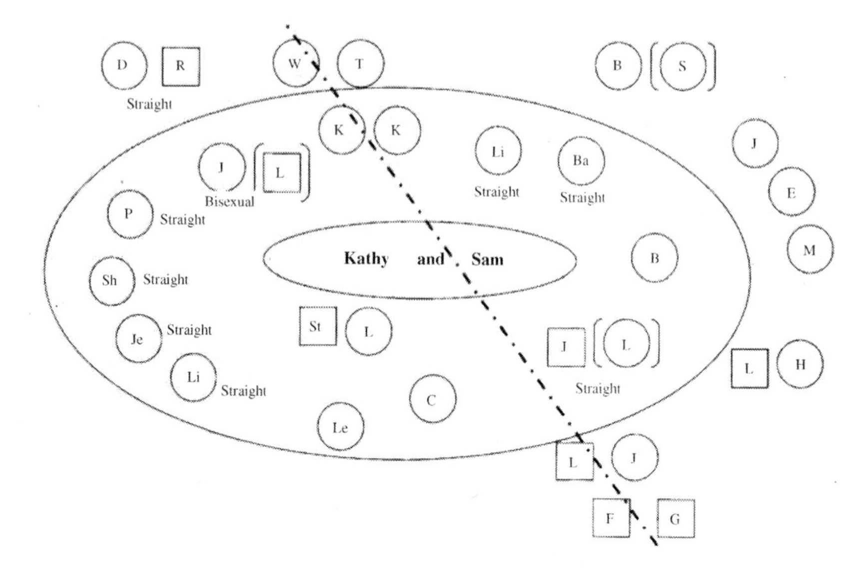

FIGURE 5.2. Sam and Kathy (Couple 6) joint genogram (final version).

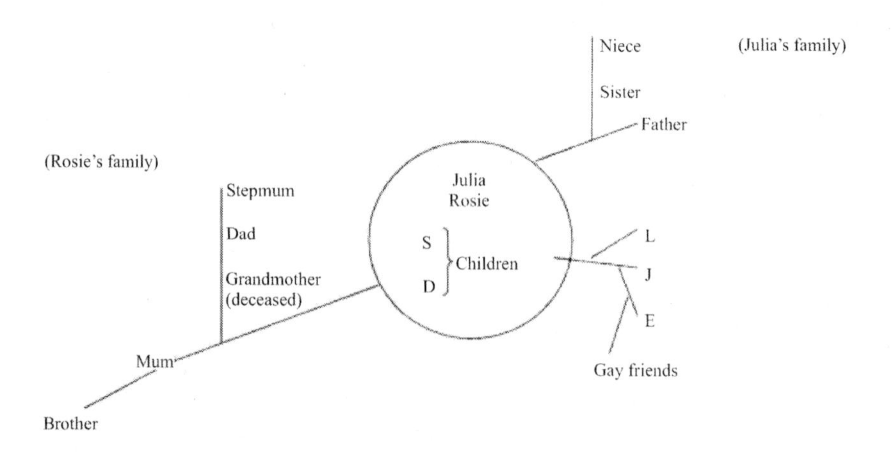

FIGURE 5.3. Rosie's individually drawn shared genogram (Couple 1).

TABLE 5.2. Grounded Theory coding of genogram interviews: Open coding concepts grouped under categories.

Category	Contributing open coding concepts
Definitions of family	• Traditional (heterosexual) family
	• No accepted symbols
	• Lack of language
	• Children defining family
	• Family of origin
	• Acceptance
	• Family history and continuity
	• Family heritage and legacy
	• Family of choice
	• Affirmation
	• Nurturing
Tiers and circles	• Emotional closeness
	• Tiers, ranking, steps
	• Pie charts
	• Circles
	• Color
Family as process	• Change over time
	• Developmental change with children
	• Family of origin changes in acceptance
	• Family of choice changes in importance
Heterosexism and homophobia	• Comparison with heterosexual families
	• Pressure from negative beliefs about lesbian families
	• Invisibility
	• Negative beliefs about lesbians having children
	• Pretend families
	• Not family

Definitions of family

All of the participants expressed dissatisfaction with the traditional genogram format, feeling that it did not fit her situation. A general feeling was that the genogram is linked to heterosexual relationship norms and excludes lesbian experience. As Carol aptly commented: "I think this works better for a traditional [heterosexual] family." Claire and Rosie felt that the usual genogram took the heterosexual married couple as its starting point. Most found the positioning of family of choice difficult with no accepted symbols and the family of origin being given a privileged position. For example, Julia found her estranged sister would be included in the traditional format while her friends would have no place. Sam felt her family of friends were excluded. These expanded concepts of family did not fit into the traditional genogram format.

Participants felt not just a lack of accepted symbols to depict family members but a fundamental lack of language to express lesbian family relationships. This lack of language was felt by all participants even when they were involved in inclusive situations. When speaking out about their family relationships to others outside the family, participants had difficulty describing their relationships, as heterosexual terms did not fit. Vonnie explained: "That's one of the things that I think is quite critical . . . we don't have a language to express our family relationships."

A lesbian relationship could be adequately symbolized on the genogram, for example, using the traditional notation of two circles with a line drawn between them. However, participants felt a lack of language to describe their relationship; for example, using the term *partner* did not necessarily denote family. Donor relationships were also complicated to describe, both linguistically and on the genogram itself. For Carol, there was no way to adequately represent the donor's relationship to their family, as he was not the father of her child but was still important in her family. Ann called their donor the father only when talking to her parents but Carol disliked this. Both Vonnie and Pat had children with unknown donors who are shown on their joint genogram. They described the unknown donors to their children by using terms relating to the meaning of donor as a "gift." Co-mothers had an especially difficult task explaining their position, both using symbols on the genogram and linguistically. For example, Vonnie and Pat did not mention that their shared genogram does not indicate which partner is the biological mother. Carol and Ann did comment on this but then decided this did not matter, wanting equality in status as mothers. "Stepmother" was used by two women to describe their relationship to their partner's child, and this could be represented on the genogram using stepfamily conventions. However, it was difficult to adequately describe the relationship linguistically. For example, Pat used the term because it was the child's choice, although she herself disliked it.

The whole network of relationships with each other's families had no accepted descriptions. Naming the family of choice was also problematic. Most participants used "aunties" to describe friends' relationships with the children but did not have a word to describe adult relationships within the family of choice, although they distinguished these from more everyday friendships.

In spite of the difficulties with fit, drawing the genograms enabled definitions of family to emerge. Children were seen as important to definitions of family. In particular, Ann argued: "I think a lot of people see as a family people with children, so I think you're much more accepted as a family if you do have children. If you're just a couple you're seen as less of a unit I think."

Other participants did not put the point as forcibly as Ann and did not make a connection to wider discourses on family. However, all participants who had children saw them as primary in their thoughts about family. Vonnie said: "Well, immediate family, that's me and Pat and the children; that's my immediate family."

Women who were living with their partners' children from previous relationships also had strong opinions about this issue. Julia had taken on a stepparenting role, and children were central to her core definition of family. Julia talked about her feelings: "Especially about Rosie's children . . . I'm like a stepmother . . . we are our own very immediate family." Rosie said: "Yeah, our kids, that's what family is to me . . . Julia and my kids first." Lin was in an ostensibly similar position in relation to Claire's children, although she had not taken on a parenting role and felt that there was a split into two family systems—as reflected in their separate genograms of their families. Women with children from previous relationships facilitated contact with male ex-partners or previous lesbian partners who had been involved in parenting. These ex-partners were also included on genograms even when the relationships between adults in the family were strained.

Mary and Peggy, who do not have children, still included children in their definition of family, and this contributed to a "not family" description of their relationship. However, Sam and Kathy, who also had no children themselves, were emphatic in rejecting this idea. Kathy said: "I mean, I define us as family, you know . . . we're obviously next of kin," while Sam added: "What, that you can't build a family without children; if you don't have children you're not a family? I don't agree with that at all."

All women included members of their family of origin in their genograms. Participants had to negotiate relationships with their own and their partner's family of origin. Everyone interviewed was having contact with members of their own family of origin. Even when they were excluded or marginalized, the belief in the importance of family of origin relationships meant that partners were supportive of each other's attempts to maintain contact. Contact with family of origin was variable; for example, Pat indicated distant relationships with family of origin were desirable: "What I've done is moved 13,000 miles away from my family, and that feels absolutely the right thing for me to be true to myself." Three couples had daily contact with a member of their families of origin, either in person or by phone. Others described significant amounts of time spent with family of origin, especially with their siblings. Contact with family of origin included caring for elderly family members as well as more social events. For example, Vonnie said: "Another reason . . . we see quite a lot of them these days, is that with my siblings and my oldest nephew, and now my niece, is that we have a rotation of care, and when my stepmother goes away we do twenty-four-hour care for my father."

Acceptance by family of origin was important to all the participants. Four couples were accepted by at least one side of their families of origin and found this supportive. Four individual participants found that although their own families of origin accepted *them,* their partners were not included. In these situations lesbianism, even when known about, was not openly acknowledged. Siblings were more likely to know (about their situation) than parents, and have more contact. Contact with family of origin and enjoyment of family gatherings was influenced by family attitudes.

ROSIE: [My stepmother] said to my dad, "If you don't accept the way Rosie is, you'll lose her."

KATHY: My family is very accepting . . . automatically the family members that did fly out (when my mum had a heart attack on holiday with us) recognised Sam as part of the family, and the spokesperson.

Acceptance also seemed to be a key aspect of lesbian family relationships for including non–family of origin members on the genograms. For example, Carol and Ann included the donor and some of his family of origin on their joint genogram. Ann commented: "And for [the donor's family of origin] it was a big acceptance as well, so I suppose it's even weirder for them than for my family in terms of what their relationship should be, because they are the biological family."

Most participants felt a sense of family history and continuity with their family of origin, and this was important in defining family. Carol summed this up by saying: "I suppose it's blood, um, blood ties, but it's also to do with shared sort of past . . . and your present . . . and goes on with you into the future." Some participants, such as Mary, had extensive knowledge of their extended family over several generations and were keepers of the family stories. Even where a participant's knowledge of her family of origin was limited, she recognized of the importance of family legacy. This aspect of family was especially apparent in discussions about culture and identity. The Jewish participants reflected on the strong connection between their Jewish heritage and their ideas about family. Lin also emphasized this: "[my parents are] quite strong about their Chinese identity; I feel very proud about that . . . there's a sort of solidarity within that unit, to fight racism." These women and their partners had incorporated some of these cultural influences into their shared lives; for example, by observing religious festivals together. Where cultural or religious beliefs seemed to hinder acceptance by family of origin, these women showed considerable understanding of their partners' need to keep in touch with their families of origin.

These women were aware of what they brought into their own families as a heritage or legacy of values from their upbringing. This included consciously continuing particular family patterns—for example, commitment to long-term relationships, friendship, and parenting skills as well as values and beliefs. Rosie mentioned her grandmother as having given her important lasting qualities: "My grandmother, who I've put deceased . . . she's taught me kindness, patience . . . the ripples that can actually give out in terms of giving people a steadfast life." As Kathy said: "I think it's important to share your history and to have something to fall back on. You know, um, because for me there's a lot of stuff that happened when I was growing up that only those people would know . . . so my mannerisms or behaviour is acceptable in my family." Sam added: "Kathy and I are in a long-term relationship, and I wonder whether or not it's because of that background we've grown up with people who've had connections for a really long time and you observe . . . you learn from it, you copy it or whatever."

Five of the couples referred specifically to friends as part of family. Only one couple did not name friends as family of choice, although they still acknowledged the importance of friendship. Three participants felt closer to their family of choice than to their family of origin. Five other participants felt that the two systems had equal though different value. These families of choice included lesbian, gay, and straight friends. The time and effort devoted to these friendship networks indicated their importance and the depth of commitment to them.

JULIA: I've got close friends in my inner circle, friends who nurture. Mostly gay men and women here . . . gay people who are like us, who nurture in a kind of gorgeous and wonderful—I'm saying we're gorgeous and wonderful! *[laughter].*

MARY: Well, I've known C for about sixteen years, and A I've known for about twenty. She's an ex-partner. I lived with her for ten years. . . . She feels like family. . . . It's taken a long time to have this kind of contact we have now, but because of all the time we spent together it feels like, I wouldn't say a blood relative, but it feels like I've spent time with my brother and sisters.

Ex-partners were included for six participants, and in two cases had become close to both women. Ex-partners were not shown on any genogram in the traditional way but always placed within the family of choice. Lesbian "aunties" were especially important to families with children, playing a hugely important family-support role. Pat and Vonnie had taken legal steps to include their friends as guardians to their child in preference to their families of origin. A number of women were still close to friends they had known since childhood; school friends were especially important to Kathy and Peggy.

Friends who become family had particular characteristics, namely that they were positive about the participants' lesbian identity and affirmed the lesbian couple or family status. These were friendships which had endured over time, and friends that the participants felt they could rely on completely in times of need. Frequency of contact was variable and not a deciding factor in inclusion in family of choice. Members of the family of choice were involved in lesbian family celebrations. They attended children's birthday parties as well as new ceremonies devised to meet lesbian family needs, such as commitment ceremonies and adapted cultural festivals.

Overall, the findings showed that lesbian couples have complex definitions of family that are generally based on inclusive rather than exclusive ideas. A key concept for defining family related to involvement in nurturing relationships—feeling nurtured and in turn nurturing others. So in this respect Sam and Julia included old friends of their parents in their genograms, and Sam also included her ex-husband and his new family. Both couples without children spoke of their pets as part of their families, but did not add them to the genogram.

Tiers and Circles

Several women used the concepts of tiers, ranking, steps, circles, or pie charts to describe their families that included emotional closeness as a level as well as kinship. Some adapted the genogram and added extra pieces where necessary for friends. Carol and Ann had three tiers and finally used a combination of circles and traditional lines to indicate inclusiveness and relational closeness to the core unit. Julia used overlapping circles because she wanted to prioritize closeness. She added qualities of friendship rather than named friends. Rosie had a central circular core with arms radiating out, again to indicate emotional space. Sam and Kathy initially produced separate traditional family trees (genograms) for their families of origin. Then they did a joint version with concentric circles representing their shared family (see Figure 5.2). Vonnie and Pat used color within a traditional genogram format to show different family subsystems, including family of choice, but did not indicate degrees of emotional closeness.

ANN: I think if you think in terms of concentric circles, so the people closest to us are put here . . . I think I'd put the nonbiological family closer to us than the biological family . . .

JULIA: If I hadn't considered your question, I'd have put the traditional family tree . . . it would be better to do a kind of pie chart, so it could kind of overlap.

SAM: I would start ranking people, giving them tiers, maybe. . . . For me [in the inner circle] would be who I feel like I could call on in a real emergency and feel like they would do something. They would feel a connection.

Both couples who did not define themselves as family produced quite traditional representations of their families of origin, basic in the case of Claire and Lin but more detailed from Peggy and Mary, who also included separate families of choice.

Family As Process

All the lesbian couples were involved in complex relationships with their families of origin, their children, and families of choice that changed over time. Consequently, the women interviewed were very aware of family as an evolving, dynamic process. The participants had all experienced changes in their couple relationships, as would be expected in relationships where partners have been together for over five years. Women were involved in different parts of their family systems to varying degrees at different times in their lives, both as a couple and separately.

For couples with children, there were developmental changes in family relationships to accommodate their changing needs. For example, Rosie's son had gone to live with his father when he was sixteen following a time when he was rejecting of her sexuality and of her partner, Julia. There was no contact for two years until he was ready to reconnect, and now, several years later, a close relationship has grown between the three. For Ann, having a child with Carol changed her relationship with her family of origin. Her mother, though still saying she did not accept their decision to have a baby, had started knitting before he was born. Ann said with admiration: "[My parents'] acceptance of us is quite sort of, absolutely amazing . . . I think they've made such an incredible journey."

Relationships with families of origin had undergone considerable change for all couples in different ways. For Julia, having a serious illness had led her to contact members of her family even though they were not accepting of her lesbianism. Sam's relationship with her parents had become distant following her coming out. However, following her mother's terminal illness, her relationship improved with her father and he ended up accepting her partner. Kathy said: "It made me feel so special in a way that he's actually recognizing that we are family . . . to think that someone of his generation has turned the tables."

Family of choice relationships were also subject to changes in importance. For example, in recent years Peggy had reconnected with friends from school. These relationships were especially important to her because her parents were dead and not many people shared her childhood memories. Vonnie and Pat were also aware of the possibility of change in relation to a member of their family of choice who had recently had her own child:

PAT: It might be that having her own family now there's not the time to have that connection with another child, at which point we need to rethink who we want to take on that responsibility.

VONNIE: I have kind of accepted that people will come in and out of [our children's] lives.

Heterosexism

Drawing a genogram drew the attention of participants to issues of homophobia and heterosexism. Participants found drawing a family tree difficult because of the inherent bias toward nuclear family norms. It led to comparisons with heterosexual families and the exclusion of lesbian families from accepted definitions and ordinary life experiences. As Sam said: "I wouldn't know exactly how to put [a family of choice relationship] down. Where, you know what a traditional family tree looks like, but when you start putting friends on there, how?"

The couples in the sample reported pressure from negative beliefs about lesbian family relationships from within their own family networks and from society. Stress was involved in being out or being invisible. Only three individual participants described themselves as fully out. The other nine were on a continuum of outness that ranged from Peggy being out only within her lesbian family and to her only brother to other participants being out except at work. For some couples, this pressure on their lesbian relationship was from their own families of origin. Pat's family could not reconcile acceptance of her lesbian family with their Christian beliefs. Two couples could not stay at family members' homes. For other couples, the main stress came from exclusion from aspects of living in society that heterosexual families take for granted. For example, Carol and Ann, when traveling with their child, were prevented from sitting together in a family-designated area, as their couple relationship was not recognized.

Invisibility had different problems that were both social and legal in nature. All families interviewed were aware of the inequality of their positions and the impact of the lack of legal sanctions for their relationships with each other and their children. None of the participants wanted to marry, but they wanted more legal rights and safeguards. Three couples mentioned the idea that they were seen as "pretend" families, echoing the statement of Clause 28 of the 1988 UK Local Government Act. This epitomized the lack of validation for lesbian family relationships, but it also was a source of defiance.

VONNIE: Because with biological family there's still always this kind of connection of well, you are related, and I think when you have nonbiological, as it were "pretend" family relationships of an extended variety, there isn't that. But maybe there is.

CAROL: And I think it does affect how I feel about us as a family because it is an unrecognised institution almost, in the broadest sense, and because it's unrecognised, I do sometimes, I really do sometimes feel like we're pretending. You know this whole thing of "pretend families" . . . Other families, they just get on with their relationships, their interrelationships.

JULIA: I'm a member of Stonewall and in that way . . . someone is fighting on my behalf who hopefully will repeal Section 28 . . . "Pretend" makes us really laugh, doesn't it? "Ooh, look at our pretend family."

The wider context of heterosexism and homophobia had also influenced some lesbian couples' decisions about having children. Three individual participants held negative views about lesbians having children together, seeing this as damaging to the children. This was partly because of discriminatory attitudes in society but also connected with their beliefs that children need an involved, biological father. These opinions went alongside deep feelings of personal loss about not having children.

All of these factors combined to make all the participants aware of the impact of homophobia on their lives and choices about family. Two couples could not define their relationships as family. Even where participants felt very positive about their own immediate family and had good relationships with their families of origin, they were aware that they were negatively viewed by wider society. Mary summed this up: "Really, it's difficult to imagine, if homosexuality was accepted, like heterosexuality is, what you would feel like. But because it isn't, there's no knowing."

DISCUSSION

This study found that even in a small sample considerable diversity exists in lesbian family relationships and describing them adequately is difficult. Using the genogram produced interesting results. None of the participants initially found it a good fit with their family but subsequently found the process of mapping their families useful. Lesbian couples, in particular those who drew shared genograms, wanted this not only to represent family relationships but also to indicate closeness and, above all, acceptance of lesbian family relationships. The solution these couples found was to redraw their genograms in terms of tiers or circles of closeness.

Drawing the genograms generated conversation, and the process of finding a more constructive format meant that definitions of family were foregrounded and whole network systems emerged. Encouraging participants to draw a genogram may have helped them take a metaposition and enabled new narratives of family connections to emerge. Drawing a lesbian family genogram also uncovered the impact of heterosexism and homophobia and helped to render the problems of both invisibility and being out available for discussion.

The study confirmed Laird's (1998) observations that lesbians connect in complex ways to their families of origin but with much variation in the quality of the relationships. The birth of children did seem to increase contact with family of origin, especially with the new grandparents, and these relationships were often supportive, confirming Lewin's study (1993). Participants were largely accepting of any negativity from family of origin, working hard to maintain relationships even where, as for one couple, exclusion was compounded by racial and cultural difference. No participant suggested that the costs of maintaining contact were greater than the benefits. It may be that the generosity shown to families of origin reflects an awareness of the difficulty of standing up against homophobia (Laird, 1998).

The participants had drawn on their early family life experiences in making their own families and wanted to keep some values and make some changes. The concept of generation as a family definition was important to four of the six couples, linked not only to having children—as in traditional genogram drawings—but also to family history. Furthermore, family of origin was important in relation to passing on cultural values for some participants, particularly in relation to incorporating Chinese and Jewish family beliefs and rituals in their couple relationships. Families also gave participants a legacy of important family values and beliefs about long-term relationships and nurturing.

The couples interviewed for this study were all connected via friendships into a wider sense of lesbian community and all said how important this was for them as individuals and as couples. Confirming the patterns noted in other studies, many of these lesbian and gay friendships were in fact more than friendships and denoted as family of choice (Weeks, 2000; Weston, 1991). Couples also included heterosexual friends as part of their family of choice. These networks, defined as qualitatively different from other friendships, were central to most lesbian families, and a true understanding of the family would not be gained if they were ignored. However, as our findings indicate, it is difficult to depict these on the traditional genogram format, and more work is needed to develop new genogram symbols to depict family of choice membership.

It was interesting to find that two couples did not describe themselves as family even though they had been together for over five years, made a home together, and, in one case, the couple were also living with children from one partner's previous marriage. This definition of "not family" seems to be important, as neither of these couples had shared networks of support and they also held negative views about lesbian parenting. In both these respects they differed from the couples who self-defined as family. This might be a useful area for further research, especially as "not family" couples expressed feelings of sadness about constraints on their life choices. This may relate to internalized homophobia (Slater, 1995), but for the couples in the present study it seemed specifically connected to their beliefs about lesbian family rather than to individual sexual identity.

Limitations

This study is limited by the small number of participants and cannot be seen as representative of the experiences or beliefs of all lesbian couples about family. Only cohabiting couples participated in the study, yet many longstanding lesbian couples choose not to cohabit. The information letter and snowball sample recruitment could have attracted responses from couples particularly interested in exploring family structure, and couples not in contact with their families of origin might have felt excluded.

The decision to interview only couples and not children or other family members has meant that the findings evaluate the usefulness of genograms from the perspective of the couple only. These do not give a complete representation of any of the lesbian families involved. Clinicians may wish to consider exploring the use of tier and circular genograms with other members of lesbian-led families, and future research might tackle the complexities of portraying lesbian families from different perspectives.

The findings are also constrained by the measures used. The use of the genogram as an interview tool could have highlighted themes of family of origin, generation, and change over time for couples. Furthermore, given the genogram's roots in family therapy, it may have overemphasized difficulties in the family relationships. Finally, the focus on evaluating the usefulness of genograms has meant that many of the rich descriptions of family life given during the interviews have not been fully explored, for example, gender issues, relationships with children, the nature of support given and received within both families of origin and choice, the impact of homophobia on relationships outside the home, and, above all, the positiveness of the couples interviewed about lesbian families (Swainson, 2000).

Recommendations

Asking the couples to draw their own genograms and not dictating the form allowed for a full description of the various family systems and discussion about relational closeness and distance, strengths, and resilience, which could be helpful in therapeutic practice. Couples were able to decide how to represent their families of choice and a donor relationship. The reconceptualization of the genogram in terms of tiers or circles might be useful in considering the support systems that lesbian families may draw upon. The extent to which the families were experiencing stress due to homophobia also emerged. We suggest that further research extend these conclusions by systematically investigating the application of genograms with lesbian couples in therapy to examine the usefulness of redrawing genograms with tiers and circles when confronting relationship problems.

The study, by drawing attention to lesbians' continual negotiations with negative attitudes regarding their relationships and families, suggests that therapists cannot ignore heterosexism and homophobia when seeing lesbian clients. Therapists need to look at their own prejudices and beliefs and neither minimize nor overemphasize the effects of homophobia for their clients. For example, Basham (1999) suggests using Hare-Mustin's (1991) alpha/beta schema to avoid the risk of bias, either by overexaggerating or by ignoring differences between lesbians and other women clients. Awareness of the protective function of choosing not to be out and not pathologizing this as a family secret while exploring any problems of hidden identity could be a vital therapeutic task (Sanders, 1993). In this study, all participants had some external validation of their sexuality and their relationships, and it seems important to explore these supports.

It is also important for therapists to be aware of the constraints on the family narratives of lesbian couples caused by the lack of accepted terms for their relationships. It is important to distinguish between the unsaid and the unsayable (Becker, 1991). These issues are particularly interesting in the context of current discussions in social constructionist and narrative theory about the role of language in the formation of identity (Laird, 1999; White, 1988).

We found redrawing to be a very useful method to generate discussion about lesbian family relationships. Using tiers and circles, together with developing new symbols for lesbian family relationships, helped to represent a diversity of family systems for couples. We suggest it may also be useful for exploring gay, bisexual, and transgender family relationships. Future work with GLBT families may create new ways of depicting family relationships in genograms.

REFERENCES

Basham, K. K. (1999). Therapy with a lesbian couple: The art of balancing lenses. In J. Laird (Ed.), *Lesbians and lesbian families: Reflections on theory and practice* (pp. 143-177). New York: Columbia University Press.

Becker, A. L. (1991). A short essay on languaging. In F. Steier (Ed.), *Research and reflexivity* (pp. 226-234). London, UK: Sage Publications.

Burnham, J. B. (1988). *Family therapy.* London, UK: Routledge.

Byng-Hall, J. (1995). *Rewriting family scripts.* New York: Guilford Press.

Carter, B., & McGoldrick, M. (1980). *The family cycle: A framework for family therapy.* New York: Gardner Press.

Carter, B., & McGoldrick, M. (1999). *The expanded family cycle: Individual, family and social perspectives.* London, UK: Allyn & Bacon.

Cogan, J. C. (1996). The prevention of anti-lesbian/gay hate crimes through social change and empowerment. In E. D. Rothblum & L. A. Bond (Eds.), *Preventing heterosexism and homophobia* (pp. 219-238). Thousand Oaks, CA: Sage Publications.

Falicov, C. J. (1995). Training to think culturally: A multidimensional comparative framework. *Family Process, 34,* 373-388.

Glaser, B. (1992). *Emergence vs. forcing: Basics of grounded theory analysis.* Mill Valley, CA: The Sociology Press.

Glaser, B., & Strauss, A. (1967). *Discovery of grounded theory.* Chicago: Aldine.

Gorell-Barnes, G. (1998). *Family therapy in changing times.* London, UK: MacMillan Press Ltd.

Green, R-J., Bettinger, M., & Zack, E. (1996). Are lesbian couples fused and gay male couples disengaged? Questioning gender straitjackets. In J. Laird & R-J. Green (Eds.), *Lesbians and gays in couples and families* (pp. 185-230). San Francisco: Jossey-Bass.

Greene, B. (1994). Lesbian and gay sexual orientations: Implications for clinical training, practice, and research. In B. Greene & G. M. Herek (Eds.), *Lesbian and gay psychology* (pp. 1-24). Thousand Oaks, CA: Sage Publications.

Hare-Mustin, R. (1991). The problem of gender in family therapy theory. In M. McGoldrick, C. M. Anderson, & F. Walsh (Eds.), *Women in families: A framework for family therapy* (pp. 61-77). New York: Norton.

Healey, T. (1999). A struggle for language: Patterns of self-disclosure in lesbian couples. In J. Laird (Ed.), *Lesbians and lesbian families: Reflections on theory and practice* (pp. 123-141). New York: Columbia University Press.

Johnson, T. W., & Colucci, P. (1999). Lesbians, gay men, and the family life cycle. In B. Carter & M. McGoldrick (Eds.), *The expanded family cycle: Individual, family and social perspectives* (pp. 346-361). New York: Allyn & Bacon.

Laird, J. (1996). Invisible ties: Lesbians and their families of origin. In J. Laird & R.-J. Green (eds.), *Lesbians and gays in couples and families* (pp. 89-122). San Francisco: Jossey-Bass.

Laird, J. (1998). Invisible ties: Lesbians and their families of origin. In C. J. Patterson & A. R. D'Augelli (Eds.), *Lesbian, gay and bisexual identities in families: Psychological perspectives* (pp. 197-228). Oxford, UK: Oxford University Press.

Laird, J. (1999). Gender and sexuality in lesbian relationships: Feminist and constructionist perspectives. In J. Laird (Ed.), *Lesbians and lesbian families: Reflections on theory and practice* (pp. 47-89). New York: Columbia University Press.

Lewin, E. (1993). *Lesbian mothers: Accounts of gender in American culture.* Ithaca, NY: Cornell University Press.

Liu, P., & Chan, C. S. (1996). Lesbian, gay, and bisexual Asian Americans and their families. In J. Laird & R.-J. Green (Eds.), *Lesbians and gays in couples and families* (pp.137-152). San Francisco: Jossey-Bass.

Lott-Whitehead, L., & Tully, C. T. (1999). The family lives of lesbian mothers. In J. Laird (Ed.), *Lesbians and lesbian families: Reflections on theory and practice* (pp. 243-259). New York: Columbia University Press.

Malley, M., & Tasker, F. (1999). Lesbians, gay men and family therapy: A contradiction in terms? *Journal of Family Therapy, 21,* 3-29.

Minuchin, S. (1977). *Families and family therapy.* London, UK: Tavistock Publications Ltd.

Mitchell, V. (1996). Two moms: Contribution of the planned lesbian family to the deconstruction of gendered parenting. In J. Laird & R.-J. Green (Eds.), *Lesbians and gays in couples and families* (pp. 343-357). San Francisco: Jossey-Bass.

Morningstar, B. (1999). Lesbian parents: Understanding developmental pathways. In J. Laird (Ed.), *Lesbians and lesbian families: Reflections on theory and practice* (pp. 213-241). New York: Columbia University Press.

Muzio, C. (1996). Lesbian co-parenting: On being/being with the invisible (m)other. In J. Laird (Ed.), *Lesbians and lesbian families: Reflections on theory and practice* (pp.197-211). New York: Columbia University Press.

Pidgeon, N., & Henwood, K. (1996). Grounded theory: Practical implementation. In J. T. E. Richardson (Ed.), *Handbook of qualitative research methods for psychology and the social sciences* (pp. 86-101). London, UK: BPS Books.

Richardson, D. (1996). Heterosexuality and social theory. In D. Richardson (Ed.), *Theorising heterosexuality* (pp. 1-20). Buckingham, UK: Open University Press.
Sanders, G. L. (1993). The love that dares to speak its name: From secrecy to openness in gay and lesbian affiliations. In E. Imber-Black (Ed.), *Secrets in families and family therapy* (pp. 215-243). New York: Norton.
Savin-Williams, R. C. (1996). Self-labeling and disclosure among gay, lesbian, and bisexual youths. In J. Laird & R-J. Green (Eds.), *Lesbians and gays in couples and families* (pp.153-182). San Francisco: Jossey-Bass.
Siegal, S., & Walker, G. (1996). Connections: Conversations between a gay therapist and a straight therapist. In J. Laird & R.-J. Green (Eds.), *Lesbians and gays in couples and families* (pp. 28-68). San Francisco: Jossey-Bass.
Simon, G. (1998). Family therapy: Whose story is it anyway? *Context, 40,* 12-14.
Slater, S. (1995). *The lesbian family life cycle.* New York: The Free Press.
Starrin, B., Dahlgren, L., Larsson, G., & Styrborn, S. (1997). *Along the path of discovery: Qualitative methods and grounded theory.* Stockholm, Sweden: Studentlitteratur.
Strauss, A., & Corbin, J. (1998). *Basics of qualitative research: Techniques and procedures for developing grounded theory* (2nd ed.). Thousand Oaks, CA: Sage Publications.
Swainson, M. (2000). Pretending? Lesbian couples define their families. Dissertation submitted for MSc Family & Systemic Psychotherapy, Birkbeck College University of London and Institute of Family Therapy, UK.
Tasker, F., & McCann, D. (1999). Affirming patterns of adolescent sexual identity: The challenge. *Journal of Family Therapy, 21,* 30-54.
Weeks, J. (1990). *Coming out.* London, UK: Quartet Books.
Weeks, J. (2000). *Making sexual history.* Cambridge, UK: Polity Press.
Weston, K. (1991). *Families we choose: Lesbians, gays and kinship.* New York: Columbia University Press.
White, M. (1988, Summer). The externalizing of the problem and the re-authoring of lives and relationships. *Dulwich Centre Newsletter,* pp. 5-28.
Willig, C. (2001). *Introducing qualitative research in psychology: Adventures in theory and method.* Milton Keynes, UK: Open University Press.

Chapter 6

Siblings and Sexual Orientation: Products of Alternative Families or the Ones Who Got Away?

Esther D. Rothblum
Kimberly F. Balsam
Sondra E. Solomon
Rhonda J. Factor

Consider the following two anecdotes:

George is a thirty-two-year-old gay man from a large, Irish-Catholic family of six siblings. Three of his brothers are gay and one of his two sisters is bisexual. When George was in first grade, his mother become romantically involved with a woman (George's first grade teacher—a nun!) and has lived with her ever since.

The three studies reported in this chapter were supported by grants from the Lesbian Health Fund of the Gay and Lesbian Medical Association and the Dean's Fund from the University of Vermont (Study 1); grants from the Lesbian Health Fund of the Gay and Lesbian Medical Association, the Scrivner Award of the American Psychological Foundation, and a University Research and Scholarship Grant from the University of Vermont (Study 2); and grants from the Gill Foundation and the University Committee on Research and Scholarship of the University of Vermont (Study 3).

This chapter was written while the first author was on sabbatical at the Lesbian Health Research Center of the University of California at San Francisco, the Women's Leadership Institute at Mills College, and the Beatrice M. Bain Center for Research on Women at the University of California at Berkeley.

The authors would like to thank Nanette Gartrell, Marny Hall, Marcia Hill, Ellyn Kaschak, Hadas Rivera-Weiss, and Penny Sablove for reading earlier versions of this chapter.

doi:10.1300/5792_07

When she was seventeen, Rebecca escaped from an arranged marriage in an ultrareligious Hasidic Jewish community. She took a bus to San Francisco, where she is currently in law school and in a relationship with another woman. Her five brothers and two sisters have all married and remain in the Hasidic community. Rebecca has little contact with them.

George and Rebecca are real people (though their names and some identifying information have been changed). Both are unusual—few families in the United States have that many children, very few people are Hasidic, and it is very rare to have so many people in one family identify as gay, lesbian, or bisexual (GLB). Yet George and Rebecca represent the extremes of what this chapter will focus on: do GLB individuals come from families that are nontraditional, or are they the ones who got away from conventional families? Our research projects find that one of these extremes is much more common than the other.

How much do most GLBs know about their friends' and lovers' siblings? Probably not too much, given that GLBs tend to socialize more with friends than with family of origin (Kurdek & Schmidt, 1987). GLBs who are closeted may never have introduced their lover or GLB friends to their siblings, so that the only information we have about those siblings is via anecdotes and photographs. In the GLB communities, we spend a lot of time discussing our parents (e.g., should I come out to them; will they accept my lover as a member of the family), but otherwise probably spend more time describing our exlovers, therapists, and pets than our relatives, including our siblings.

Yet something is fascinating about GLBs and their siblings. Most people are the same general age as their siblings and also the same race and ethnicity. They were raised in the same religious tradition. Despite the increasing divorce rate and concomitant blended families, most siblings grew up in the same household and attended the same schools at least for a while. The parent(s) or other adults who took care of them had a particular income, educational level, and occupation, so that siblings, especially if close in age, came from similar socioeconomic backgrounds. However now, in adulthood, one of those siblings identifies as GLB and one as heterosexual. How did this come about? What other factors are different (or similar) among siblings who differ in sexual orientation?

SIBLINGS AS A COMPARISON GROUP FOR GLBs: THE STUDIES

We did not set out to conduct a profile of GLB and heterosexual siblings. Instead, we were looking for a good way to find heterosexuals who could serve as a comparison group for GLBs. Researchers who study GLBs and want to compare them with heterosexuals face a number of methodological obstacles. One way to find large numbers of GLBs is to distribute questionnaires at GLB community events (such as gay pride marches) or organizations (such as lesbian bars) or place advertisements asking for participants in GLB newsletters or magazines. The problem is that such sources do not yield many heterosexual participants. Conversely, if researchers use general sources (e.g., random telephone calls, ads in city newspapers), only a tiny fraction (1 to 2 percent) of participants will identify as GLB. This necessitates contacting thousands of participants to obtain even a small sample of GLBs. Finally, it is possible to recruit participants from GLB community sources and just compare the results to published studies of the general population, presumed heterosexual. This too has some weaknesses—the two samples have often been collected in different ways or at different times. Also, GLBs are usually demographically different from general survey data, so the researchers have to control statistically for these differences.

One solution we had to this methodological dilemma was the idea of recruiting GLBs via community sources and then asking them to recruit their heterosexual siblings. That way, GLB and heterosexual participants would be surveyed via the same methods, during the same time period, and using the same measures. Our first study was designed to focus only on lesbians and their heterosexual sisters. We knew that we wanted to include lesbians who were not out to their heterosexual sisters so we made sure that the questionnaires did not state anywhere that ours was a study of sexual orientation. Among many demographic items and other subscales in the questionnaire were two items about sexual orientation (versus, for example, three about religion). Our main interest was the feasibility of the study—for instance, would enough heterosexual sisters participate?

This first study (Rothblum & Factor, 2001) taught us a number of things. In many cases lesbians had multiple sisters and all of them wanted to participate. In hindsight, this had a major benefit: the response rate of the index participants (the original participants who contacted us) was much higher than those of their sisters. However, with multiple sisters, we ended up with nearly identical numbers of lesbians (314) and heterosexual women (315). Furthermore, some of the respondents (133) were bisexual so we could compare bisexual women with lesbians and heterosexual women. Finally, some index participants had sisters who were themselves lesbian or bisexual. This allowed us to compare index participants with siblings who were similar in sexual orientation to see if recruitment method (e.g., bisexual women who actively sought us out versus those dragged into the study by their sisters) made a difference (it did not).

Our second study (Rothblum, Balsam, & Mickey, in press) recruited lesbians, gay men, and bisexual women and men, and their siblings (whether heterosexual or GLB). Once again, we wanted to include GLBs who were not out to their siblings but we also wanted to survey GLBs about a number of issues specific to the coming-out process. Consequently, we sent every participant a questionnaire printed on white paper, and sent GLB participants an additional questionnaire on lavender paper with items about the GLB experience. Based on the self-rating of sexual orientation, 348 heterosexual women, 125 bisexual women, 332 lesbians, 185 heterosexual men, 38 bisexual men, and 226 gay men participated in this study.

The third study took advantage of the same-sex civil union legislation in the state of Vermont. We obtained copies of all civil union certificates from the first year of this legislation (July 1, 2000, to June 30, 2001) and wrote to all the couples. We also wanted to compare these civil union couples (two-thirds of whom were lesbians, 10 percent people of color, and 80 percent from outside Vermont) to same-sex couples in their friendship circle who had not had civil unions, and also with heterosexual married siblings and their spouses. The analyses we will report here are only those of civil union couples and heterosexual married couples recruited from their siblings (that is, we will not be discussing results of same-sex couples not in civil unions). This sample consisted of 212 lesbians in civil unions, 219 married heterosexual women, 123 gay men in civil unions, and 193 married heterosexual men.

This study (Solomon, Rothblum, & Balsam, 2004) differed from our first two studies in several ways. First, we had access to a whole population (rare in GLB research, where many participants are closeted or unknown to the research team), although we had limited funding and thus sent questionnaires to only a subset of this sample. Furthermore, the civil union certificates also contained some information (year of birth of both partners, their race and ethnicity, educational level, where they lived, and whether they had been married heterosexually) that allowed us to compare characteristics of our sample with the whole population. This study was limited to couples in legal relationships (whether lesbian, gay, or heterosexual). Unlike the first two studies, we included only lesbian and gay male couples in civil unions who were out to their heterosexual married siblings.

The results of these studies point out many differences among lesbian, gay, bisexual, and heterosexual siblings (whenever we refer to *differences* we mean those that were statistically significant). A few words of caution are in order. Not all of the following variables were included in all three studies. We compared participants separately by gender. Thus, heterosexual men were compared with gay men (and in Study 2 to a very small sample of bisexual men). Heterosexual women were compared with lesbians and in Study 2 with bisexual women (Study 1 also included bisexual women in some analyses). We will present the results in three general areas: (1) education and moving away from the family of origin; (2) relationships, children, and division of labor; and (3) religion and politics.

EDUCATION AND MOVING AWAY FROM THE FAMILY OF ORIGIN

Lesbians and bisexual women have higher levels of education than do heterosexual women; this effect is weaker for gay men. Prior convenience studies have found lesbians to be highly educated (e.g., Bradford, Ryan, & Rothblum, 1994; Morris & Rothblum, 1999). This fact was often interpreted as the result of convenience sampling; for example, it was assumed that educated individuals would be more likely to subscribe to GLB periodicals and thus see ads about research. However, our research shows this effect even when lesbians are compared with their heterosexual sisters. In all three studies, lesbians have higher educational levels than heterosexual women. In the two studies that included bisexual women, they too surpass the educational levels of heterosexual women. On average, lesbians and bisexual women have a college degree or some graduate training whereas heterosexual women have some years of college but not a degree.

Our studies were not longitudinal, so we cannot identify which came first—coming out as lesbian or bisexual versus obtaining higher education. For example, heterosexual women may have married or had children at a young age (more about these variables later). Thus, heterosexual women may have dropped out of college or started college at a later age. Furthermore, universities in most countries are located in major cities, but in the United States these can also be in rural or isolated locations, including prestigious colleges (e.g., Cornell) and land grant universities (e.g., University of Illinois) that have graduate departments. Many variables are involved in attending a particular college, such as identifying a college that offers what you want, being accepted by that college, and being able to afford attending that college. Women with husbands and children might be less likely to uproot their families in search of higher education.

Lesbians may seek out education particularly because they are aware that they will not marry a man with a higher salary to support them or supplement what they earn. Thus, they need to think seriously of their education preparing them for a job or career (see Dunne, 1997, 1998, for lesbians' career preparations and choices).

These possibilities assume that higher education follows coming out as lesbian or bisexual. The converse may be true as well. Faderman (1991) has argued that colleges expose women to feminism and lesbianism. In that case, the sibling who attended college is the one more likely to come out as a sexual minority. Or, are there ways in which the daughter who moves away to attend college or who seeks a higher level of education than her siblings or parents is already predisposed to be more independent or to seek out novel experiences? Either way, a lesbian or bisexual sexual orientation is associated with higher education.

Education was not as strongly associated with sexual orientation among men. Gay men have higher levels of education in one study but not the other. Bisexual men have similar levels of education to heterosexual men (and thus lower levels than gay men). It is likely that for heterosexual men, marriage and children are not barriers to higher education the way they are for heterosexual women. Furthermore, the possibility that colleges may be a way that students learn about GLB issues may be less salient for men, because gay men reach developmental milestones in the sexual-identity process at earlier ages than do women (Garnets & Kimmel, 2003).

GLBs are underpaid relative to their educational level. Despite higher educational levels, we found no significant differences in income between GLB and heterosexual siblings. In the general population, income and educational levels are correlated (on average, people with more education earn more money). This means that GLBs are underpaid for their educational level. It is possible that GLBs face discrimination in the workplace or in hiring practices so that their income is not commensurate with their abilities (Badgett, 2001). It is also possible that GLBs prioritize workplace factors other than income such as choosing to work for a company with gay-affirmative practices or one that is in a liberal location. Or, GLBs may select jobs that have a social justice component rather than those aimed at advancement or high incomes. Whatever the cause, it is important to point out that the comparable income between GLBs and heterosexual siblings counters the stereotype in the media that GLBs (especially gay men) are financially very well-off.

Heterosexual women are more likely to be homemakers. The role of homemaker is reserved almost exclusively for women who are heterosexually married. In all three studies, about one-fifth to one-quarter of heterosexual women are homemakers, which is not a role that has high status in our society. For men and also for women who are not married, very few identify with the role of homemaker.

Gay men have moved to large cities. Both convenience surveys and nationally representative studies have found a high proportion of gay men live in large urban areas (e.g., Laumann, Gagnon, Michael, & Michaels, 1994). It is difficult to know from those studies whether gay men have moved to large cities or whether those researchers were disproportionally targeting urban gay men (e.g., by using snowball sampling or distributing surveys at large gay events). However, our research consistently shows that gay men live in large cities about twice as often as do heterosexual men recruited from siblings who presumably grew up in the same place. Thus, it is likely that gay men gravitate from rural areas and smaller cities to the large, urban areas known for their gay communities.

Lesbians, too, have moved away from their families of origin. In Study 1, lesbians were found to live farther in miles from their mother and father than their heterosexual sisters. They have also moved to their current location from a greater distance than have their heterosexual sisters. In Study 2, lesbians were found to have attended colleges that were farther from home than the ones that heterosexual women attended.

Lesbian, bisexual, and heterosexual women move to a new location for different reasons. We asked participants how long they had lived in their current location and their reasons for moving there. Lesbians and bisexual women are more likely than heterosexual women to report that they had moved for their own education. Conversely, heterosexual women are more likely than lesbians or bisexual women to indicate that they had moved for their partner's job or their child's education. Heterosexual women have lived in their current location for more years than lesbians or bisexual women. These results point to ways that lesbians prioritize their own lives, whereas heterosexual women move for husbands or children. One could speculate that gender roles in heterosexual relationships do not allow women as much choice over geographic moves for their own career or education to the extent that men have. Gay, bisexual, and heterosexual men do not differ on these variables.

Lesbians perceive less support from family than do heterosexual women, and gay men perceive more support from friends than do heterosexual men. Study 3 asked couples about perceived social support from family and friends. Heterosexual married women perceive more support from their families of origin than do lesbians in civil unions (gay men do not differ from heterosexual men on this measure). However, gay men perceive more support from friends than do heterosexual married men (lesbians do not differ from heterosexual women on this measure).

These results fit with the results described previously that lesbians attended a college that was farther away and also live farther from their parents in adulthood. Thus, lesbians may leave home because there is less to lose or else lesbians may drift apart emotionally from their families of origin because they live farther away. Gay men may also move to large cities to find friends or else have more friends because they live in a large city. Traditional male gender roles may not allow heterosexual men to have close friendships, whereas male friendships are highly valued in gay male communities. These geographic moves may enable lesbians and gay men to be more out (for example, to friends and co-workers) without the knowledge of their families.

Heterosexual couples have more contact with families of origin than do same-sex couples. Study 3 asked a number of questions about contact with family of origin. Heterosexual married women have more contact with their mothers than do lesbians in civil unions and also initiate more contact with their parents-in-law. Heterosexual married men initiate more contact with their fathers-in-law, and also report that their fathers-in-law make them feel "part of the family," compared with gay men in civil unions. These results mesh with the findings that GLBs have moved farther away from their parents. Parents may be less supportive of their GLB children, so that GLBs have less reason to visit or contact their parents. GLBs also may not be "out" to their parents and thus would not want to introduce their partners to their parents or meet their partners' parents. Finally, GLBs may have less in common with their families of origin (e.g., values, politics, lifestyle, and so on) and thus spend less time with them.

RELATIONSHIPS, CHILDREN, AND DIVISION OF LABOR

Heterosexuals have been in relationships longer than GLBs. Studies 1 and 2 did not focus specifically on couples. In those studies, lesbians are no less likely than heterosexual women to be in a partnered relationship. When we looked only at women in partnered relationships, lesbians have been in their current relationship for a shorter duration (six to seven years on average) than heterosexual women (twelve years on average). Bisexual women are less likely to be in a partnered relationship than either lesbian or heterosexual women, and those in relationships have been so for a shorter duration (five years on average) than heterosexual women. For men, the results are somewhat different. Gay men are less likely to be in partnered relationships than are heterosexual or bisexual men. However, when we looked only at men who were in partnered relationships, the difference in length of relationship among gay (nine years), bisexual (seven years), or heterosexual (ten years) men was not significant. In Study 3, which focused only on couples in legalized relationships, couples were asked when they first met, when they began dating, and when they moved in together. On all these measures, heterosexual married couples report more years than do lesbian or gay male couples in civil unions. For example, heterosexual married couples have lived together for fifteen years on average, compared with nine years for lesbians and twelve years for gay men in civil unions.

A number of factors may influence relationship longevity. For heterosexuals, marriage is not only personally desirable but something that family and friends encourage and support. GLBs may not have the support of their families to enter into same-sex relationships, and in fact family members may even be relieved when the same-sex relationship breaks up (for example, hoping that the next partner will be heterosexual). Whereas heterosexual marriage is a federal, legal institution, this is not the case for same-sex marriage. Thus, same-sex couples can break up without a legal divorce (even for same-sex couples joined in civil unions in Vermont, 80 percent are from out of state, where the legality of the relationship is not recognized).

Gay men are less monogamous than heterosexuals or lesbians. Study 3 asked couples whether they had had sex outside their relationships and also whether they had an agreement that nonmonogamy was permitted under certain circumstances. Relatively few lesbians in civil unions or heterosexual married women or men report this. However, 40 percent of gay men in civil unions have an agreement that nonmonogamy is permitted and over half have had sex outside their current relationship. Prior research has also found that nonmonogamy is an accepted part of gay male culture (Blumstein & Schwartz, 1983; Peplau, Fingerhut, & Beals, in press) and that gay male couples had a specific agreement about sex outside their relationships (Hickson et al., 1992).

GLBs are less likely to have children than heterosexuals. Despite the media focus on lesbian and gay parents, GLBs are less likely to have children than heterosexual siblings. In Study 2, over half of heterosexual women and men have children, compared with 34 percent of bisexual men, 19 percent of lesbians, 14 percent of bisexual women, and 9 percent of gay men. Among couples in Study 3, 80 percent of married heterosexuals have children, compared with 34 percent of lesbians and 18 percent of gay men in civil unions. The fact that heterosexuals are more likely to have children may also explain why they remain in relationships for a longer duration—perhaps even staying in unhappy relationships for the sake of the children. However, there are increasingly more options for GLBs wanting to become parents and societal support (both emotional and tangible, such as laws allowing adoption by two same-sex parents) is increasing. Thus, this difference may be minimized in the future.

Same-sex couples share housework, child care, and finances more than heterosexual couples. Study 3 included subscales of housework and finances (whose income pays for specific items such as rent or groceries). We also asked participants with children what proportion of the child care they do. Not surprisingly, given prior research (Peplau & Spalding, 2000), lesbian and gay male couples share these activities equally, whereas heterosexual married couples are more polarized, with women doing most of the child care and housework and men paying for more items. These results are particularly interesting because all heterosexuals in that study had a lesbian or gay sibling or in-law so they were benefiting from a couple in their immediate family who could serve as a model for equality. Thus, it seems that male/female gender roles and scripts are difficult for heterosexual married couples to escape. In contrast, lesbians and gay men are less traditional because there are no scripts for male-male or female-female couples.

RELIGION AND POLITICS

GLBs are less religious than heterosexuals. We asked participants to indicate their religion while growing up, their current religion, the importance of religion, and how often they attend religious services. Not surprisingly, GLB and heterosexual siblings do not differ in childhood religion—over three-quarters were raised in a formal religion, usually Catholic or Protestant. In adulthood, heterosexuals are generally still practicing the religion in which they were raised. However, GLBs are more likely to report that their spiritual beliefs in adulthood do not fit a formal religion, or that they have no religion. GLBs raised Jewish (about 10 percent) still identify as Jewish in adulthood, possibly because being Jewish is viewed as a cultural and ethnic identity as well as a religious one.

Lesbians and bisexual women also report a lower frequency of attending religious services than heterosexual women. We did not find this difference for men, although gay male couples rate religion as less important to them compared with heterosexual married men. It is not surprising that GLBs have moved away from traditional religions in adulthood. The same factors that permit some individuals to question a conventional sexual orientation may also result in questioning of conventional religious practices. In addition, most formal religions are not supportive of being GLB, resulting in many GLBs feeling alienated by their church or synagogue.

GLBs are more politically liberal than heterosexuals. Only Study 3 asked participants about their political views. One question asked how participants would describe their political outlook, from extremely liberal to extremely conservative. Another asked how sympathetic participants felt toward the feminist movement. GLBs are more liberal and profeminist than heterosexuals, who are closer to the midpoint on these items.

WHICH SIBLINGS BECOME GAY, LESBIAN, BISEXUAL, OR HETEROSEXUAL?

Who Is More Typical: George or Rebecca?

Our studies do not show that GLBs typically come from nontraditional families (although this had been our guess before we began this research). Quite the contrary, strong evidence suggests that GLBs are the outliers (no pun intended!) among their siblings. They are the ones who get away, both geographically and emotionally. Gay men end up in large cities and receive their social support from friends rather than family. Lesbians and bisexual women move for their own education, attend colleges that are farther from home than those that heterosexual women attend, and are more highly educated than their sisters. In sum, although Rebecca in the anecdote at the beginning of this article is an extreme case (with many siblings and from an ultrareligious family), GLBs are more likely to come from traditional families such as hers.

How do lesbians and gay men, reared in traditional families, become different and get away (or get away and then become different)? It will always be challenging to conduct longitudinal research on the coming-out process for lesbians and gay men. Many GLBs report feeling different even at a young age, though they may not have come out until adulthood. However, many heterosexuals report feeling different in adolescence as well. The number of GLBs in the general population (or at least those willing to identify as such to researchers) is very small (Laumann et al., 1994), so extremely large numbers of adolescent and young-adult sibling groups would have to be followed over time for even small samples of GLBs to be identified eventually.

A host of demographic factors in our research studies differentiate GLBs and heterosexual siblings, so it is difficult to know the progression of these factors. Do GLBs go to liberal colleges or progressive cities and then become less traditionally religious? Or, do less religious siblings obtain higher education because they feel less pressure to get married? Does lower support from families and less contact with these families precede or follow moving away? Does being GLB result in less family support? Do liberal politics precede or follow coming out as GLB?

We do not want to ignore GLBs who come from alternative families. George, in the anecdote at the beginning of this article, comes from an unusual family; however, most of us know GLBs who have another GLB sibling or GLB parent or whose siblings are themselves quite nontraditional in other ways. For example, more children are being reared by GLB parents who are out about their own sexual orientation. Recently, Stacey and Biblarz (2001) reviewed the literature on children reared by lesbian mothers. Even though the sample sizes are small and the children were often still quite young when the research was conducted, the evidence suggested that, overall, the children of lesbians may be more nontraditional than those of heterosexuals.

We are also aware that traditional families are declining in frequency. U.S. Census data indicate that 5.5 million Americans were living together and not married in 2000, compared with 1.1 million in 1970, and nearly half of single mothers in 2000 had never been married (Eskridge, 2001). More than half of all marriages ultimately end in divorce. Thus, children who come from traditional families are becoming the exception rather than the norm.

Who Becomes Bisexual?

Even in Study 2, where we made a concerted effort to recruit bisexuals, we ended up with fewer bisexual women than lesbians or heterosexual women and a very small sample of bisexual men. Nevertheless, even these small samples show many statistically significant effects, illustrating the importance of not generalizing from lesbians and gay men to bisexuals.

Looking across these results, bisexual women are more like lesbians than heterosexual women on many variables, including educational level, religion in adulthood, duration of their current relationship, children, years they have lived in their current location, and reasons for moving. Like lesbians, over 70 percent of bisexual women have never been married to men. However, bisexual men are more like heterosexual men than gay men, including educational level, currently being in a relationship, having children, and size of city or town. About half of bisexual men had ever been married compared with only 13 percent of gay men.

What could explain these differences between bisexual women and men? Possibly, bisexual women are more connected with lesbian organizations, events, and communities so that bisexual women are (or become) more demographically similar to lesbians (for example, by knowing more women in their communities who are highly educated or not religious). Maybe more women than men identify as bisexual (accounting for the larger number of bisexual women in our sample). It is possible that more organizations exist for bisexual women than men, or that women are more likely to join these groups. Or, bias against bisexual men may be stronger than it is against bisexual women in the dominant society.

Who Becomes Heterosexual?

Our research consistently finds that GLBs have heterosexual siblings who are, on the whole, quite traditional. Thus, GLBs have siblings who are married, have children, and live closer to where they grew up. These heterosexual siblings belong to formal religions and attend religious services. Their educational level is more in line with U.S. Census data. They are emotionally closer to their family of origin. The women do housework and child care, and the men take care of the finances.

Although it may not seem surprising that heterosexuals come from traditional families, our research raises the question of how heterosexuals remain traditional even when they have an GLB sibling. Why are these heterosexual siblings not tempted to move farther away from home or to attend graduate school? Are they out to their local community about having an GLB sibling? Is there extra pressure by parents on siblings to remain faithful to family values when one child has come out as GLB?

Other researchers have shown that siblings may experience the same family environment quite differently. Feinberg and Hetherington (2001) argue that parents treat children in different ways on variables such as warmth and negativity so that parenting should be viewed as a within-family variable. In addition, siblings may emphasize characteristics that highlight their own uniqueness in order to deidentify with one another (e.g., Schachter, 1985).

A recent book (Conley, 2005) focuses on how siblings within the same family can have such different life paths. Using large databases, the author found that birth order is less important in predicting success than family size, attention and quality time from parents, and how much of the family's economic resources are devoted to the sibling. Based on interviews, Conley speculates that sexual orientation interacts with family income to influence siblings. Those siblings who are GLB and from wealthy families will be downwardly economically mobile (e.g., less likely to inherit the family business) whereas those from poor families will be upwardly mobile (leaving home to find the middle-class GLB communities). Rebecca's father was on welfare when she was growing up. She has had more formal secular education than her siblings or parents, so her story fits in with Conley's theory. However, regardless of how society defines success, Rebecca's Hasidic family would consider her a failure since she has not married a man or had children, and she is no longer religious. Also, in many traditional families, being married, having children, being religious, living close to the family of origin, engaging in strict gender roles, and following the politics of the religious leader are the norm. Thus, it could be argued that Rebecca's siblings may be nontraditional in other ways that were not the focus of the present studies.

These studies also are not representative of people of color, since the overwhelming majority (about 90 percent) of respondents in each study were white. Consequently, people who are African American, Latina/o, Asian American, Pacific East Islander, Native American, or of non-American origin are underrepresented. In Study 3, in which we have data about everyone who had a civil union in Vermont, the percentage of respondents of color in our sample who had had civil unions was the same as people of color in the whole civil union population. Perhaps fewer lesbians and gay male couples of color who desired to be joined in civil unions were willing to travel to Vermont, a state that is known to be particularly (i.e., 95.5 percent) white. Also, gays and lesbians of color may not have the same financial resources as their European-American cohorts. This would inhibit their ability to pay for the travel and lodging costs of a trip to Vermont. Similarly, in Studies 1 and 2, fewer participants of color may have been able to afford subscriptions to GLB magazines (where we placed our ads about the study) or gone to GLB bars or bookstores (where our study announcements were posted).

Our research just scratches the surface of all the ways in which sexual orientation of siblings may affect their lives. We have focused mainly on demographic factors, and we suspect that there are a host of developmental, psychological, sociopolitical, and economic factors as well. We do not know which factors precede others, nor do we know which ones precede or follow coming out as GLB versus being heterosexual. However, we do know that siblings are a rich source of data, as well as a methodological innovation for comparing GLBs with heterosexuals who grew up in similar environments yet are different in adulthood.

REFERENCES

Badgett, M. V. L. (2001). *Money, myths, and change: The economic lives of lesbians and gay men.* Chicago: The University of Chicago Press.

Blumstein, P., & Schwartz, P. (1983). *American couples: Money, work, sex.* New York: William Morrow.

Bradford, J., Ryan, C., & Rothblum, E. D. (1994). The National Lesbian Health Care Survey: Implications for mental health. *Journal of Consulting and Clinical Psychology, 62,* 228-242.

Conley, D. (2005). *The pecking order: A bold new look at how family and society determine who we become.* New York: Knopf.

Dunne, G. A. (1997). *Lesbian lifestyles: Women's work and the politics of sexuality.* Toronto, Canada: University of Toronto Press.

Dunne, G. A. (1998). *Living "difference": Lesbian perspectives on work and family life.* Binghamton, NY: Harrington Park Press.

Eskridge, W. N. (2001). *Equality practice: Civil unions and the future of gay rights.* New York: Routledge.

Faderman, L. (1991). *Odd girls and twilight lovers: A history of lesbian life in twentieth-century America.* New York: Columbia University Press.

Feinberg, M., & Hetherington, E. M., (2001). Differential parenting as a within-family variable. *Journal of Family Psychology, 15*(1), 22-37.

Garnets, L., & Kimmel, D. (2003). *Psychological perspectives on lesbian, gay, and bisexual experiences* (2nd ed.). New York: Columbia University Press.

Hickson, F. C. I., Davies, P. M., Hunt, A. J., Weatherburn, P., McManus, T. J., & Coxon, A. P. M. (1992). Maintenance of open gay relationships: Some strategies for protection against HIV. *AIDS Care, 4,* 409-419.

Kurdek, L. A., & Schmitt, J. P. (1987). Perceived emotional support from family and friends in members of homosexual, married, and heterosexual cohabiting couples. *Journal of Homosexuality, 14,* 57-68.

Laumann, E. O., Gagnon, J. H, Michael, R. T, & Michaels, S. (1994). *The social organization of sexuality: Sexual practices in the United States.* Chicago: University of Chicago Press.

Morris, J. F., & Rothblum, E. D. (1999). Who fills out a "lesbian" questionnaire?: The interrelationship of sexual orientation, years out, disclosure of sexual orientation, sexual experiences with women, and participation in the lesbian community. *Psychology of Women Quarterly, 33,* 537-557.

Peplau, L. A., Fingerhut, A., & Beals, K. P. (in press). Sexuality in the relationships of lesbians and gay men. In J. Harvey, A. Wenzel, & S. Sprecher (Eds.), *Handbook of sexuality in close relationships.* Mahwah, NJ: Lawrence Erlbaum Associates, Inc.

Peplau, L. A., & Spalding, L. R. (2000). The close relationships of lesbians, gay men, and bisexuals. In C. Hendrick & S. S. Hendrick (Eds.), *Close relationships: A sourcebook* (pp. 111-124). Thousand Oaks, CA: Sage.

Rothblum, E. D., Balsam, K. F., & Mickey, R. M. (in press). Brothers and sisters of lesbians, gay men, and bisexuals as a demographic comparison group: An innovative research methodology to examine social change. *Journal of Applied Behavioral Science.*

Rothblum, E. D., & Factor, R. J. (2001). Lesbians and their sisters as a control group: Demographic and mental health factors. *Psychological Science, 12*(1), 63-69.

Solomon, S. E., Rothblum, E. D., & Balsam, K. F. (2004). Pioneers in partnership: Lesbian and gay male couples in civil unions compared with those not in civil unions, and heterosexual married siblings. *Journal of Family Psychology, 18,* 275-286.

Stacey, J., & Biblarz, T. J. (2001). (How) does the sexual orientation of parents matter? *American Sociological Review, 66,* 159-183.

Chapter 7

Stress and Adaptation Among Families of Lesbian, Gay, and Bisexual Youth: Research Challenges

Anthony R. D'Augelli

Considerable interest has been focused on the stresses GLB (gay, lesbian, bisexual) youths experience in their development toward adulthood, and increasing attention has been directed toward the relationship between GLB youths and their families because of the centrality of families in youths' lives. Much GLB youth research has focused in a fairly limited way on personological perspectives—youths' singular view of the development of their sexual orientation, particularly the correlates and consequences of their increasing awareness of their same-sex attractions, the subsequent processes of disclosing their sexual orientation or having their sexual orientation discovered, and the ensuing personal, social, and interpersonal challenges and opportunities. Although historically considerable attention has rightfully been placed on risk factors associated with GLB youth development, such as suicide (Russell, 2003) and HIV infection (Grossman, 2001), considerations of their normative development (Graber & Archibald, 2001) as well as patterns of coping and resilience have also been increasing. The issues raised by understanding the development of GLB youth in a family context are substantial, and research on these issues is especially difficult. In this chapter, I will briefly discuss the current status of research on GLB youth and their families and

The completion of this chapter was facilitated by grant RO1-MH58155 from the National Institute of Mental Health.

doi:10.1300/5792_08

suggest directions for future research. To assist with developing future research questions, a general conceptual model of GLB youth development that suggests areas needing future research will be presented.

STRESS AND THE DISCOVERY OF GLB YOUTHS' SEXUAL AND GENDER IDENTITIES

Nearly two decades of research have shown that GLB individuals experience stress as a result of various types of stigma and victimization (D'Augelli, 1998; Herek, 1995; Otis & Skinner, 1996; Rivers & D'Augelli, 2001). This *minority stress* (Meyer, 1995) results from experiencing individuals' and society's negative reactions to same-sex sexual attractions and their expression. Although many GLB individuals cope successfully with the stresses associated with their sexual orientation, others have more difficulties, which may result in physical and mental health consequences. For example, Mays and Cochran (2001) used a nationally representative sample to find that adults identifying as GLB were more frequently discriminated against based on their sexual orientation than heterosexually identified participants. Perceived discrimination was associated with more mental health problems, suggesting that such victimization may be partly responsible for the elevated mental health problems consistently found among GLB adults in epidemiological research (Cochran, 2001). It is a reasonable presumption that the negative consequences of stigma and victimization shown in the adult sexual orientation research findings would be more severe for GLB youths than for GLB adults. The accumulated research on GLB youths, derived from a variety of sources, shows that they demonstrate more mental health problems than their heterosexual peers. Almost no empirical literature exists on the lives of transgender[1] youths, although some evidence suggests that they too experience stress and victimization (Grossman, D'Augelli, & Salter, in press). Because of the paucity of research on transgender youths and their families, this chapter will focus only on GLB youths.

GLB youths' disclosure of their nonheterosexual orientation not only creates substantial stress for them but also creates crises in their families, especially for parents and siblings. The family stress in these situations emanates from the family members first told or the family members who first discover youths' sexual orientation to others in the family, including spouses/partners, siblings, grandparents, and extended family, following typical patterns of family dispersion (or withholding) of highly personal information. In essence, the disclosure process reflects families' communication routines and fault lines, that is, both the known, practiced ways in which family members share information, as well as more complex, indirect patterns of communication. Little is known about the nature of the family stress itself—its characteristics, how many family members are affected, or how different family members respond, including extended family members and others who are de facto family members as a result of closeness to the family. Even less is known about how familial responses and youths' development influence one another. For instance, it is unlikely that a youth who self-identifies as GLB upon entering junior high school or middle school will provoke the same response from family members as an eighteen-year-old, and a youth who discloses his or her sexual orientation to a tightly knit, socially and religiously conservative family will be treated differently than a similarly aged youth from a more liberal family whose members are dispersed across the country and have little direct contact.

Geographical context is a powerful element in the variability of familial disclosure and reaction patterns. We do not know the developmental differences between a young lesbian living in an isolated rural community—an only child, who tells middle-aged parents and who does not live near extended family—compared to another young lesbian, living in a major metropolitan area with two older male siblings, one younger female sibling, two foster siblings, and grandparents who are raising the youth. To assume similar developmental trajectories (Rotheram-Borus & Langebeer, 2001) for GLB youths who disclose their sexual orientation at the same chronological age in very different family contexts is as simplistic as presuming similar family responses to youth who disclose at different ages to parents from different cultural backgrounds.

Individual psychological growth curves may be found in the development of sexual orientation: youths' families differ and people within each family differ from one another, and major differences exist between families at different parts of the family life cycle as well. Thus, a typical family response to youth disclosure of sexual orientation does not exist. Nonetheless, it is important to learn about the adaptational processes used by these diverse youths and their families in coping with youths' new status as GLB, integrating them into the family structures, and enabling the families to emerge as families with a GLB member in the local community. Such an emergence, of course, can occur when the youth is forced to leave the family, whether by relocating to another family member's home or to the streets. Such a *gay cleansing* may well be rare, but its prevalence is unknown. In short, when a GLB youth self-identifies or is discovered, his or her family changes and his or her relationship to the family changes. Learning how much or how little change occurs within families over time is a major challenge for researchers in this field.

RECENT FINDINGS CONCERNING GLB YOUTH AND THEIR FAMILIES

Varieties of Familial Reactions

Many GLB individuals fear that their families will reject them when they disclose their sexual orientation. In a study of thirty-two gay and lesbian adults, Ben-Ari (1995) found that 52 percent feared rejection from their parents prior to disclosure of their sexual orientation. In a qualitative study of 748 Australian same-sex-identified adolescents, Hillier (2002) reported that youths feared rejection from their parents upon disclosing same-sex sexual identity and were concerned that disclosure would hurt their parents' feelings. Many reported engaging in a monitoring process by which they would seek indications of homophobia prior to disclosing their sexual orientation. In an analysis of data from 542 GLB youths, D'Augelli (2002) found that telling families about sexual orientation was seen as extremely troubling by 23 percent, very troubling by 19 percent, somewhat troubling by 28 percent, and "no problem" by only 29 percent. In addition to worry about parental reactions, youths living at home who told their parents that they are GLB experienced more victimization by their families (D'Augelli, Hershberger, & Pilkington, 1998). Pilkington and D'Augelli (1995) found that over one-third of their GLB youth sample had been verbally abused by a family member and that 10 percent were physically assaulted by a family member because of sexual orientation. In a study of 206 young lesbian and bisexual females, D'Augelli (2003) found that mothers more often (14 percent) verbally abused their daughters than fathers (4 percent) and that mothers more often physically hurt their daughters (7 percent versus 2 percent of fathers). This differential may be partly due to the finding that more mothers than fathers knew of their daughters' sexual orientation (nearly three-quarters of the mothers compared to half of the fathers).

The research on parental reactions to disclosure of sexual orientation, most of which uses participants' recollection of parents' responses, suggests that parents are initially upset, although negative reactions generally become more positive over time (Savin-Williams & Dubé, 1998). Cramer and Roach (1988), using an adult gay male sample, found that 55 percent of the men's mothers and 42 percent of their fathers initially had a negative response. Robinson, Walters, & Skeen (1989) sampled parents of lesbian and gay adults through a national support group for parents and found that most reported initial sadness (74 percent), regret (58 percent), depression (49 percent), and fear for their children's well-being (74 percent). Neither study focused specifically on parents of GLB youths, however. In contrast, Boxer, Cook, & Herdt (1991) studied youths aged twenty-one and younger and a sample of their parents. More youths had disclosed their sexual orientation to their mothers than to fathers. Of the lesbian youths, 63 percent had told their mothers and 37 percent fathers; of the males, 54 percent had told mothers and 28 percent fathers. Parents reported a period of considerable family disruption. D'Augelli and Hershberger (1993) found that 11 percent of a sample of GLB youths received a positive response from parents upon disclosure. Of parents aware of their children's orientation, 20 percent of mothers and 28 percent of fathers were either intolerant or rejecting. Parents' reactions or youths' fear of their reactions have been found to be associated with more mental health symptoms among GLB youths (D'Augelli, 2002). The same report showed that 30 percent of GLB youths feared verbal abuse at home, with more males experiencing this fear. Fear of verbal abuse at home was significantly associated with youths' mental health symptoms.

Hillier (2002) found that if parents questioned youths about their sexual identity, parents' responses were positive if parents had assumed that their child really did have a same-sex orientation. If, however, parents did not expect their child to be GLB and the child acknowledged a same-sex orientation, then parents' reactions were negative. Hillier (2002) also reported that none of the adolescents reported that their parents embraced their GLB identity. Savin-Williams (2001a) interviewed 164 GLB youths and young adults (from seventeen to twenty-five years of age), finding that about two-thirds had told mothers and one-third had told fathers. About half of the mothers were positive, whereas one-quarter of the fathers were positive. The participants reported that the primary reason for not telling fathers was because they were not close to fathers. Some daughters reported that the only reason to tell their fathers was to hurt them. Relationships with mothers were generally more positive; the most common reason reported for telling mothers was to share this new aspect of their lives. Overall, participants had felt that their parents would react negatively to disclosure of same-sex attraction. However, this was not always the case. The initial reaction of fathers was positive for sons and daughters but the initial reaction of mothers was positive for daughters and negative for sons. Sons were more likely to report improvement in their relationships with parents, but daughters reported that relationships with parents remained the same.

The wide variety of parental responses is the result of personal characteristics of the parents and youths and the social contexts of the families. Little research has linked parents' responses to youths' sexual-orientation development. Waldner and Magruder (1999) examined the effect that perceived family relationships, perceived GLB resources, and identity expression had on identity disclosure. In a sample of 172 GLB adolescents, they found that disclosure of sexual orientation to parents was affected by perceptions of available gay-supportive resources and perceptions of getting along well with parents. An indirect relationship was found between the quality of family relationships and identity disclosure. Positive family relationships negatively influenced identity expression and the perceptions of available gay and lesbian resources. The mechanism through which positive family relations affected identity expression was that youths who viewed their relationships with families as positive were less likely to attend GLB organizations or to engage in same-sex sexual relationships. Waldner and Magruder (1999) concluded that these youths did not wish to jeopardize relationships with parents. Youths who have positive family relationships are less likely to seek GLB support elsewhere, a finding that is consistent with some views that GLB youths who are sampled from GLB social, recreational, or counseling settings may not be representative of GLB youths in general (Savin-Williams, 2001b).

Why particular parents react negatively and others respond positively has not been studied extensively. Several parent characteristics have been related to parental reactions. Floyd, Stein, Harter, Allison, & Nye (1999) found a significant relationship between maternal attitudes toward youths' sexual orientation and youths' depressive symptoms. Sampling parents recruited through support groups for parents with GLB children, Serovich, Skeen, Walters, & Robinson (1993) found that parents' prior attitudes toward homosexuality and their socioeconomic status were related to their reactions when children disclosed same-sex orientation. Parents' religiosity and the length of time that parents had known about the child's sexual orientation did not affect parental acceptance. Newman and Muzzonigro (1993) surveyed twenty-seven gay male youth and found that traditional family values played an important role in determining when youths disclosed their sexual orientation to their families. Families with more traditional values (operationalized as considering religion important, having an interest in having children, and use of a language other than English at home) were less accepting than other families.

Patterns of Familial Reactions

In addition to describing the relatively positive or negative nature of parents' responses, some research has attempted to identify familial response patterns, treating the family as a unit or system. Most often, such work takes the form of articulating stages or steps in familial assimilation (absorbing the new information) and accommodation (moving toward a stable familial response, which can vary from very positive to very negative). This is an underdeveloped area of research with considerable potential to help understand how families as collectives construct social rules that regulate youths' sexual orientation within the family context. In a small study of parents who were members of GLB parents' support groups, Muller (1987) identified four types of parental reactions to their children's disclosure of same-sex orientation. *Loving open* was a positive reaction that was characterized by parents who exhibited limited denial, who told some friends and extended family about the sexual orientation of their sons or daughters. Another positive reaction was termed *loving denial,* typified by parents who did not disclose to others outside the immediate family that their sons or daughters were GLB. These parents usually accepted the sons or daughters and their partners, but set some boundaries on the nature of their acceptance. *Resentful denial* was a reaction in which parents refused to acknowledge their child's same-sex orientation. If or when the parents did acknowledge children's sexual orientation they did so in a negative manner. The last reaction, also negative, was termed *hostile recognition,* in which parents reacted with verbal and/or physical aggression. Four parental reactions similar to these described by Muller (1987) were found by Merighi and Grimes (2000), who interviewed fifty-seven adult gay men about families' reactions to disclosure. Herdt and Koff (2000) interviewed fifty parents of gay men and lesbians. Herdt and Koff identified three stages of acceptance parents go through when their sons or daughters disclose a same-sex orientation. The first was termed *disintegration,* during which parents feel shame and guilt when they learn of their child's sexual orientation. In many cases parents had suspicions earlier in the child's development but kept silent. When the child broke the silence, a disintegration of the family's secret occurred. Next, the parents moved into a state termed *ambivalence.* During this time the parents attempted to integrate their newly disclosed GLB child into their lives, viewing some positive aspects of their child's sexual orientation. Finally, parents moved to *integration,* in which they realized that they did not have the option of changing their children's sexual orientation and integrated their children into the family as a whole.

In a qualitative study, Fields (2001) observed several themes among sixteen parents of GLB children who were attending a parents' support group. The first theme was that parents felt they lacked a script to help them react to their son's or daughter's disclosure. They also felt that they needed to recover from a feeling of loss they experienced when they heard the news. A third theme was parents' interest in emphasizing behaviors of their children that conformed to heterosexual norms and separated their children from more stereotypical GLB people. Finally, parents felt that the concept of normalcy for sexual expression should be changed to include their children. In another qualititative study, Beeler and DiProva (1999) interviewed four families recruited from support groups for parents with gay or lesbian children. Researchers identified twelve themes evident in families following the same-sex disclosure of a family member. The themes included setting informal rules about topics that could be discussed openly, seeking information about homosexuality, dealing with heterosexual conventions such as commitment ceremonies and how to introduce partners, parents having to come out to extended family and friends, and coping with homophobic comments by others who do not know that they have a gay or lesbian child.

Anecdotal data suggest that families have considerable difficulty telling others in their communities about their offspring, thus increasing intrafamilial stress. Families may erect their own closets by which they avoid social discomfort and others' rejection; the mental health costs of this coping strategy remain untested (Boxer et al., 1991). Indeed, it is crucial to remember that having a GLB youth (or a GLB person of any age, for that matter) in a family can be a negative, positive, or neutral event for different family members. For some parents, having a lesbian daughter may be of little concern; for other parents, such a daughter might be seen as a major problem resolved only if the youth changes her sexual orientation; for other families, albeit rare, such circumstances can be seen as positive. One should not assume that GLB family members are intrinsically burdensome to families; yet, no evidence suggests that parents and families actively celebrate the discovery of a GLB youth in the family. The youth's violation of presumed heterosexuality, which is fueled by cultural heterosexism, is not a casual one, as the change in identity status has very real implications for the family. However, stress is not inevitable; stress may vary considerably in duration between families. We do not know the family processes that are associated with supportive and affirming responses. Families especially concerned about others' reactions are likely to be particularly negative. In an interesting analog study, Armesto and Weisman (2001) provided college students with the scenario of their future children disclosing a same-sex orientation and asked their potential reactions. Students who were more prone to experience shame and who viewed same-sex orientation as controllable were likely to be negative about having a GLB child.

It should be noted that these patterns do not include siblings or other family members such as grandparents, despite the likelihood that reactions of these other family members partially shape parental responses, and parental responses, in turn, partially shape the reactions of others in the family. Parents' management of youths' disclosure within the family (to siblings, other relatives, and so on) and to community members can vary tremendously. Variations in the dimensions of the youth's disclosure, the nature of the parent-adolescent relationship, parents' management of the information within the family, and parents' discussion of the issue in their communities influence variability in parental stress related to the sexual orientation of their children and associated parental mental health problems.

PROBLEMS WITH RESEARCH ON FAMILIAL REACTIONS TO DISCLOSURE OF GLB YOUTHS' SEXUAL ORIENTATION

The available research has many limitations related to GLB youths and their families. In an excellent review of empirical research on the processes of disclosure of sexual orientation to families, Savin-Williams and Esterberg (2000) identified important gaps in this literature. These include information about what circumstances provoke someone to come out to family, details of conversations within the family about sexual orientation, and the consequences of disclosure within the family. Savin-Williams and Esterberg also pointed out that little is known about whether mothers and fathers are told in different ways, what expectations individuals have about parents' possible reactions, and how parents actually react. Furthermore, details such as the age, socioeconomic status, religiosity, and personality characteristics of parents have not been included in most studies, and these factors surely account for some of the diversity of familial responses. Another common feature of available GLB research is that it depends on information obtained from GLB youths that is not independently confirmed, so there is no cross-validation of GLB youths reports of their families' reactions. Also, we do not know the effect of having a child or adolescent who is GLB on particular family members. This is a crucial issue, as increasing numbers of GLB youths are coming out to families at earlier ages and more families must deal with the issue of same-sex sexual expression and atypical gender expression within the family, including relationships among siblings and extended family. We lack basic information needed to understand the characteristics of the stressors in families such as who knows, who does not know, what kinds of problems the knowledge generates, and how different family members respond. In some families, for instance, only one parent is told of the youth's sexual orientation, which may place excessive stress on that individual who not only has to accommodate the disclosure himself or herself but also must determine how to manage the information among other family members. In addition, we have no information about how families with GLB youths are treated by their social networks of friends, neighbors, co-workers, religious authorities, and so on. How do others in communities react, if at all, to families in which there is a GLB youth? It is certainly probable that, in most communities, some discomfort for others would occur when discussing a family's GLB members, but in other communities having a GLB child would be kept a well-guarded secret.

Another serious omission in the current literature is an examination of the role of ethnicity and race in the families of GLB youths (Morales, 1989). In discussing ethnic-minority lesbians and gay men, Greene (1997) emphasized the importance of an understanding of the extent to which parents or families of origin control or influence family members and the importance of the family as a tangible and emotional source of support. Other factors in need of examination, according to Greene (1997), include:

1. the importance of procreation and the continuation of the family line;
2. the nature, degree, and intensity of religious values;
3. the importance of ties to the cultural community; and
4. the history of discrimination or oppression the particular group has experienced from members of the dominant culture.

Tremble, Schneider, and Appathurai (1989) noted that some parents from various cultural backgrounds adjusted to their offspring's homosexuality by reinterpreting their traditional values, maintaining that they would support their children "no matter what" (p. 259). Other parents who accepted their GLB children found precedents for youths' homosexuality among their own gay and lesbian family members and friends.

A HUMAN DEVELOPMENT MODEL OF GLB YOUTH DEVELOPMENT IN THE FAMILY CONTEXT

In an earlier analysis (D'Augelli, 1994), I described the advantages of a human development model for understanding GLB lives. Such a model makes several assumptions about individual development, family development, and changes in communities over time. Assumptions about individual development include the following:

1. Individuals develop and change over the entire life span.
2. Human development is characterized by considerable plasticity in human behavior and functioning.
3. Important interindividual differences exist in intraindividual behavioral development.
4. Individuals have considerable control over the circumstances that shape their development over time.
5. Research designs must reflect the complex, changing nature of individuals over the life span, with longitudinal designs preferred to cross-sectional designs.

These propositions are complemented by family-level assumptions in the model such as the following:

1. Families are complex collectives of individuals at different developmental phases that change over time, most importantly with the addition and loss of family members.
2. Considerable flux occurs in family processes, and both general family processes and domain-specific processes must be considered.
3. There are important interfamilial differences in how families function and change over time.
4. Families are not passive social groups, but operate as different members act in ways to influence other members.
5. Family research must include consideration of all family members, their developmental statuses, and their interrelationships.

Parallel principles of community change include the following:

1. Communities undergo change over time, as demographic and cultural trends affect local settings.
2. Communities can vary in terms of how they change over time.
3. Some communities change quickly, whereas others maintain stability and tradition over long periods of time.

4. Efforts to affect community change will be challenging, but not impossible.
5. Research on communities must contain representative samples from diverse community groups, and longitudinal analyses of community change are important.

Embodying these principles, a general human development model that can help guide research on GLB youths appears in Figure 7.1. This version of a social-ecological model views the youth and his or her family as embedded in mutually influencing spheres of influence or systems (Bronfenbrenner, 1977; Lerner, 1984). At the center of the model are individual youths, individuals at certain developmental levels on various developmental dimensions (e.g., formal operations in the realm of cognitive development, self-identification as GLB in

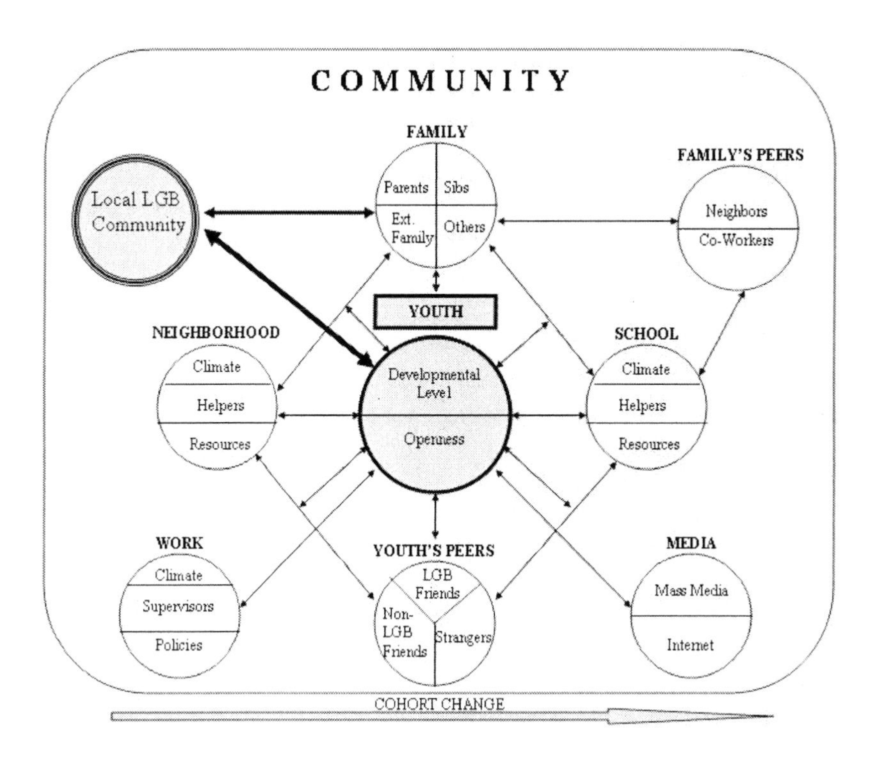

FIGURE 7.1. A human development model for the analysis of sexual orientation and gender identity among youth in families.

the realm of sexual-identity development), who are open about their sexual orientations with others to varying degrees. Youths' development after childhood occurs on many dimensions in addition to those related to sexual identity. Various developmental domains, such as biological, cognitive, and social, are also changing.

Important direct spheres of influence are families, schools, peers, and neighborhoods. As an example, a thirteen-year-old female adolescent self-identified as lesbian will be influenced by her family's structure and functioning, especially in terms of various family members' comfort with her sexual orientation. Certain family members may be highly positive, some may be highly negative, some may be ambivalent, and others may not know or suspect. The influence is reciprocal in that the youth's openness or reluctance to disclose her identity will shape the family's views of her. If she is unable to discuss her feelings with anyone, the family's attitudes will remain unchallenged; if she shares her feelings with family members, they will be forced to deal with her, and their heterosexist assumptions may change.

Adolescents' peers are crucial to their successful transition to early adulthood. For GLB youths, peers' reactions to their knowledge of youths' sexual orientation can be profoundly important. Loss of close friends and even acquaintances can exacerbate feelings of isolation that many GLB youths report. In addition, the complex social worlds of adolescent peers heighten the chance that the nature of the reactions of some peers will be magnified through tightly knit peer networks. Unfortunately, few adolescents are educated about homosexuality and, therefore, maintain myths and negative stereotypes. In addition, most victimization of GLB youths is perpetrated by peers, many of whom are acquaintances or strangers.

The nature of the thirteen-year-old's neighborhood can also strongly impact her development. A very conservative neighborhood will likely prompt less openness than a neighborhood that is more liberal; a neighborhood with open GLB people will be a very different context than one in which no GLB person is visible. Individuals can change neighborhoods by being open about their sexual orientation and challenging heteronormativity. Such a challenge is difficult for many GLB adults and even more difficult for youths. Neighborhoods differ in the overall climate for GLB people, the availability of supportive helpers (some neighborhoods have community centers for GLB people, although most do not), and the resources available for

GLB people (e.g., some towns have PFLAG groups for parents with GLB offspring as well as recreational opportunities for GLB youths, whereas others have no resources).

As schools are the social contexts in which adolescents spend much of their time and serve as the sites for developmental processes, the nature of the girl's school and its personnel can be immensely important in her development as a young lesbian. Evidence suggests that GLB youths not only are victimized in schools but also observe considerable victimization of others like themselves (D'Augelli, Pilkington, & Hershberger, 2002). An obvious contrast is between schools with and without exposure to and experience with GLB youths. Schools differ tremendously in the visibility of GLB students, although increasing numbers of schools are supporting Gay-Straight Alliances (GSAs), informal social groups which advocate for GLB students (Perrotti & Westheimer, 2001). Other schools not only do not have such groups but may be characterized by high levels of homophobia among both students and staff. It is reasonable to assume that schools with active GSAs, supportive staff, and supportive administrators will provide a more conducive developmental context than schools in which fears of victimization and indifference from authorities are norms. Some schools have counselors trained in GLB issues (as well as gay-friendly HIV-prevention programming) and will have current materials in their libraries for GLB youth to access. Other schools have none of these resources. A conceptual analysis of how various subsystems of schools affect GLB youths has been recently provided by Chesir-Teran (2003).

Other less proximal influences are work settings and the media. As many adolescents work, these settings can provide difficulties for GLB youths. Many areas still do not provide discrimination protection for GLB people, so youths who are GLB or who are suspected to be GLB may be subject to arbitrary treatment. Supervisors will vary in their attitudes about homosexuality and workplaces differ in their commitment to diversity. Some companies, although not required to by state or local legislation, have antidiscrimination policies that include sexual orientation, but most do not. To the degree that this thirteen-year-old needs the income the job provides, she will be more cautious about disclosing her sexual orientation, especially if her coworkers and supervisors are observed to be homophobic. As for the media, considerable change has occurred in the past decade in the portrayal of GLB adults and youth in mass media with the advent of such mainstream television programs as *Will & Grace* and the appearance of GLB characters in many programs watched by younger audiences, for example, MTV's *The Real World.* The increasingly positive portrayals in the media are more conducive to positive GLB youth development than negative imagery or no images at all.

The Internet is another form of mass communication that can have a profound effect on GLB youths. For the first time in history, a young person can readily obtain information about sexual orientation without having to rely on local resources. This substantially decreases the isolation of GLB youths and provides them with opportunities to discuss their lives with others like themselves. We have gone from a situation in which this young lesbian could find no accurate information at all about GLB people in her local library, her school library, or on television, to a point in which information is a few keyboard strokes away and positive images can be observed with regularity on the Internet, on television, and in films.

An important, somewhat proximal set of influences are the youths' families' peer groups. Neighbors, co-workers, people with whom family members attend religious activities, and others with whom they have regular contact can have a very important influence on the youth, as mediated through families. A young lesbian whose family attends services at a very orthodox Jewish congregation will have a difficult challenge because her family's attitudes will likely reflect those of their religious reference group.

The darkened circles and arrows in Figure 7.1 highlight the youth's individual development and its relationship to the local GLB social context. The arrows suggest reciprocal influences between spheres. The entire set of recursive interactions occurs within a community (which has its own history and current functioning); the community and its residents are all living at a particular historical time in a particular birth cohort. Cohorts can have a substantial impact on the entire set of systems and, in turn, youth development. For instance, the pre-Stonewall cohort of individuals were youths or adults at a time when homosexuality was illegal, the cohort of the mid-1970s came of age when homosexuality was removed from the official list of mental disorders, and the post-HIV/AIDS cohort born in the early 1980s have lived for more than twenty years with an epidemic that is a historical anomaly. It may well be that the current cohort, starting with 2000, will be the cohort most associated with the prominence of gay marriage. In each cohort, changing concepts of lesbian, gay, and bisexual people and of gender and gender identity have ripple effects that influence the youths' diverse social systems. As attitudes about homosexuality become more tolerant (cohort effect), more positive media images are seen, neighborhoods become less dangerous, schools see more young people disclosing their sexual orientations, and parents are better prepared to deal with their children's sexual orientations. Although there are surely developmental limits on the emergence of sexual identities, the entire movement forward through history is one of accelerating GLB development, a phenomenon seen in the dropping age that many come out, the widespread acknowledgment of same-sex couples, and the provision of legal protections from discrimination.

Thus, GLB youths' development and mental health are the complex result of relationships with family, peers, people in school, people in religious communities, people in work settings, and people in neighborhoods. GLB youth development is affected by characteristics of the local GLB community, distal factors such as media portrayals of GLB people, and by historical-cohort changes in attitudes about homosexuality. Important characteristics of youth and their families lead to differential developmental outcomes, with the family serving as a mechanism through which social circumstances affect mental health. The family is the critical link in the process of successful adaptation to sexual orientation disclosure among adolescents.

The relationship of families to their social networks is crucial for family functioning and indirectly impacts youth. Jencks and Mayer (1990) conceptualized approaches to linking child outcomes with neighborhoods; several of which have conceptual relevance to this chapter. The *neighborhood resources model* focuses on available social resources (Are any gay-affirming resources available for families in a neighborhood?). The *collective socialization model* focuses on the availability of adult socialization figures (Do GLB youths have any GLB adults to turn to as role models?). The *contagion model* emphasizes the role of peers in promoting or discouraging prosocial behavior (How much support is given by peers in the neighborhood, and how much do peers victimize GLB youths?). How families assist GLB youths in navigating the psychosocial terrain of their neighborhoods is a domain that has never been studied.

Parents, too, are influenced by multiple factors in their reactions to homosexuality and to their reactions to their son's or daughter's disclosure of a GLB identity. As the model suggests, parents deal with their own peers, with schools, and with people in their neighborhoods. For instance, highly religious parents who live in a densely populated urban neighborhood with close attachments to neighbors who harbor negative views about homosexuality would have a very different experience dealing with their children's disclosure than nonreligious suburban families who have loose ties to neighbors and are knowledgeable about homosexuality. This model is based on a reciprocal, interactive influence perspective on human development, which posits that both parents and children mutually influence their interactions and subsequent development.

DIRECTIONS FOR FUTURE RESEARCH

Clearly, many factors contribute to the developmental advancement of GLB youths as well as to the impediments to their moving toward healthy young adulthood. These youths experience the challenges of adolescence, as do all youths, with the associated fluctuations of self-esteem. Adolescence is the transition from childhood to adulthood and entails the negotiation of major developmental complexities related to the articulation of personal identity. Identity issues in adolescence occur during the course of biological changes, reorganization of peer social networks, and changes in family relationships. The family is of major importance in understanding the development of youths, including GLB youths, despite the developmental movement from families toward peers as major sources of influence. As more youths disclose their sexual orientations at earlier ages, they will do so when they still reside at home. Often, this means that they and their families will be dealing with issues related to their sexual orientation for several years while they remain at home during junior high school/middle school and high school. Despite all the progress that has occurred, many youths find disclosure to their parents to be difficult. Once the youth is known to be GLB, family stress and coping occur, processes that have yet to be studied in detail. Knowledge of normative patterns of familial reactions associated with differing levels of family conflict will be important for professionals working with GLB youths and their families. Characteristics of youths, parents, and families associated with positive reactions to youths' disclosure are especially crucial to identify. Such information can form the basis for preventive interventions, few of which have been directed to the families of GLB youths.

Future research on GLB youths and their families should be focused on

1. determining how parents learn about youths' sexual orientation and how much about a youth various family members know;
2. assessing parental and family members' reactions to milestones in the development of youths' sexual orientation—youths' growing awareness of sexual orientation, self-identification as GLB, disclosure of sexual orientation, and integrating sexual identity into other aspects of identity;
3. identifying the stressors that parents experience as a consequence of the disclosure of youths' sexual orientation;
4. examining family communication patterns about youths' sexual orientation and familial responses to disclosure;
5. assessing the family emotional climate after disclosure;
6. identifying the relationship between negative parental attitudes about homosexuality and parents' treatment of GLB youths;
7. determining the factors distinguishing families who react positively and those do not; and
8. examining the impact of the families' coping, resources, and strengths on youth development.

These suggestions are made in full awareness of the difficulties inherent in conducting research on GLB youths, no less their families. However, it is perhaps timely that researchers turn their attention from youths to the people who raise them and with whom they spend so many years of their lives.

NOTE

1. Mathy (2003, p. 791) defines transgender individuals as "people who live full or part time as members of the opposite sex. Their presentation as members of the opposite sex may occur temporarily, permanently, or by alternating their presentation as a man or a woman at different times or in varying places."

REFERENCES

Armesto, J. C., & Weisman, A. G. (2001). Attributions and emotional reactions to the identity disclosure ("coming out") of a homosexual child. *Family Process, 40,* 145-161.

Beeler, J., & DiProva, V. (1999). Family adjustment following disclosure of homosexuality by a member: Themes discerned in narrative accounts. *Journal of Marital and Family Therapy, 25,* 443-459.

Ben-Ari, A. (1995). The discovery that an offspring is gay: Parents', gay men's, and lesbians' perspectives. *Journal of Homosexuality, 30*(1), 89-112.

Boxer, A. M., Cook, J. A., & Herdt, G. (1991). Double jeopardy: Identity transitions and parent-child relations among gay and lesbian youth. In K. Pillemer & K. McCartney (Eds.), *Parent-child relations throughout life* (pp. 59-92). Hillsdale, NJ: Erlbaum.

Bronfenbrenner, U. (1977). *The ecology of human development: Experiments by nature and design.* Cambridge, MA: Harvard University Press.

Chesir-Teran, D. (2003). Conceptualizing and assessing heterosexism in high schools: A setting-level approach. *American Journal of Community Psychology, 31,* 267-279.

Cochran, S. D. (2001). Emerging issues in research on lesbians' and gay men's mental health: Does sexual orientation really matter? *American Psychologist, 56,* 931-947.

Cramer, D. W., & Roach, A. J. (1988). Coming out to Mom and Dad: A study of gay males and their relationships with their parents. *Journal of Homosexuality, 15,* 79-92.

D'Augelli, A. R. (1994). Identity development and sexual orientation: Toward a model of lesbian, gay, and bisexual development. In E. J. Trickett, R. J. Watts, & D. Birman (Eds.), *Human diversity: Perspectives on people in context* (pp. 312-333). San Francisco: Jossey-Bass.

D'Augelli, A. R. (1998). Developmental implications of victimization of lesbian, gay, and bisexual youths. In G. M. Herek (Ed.), *Stigma and sexual orientation: Understanding prejudice against lesbians, gay men, and bisexuals* (pp. 187-210). Thousand Oaks, CA: Sage.

D'Augelli, A. R. (2002). Mental health problems among lesbian, gay, and bisexual youths ages 14 to 21. *Clinical Child Psychology and Psychiatry, 7,* 439-462.

D'Augelli, A. R. (2003). Lesbian and bisexual youths aged 14 to 21: Developmental challenges and victimization experiences. *Journal of Lesbian Studies, 7*(4), 9-29.

D'Augelli, A. R., & Hershberger, S. L. (1993). Lesbian, gay, and bisexual youth in community settings: Personal challenges and mental health problems. *American Journal of Community Psychology, 21,* 421-448.

D'Augelli, A. R., Hershberger, S. L., & Pilkington, N. W. (1998). Lesbian, gay, and bisexual youths and their families: Disclosure of sexual orientation and its consequences. *American Journal of Orthopsychiatry, 68,* 361-371.

D'Augelli, A. R., Pilkington, N. W., & Hershberger, S. L. (2002). Incidence and mental health impact of sexual orientation victimization of lesbian, gay, and bisexual youths in high school. *School Psychology Quarterly, 17,* 148-167.

Fields, J. (2001). Normal queers: Straight parents respond to their children's "coming out." *Symbolic Interaction, 24,* 165-187.

Floyd, F. J., Stein, T. S., Harter, K. S. M., Allison, A., & Nye, C. L. (1999). Gay, lesbian, and bisexual youths: Separation-individuation, parental attitudes, identity consolidation, and well-being. *Journal of Youth and Adolescence, 28,* 719-739.

Graber, J. A., & Archibald, A. B. (2001). Psychosocial change at puberty and beyond: Understanding adolescent sexuality and sexual orientation. In A. R. D'Augelli & C. J. Patterson (Eds.), *Lesbian, gay, and bisexual identities and youth: Psychological perspectives* (pp. 3-26). New York: Oxford University Press.

Greene, B. (1997). Ethnic minority lesbians and gay men: Mental health and treatment issues. In B. Greene (Ed.,) *Ethnic and cultural diversity among lesbians and gay men* (pp. 216-239). Thousand Oaks, CA: Sage.

Grossman, A. H. (2001). Avoiding HIV/AIDS and the challenge of growing up gay, lesbian, and bisexual. In A. R. D'Augelli & C. J. Patterson (Eds.), *Lesbian, gay, and bisexual identities and youth: Psychological perspectives* (pp. 155-180). New York: Oxford University Press.

Grossman, A. H., D'Augelli, A. R., & Salter, N. P. (in press). Male-to-female transgender youth: Gender expression milestones, gender atypicality, victimization, and parents' responses. *Journal of GLBT Family Studies.*

Herdt, G., & Koff, B. (2000). *Something to tell you: The road families travel when a child is gay.* New York: Columbia University Press.

Herek, G. M. (1995). Psychological heterosexism in the United States. In A. R. D'Augelli & C. J. Patterson (Eds.), *Lesbian, gay and bisexual identities over the lifespan* (321-346). New York: Oxford University Press.

Hillier, L. (2002). "It's a Catch 22": Same sex attracted young people on coming out to parents. In S. Feldman & D. Rosenthal (Eds.), *Talking sexuality: Parent-adolescent communication* (pp. 75-91). San Francisco: Jossey-Bass.

Jencks, C., & Meyer, S. E. (1990). The social consequences of growing up in a poor neighborhood. In L. E. Lynn & M. G. H. McGeary (Eds.), *Inner-city poverty in America* (pp. 111-186). Washington, DC: National Academy Press.

Lerner, R. M. (1984). *On the nature of human plasticity.* New York: Cambridge University Press.

Mathy, R. M. (2003). Transgenderism. In M. Kimmel & A. Aronson (Eds.), *Men & masculinities: A social, cultural, and historical encyclopedia* (pp. 792-793). Santa Barbara, CA: ABC-CLIO Press.

Mays, V. M., & Cochran, S. D. (2001). Mental health correlates of perceived discrimination among lesbian, gay, and bisexual adults in the United States. *American Journal of Public Health, 91,* 1869-1876.

Merighi, J. R., & Grimes, M. D. (2000). Coming out to families in a multicultural context. *Families in Society, 81,* 32-41.

Meyer, I. H. (1995). Minority stress and mental health over gay men. *Journal of Health and Social Behavior, 36,* 38-56.

Morales, E. S. (1989). Ethnic minority families and minority gays and lesbians. *Marriage & Family Review, 14,* 217-239.

Muller, A. (1987). *Parents matter: Parents' relationships with lesbian daughters and gay sons.* Tallahassee, FL: Naiad Press.

Newman, B. S., & Muzzonigro, P. G. (1993). The effects of traditional values on the coming out process of gay male adolescents. *Adolescence, 28,* 213-226.

Otis, M. D., & Skinner, W. F. (1996). The prevalence of victimization and its effect on mental well-being among lesbian and gay people. *Journal of Homosexuality, 30*(3), 93-121.

Perrotti, J., & Westheimer, K. (2001). *When the drama club is not enough: Lessons from the Safe Schools Program for gay and lesbian students.* Boston: Beacon Press.

Pilkington, N. W., & D'Augelli, A. R. (1995). Victimization of lesbian, gay, and bisexual youth in community settings. *Journal of Community Psychology, 23,* 34-56.

Rivers, I., & D'Augelli, A. R. (2001). Victimization of lesbian, gay, and bisexual youths. In A. R. D'Augelli & C. J. Patterson (Eds.), *Lesbian, gay, and bisexual identities and youth: Psychological perspectives* (pp. 199-223). New York: Oxford.

Robinson, B. E., Walters, L. H., & Skeen, P. (1989). Response of parents to learning that their child is homosexual and concern over AIDS: A national survey. *Journal of Homosexuality, 18,* 59-80.

Rotheram-Borus, M. J., & Langebeer, K. A. (2001). Developmental trajectories of gay, lesbian, and bisexual youths. In A. R. D'Augelli & C. J. Patterson (Eds.), *Lesbian, gay, and bisexual identities and youth: Psychological perspectives* (pp. 97-128). New York: Oxford University Press.

Russell, S. T. (2003). Sexual minority risk and suicide. *American Behavioral Scientist, 46,* 1241-1257.

Savin-Williams, R. C. (2001a). *Mom, Dad. I'm gay: How families negotiate coming out.* Washington, DC: APA Books.

Savin-Williams, R. C. (2001b). Suicide attempts among sexual minority youth: Population and measurement issues. *Journal of Consulting and Clinical Psychology, 69,* 983-991.

Savin-Williams, R. C., & Dubé, E. M. (1998). Parental reactions to their child's disclosure of a gay/lesbian identity. *Family Relations, 47,* 7-13.

Savin-Williams, R. C., & Esterberg, K. G. (2000). Lesbian, gay, and bisexual families. In D. H. Demo, K. R. Allen, & M. A. Fine (Eds.), *Handbook of family diversity* (pp. 197-215). New York: Oxford University Press.

Serovich, J. M., Skeen, P., Walters, L. H., & Robinson, B. E. (1993). In-law relationships when a child is homosexual. *Journal of Homosexuality, 26*(1), 57-76.

Tremble, B., Schneider, M., & Appathurai, C. (1989). Growing up gay or lesbian in a multi-cultural context. *Journal of Homosexuality, 17*(3), 253-267.

Waldner, L. K., & Magruder, B. (1999). Coming out to parents: Perceptions of family relations, perceived resources, and identity expression as predictors of identity disclosure for gay and lesbian adolescents. *Journal of Homosexuality, 37*(2), 83-100.

PART II: SPECIAL ISSUES IN GLBT FAMILY STUDIES

Chapter 8

Polyamory and Gay Men: A Family Systems Approach

Michael Bettinger

A starting point for many in trying to understand gay male families and relationships is to begin with the Western model of the heterosexual family and to try to understand gay families and relationships from this perspective. This is not a good strategy. Gay families and relationships differ in characteristics and values in significant ways. Gay families and relationships need to be looked at for what they are with the understanding that gay male and heterosexual mating patterns are different.

An important difference between gay men and heterosexuals is that the majority of gay men in committed relationships are not monogamous (Bell & Weinberg, 1978; Blumstein & Schwartz, 1983; McWhirter & Mattison, 1984; Saghir & Robins, 1973). Some of these men are polyamorous. *Polyamory,* which literally means many loves, may better be understood as responsible nonmonogamy (Anapol, 1997). Monogamy is a morally neutral subject within the gay male community.

Thinking of gay male relationships only in terms of dyadic domestic partnerships is too narrow. It assumes a duality that is not always the reality. The sexual and romantic mating patterns of gay men are more complex than domestic partnership connotes. The lack of monogamy results in some gay men having primary and secondary partners—concepts that will be further discussed later in the capter. In addition, there may be more than one primary or secondary partner.

Until recently, most of the literature on gay male families and relationships has concentrated on the dyadic couple's relationship while occasionally noting that most of the men were not monogamous.

doi:10.1300/5792_09

Little discussion has focused on the structure or impact of these relationships. Coleman and Rosser (1996) indicate that although the majority of gay male couples are not sexually monogamous they are emotionally monogamous. However, some gay men in committed relationships develop other sexual relationships that also involve a degree of emotional intimacy, commitment, and/or longevity. Research has not yet been done to understand how frequent polyamory is among gay men, but it does exist. Polyamory also exists in the lesbian community (Munson & Stelbourn, 1999).

MODELS OF POLYAMORY

Polyamory may take different forms (Anapol, 1997; Labriola, 1999; Weitzman, 1999), each of which may be called a model of polyamory. Often within a related network of polyamorous individuals, couples and families one will find a combination of these models being practiced. To understand this better, I will describe four models of polyamory. To understand these models, one needs to understand a distinction between *primary* and *secondary* partners.

Primary partners are closely related to the concept of domestic partner. The couple often lives together as a family unit, and their relationship generally takes precedence over the other relationships that either may have. Generally, the primary partner has to be considered when making important life decisions. The primary partner often has considerable power and authority regarding the secondary partners. Usually a high level of commitment exists between primary partners.

Secondary partners cover a much wider range. The secondary partner may be a committed or casual relationship, and generally the person who is a secondary partner has little power or authority regarding the primary relationship. Although the level of commitment may vary, the distinguishing factors that make these partnerships special is that these relationships usually involve sexuality and emotionality, and they endure over time.

The first model is called the *Primary/Secondary Model.* In this model, a dyadic relationship is primary and the other relationships are considered secondary to that primary relationship. More than one secondary relationship may exist for either or both partners, or one may have one or more secondary relationships while the other only has a primary relationship. A commonly understood version of this model is the V pattern, where a person has both a primary and a secondary partner. The emotional intensity of either relationship may be stronger than the other.

A second and probably less-common form of polyamorous relationships is known as the *Multiprimary Individual Model.* The essential feature of this model is that one individual has a primary relationship of equal commitment with two (or in rare occasions, three) individuals. The two (or more) individuals, however, do not have a primary relationship with each other, though they may have a secondary relationship. Each of these primary relationships is considered to be of equal weight. The individual is obligated to consult with both partners regarding major changes in his or her life.

A third model is called the *Multiprimary Family Model.* Here, three or more individuals have a primary relationship—each with all the other people in the family. One common form of this model is a triad of three individuals, all of whom may consider themselves to be married to the other two. A fourth or fifth person may be added but as the numbers get larger, the number of these relationships become less frequent. Some multiprimary families of four people begin as two couples who then become a multiprimary family. Others build the families one person at a time.

Within the multiprimary family model are two variations. One is an open model, where individuals within the family are allowed to have other relationships generally along a primary/secondary model. In other multiprimary families, monogamy is the rule within the family and individuals agree to not have outside sexual or romantic relationships.

A fourth variation is the *Multisecondary Relationship Model.* In this model, an individual may have more than one relationship, though none of these relationships rise to the level of commitment one has with a primary partner. Often the individual does not live with any of these secondary partners. The secondary partners are usually not required to be consulted regarding changes in the life of the individual, yet each relationship is stable and ongoing with a level of commitment that is either explicit or implicit. Some gay men who practice this model are mistakenly considered by unknowledgeable others to be single.

Mixing of the models is also not uncommon, in fact, this is often the case. In some of these families, the rules and relationships change over time. In order to help the reader understand how polyamory functions, I will later describe a complex multicouple polyamorous family built on the primary/secondary and the multiprimary individual model. The reader, along with the members of these families, needs to be able to deal with ambiguity in understanding these relationships, as there are always exceptions to the rules.

MAKING IT WORK: ESSENTIAL SKILLS

The stability and functionality of a polyamorous family depends on how well or poorly the individuals, dyads, triads, and so on handle a number of important skills. Some of the skills are similar to those needed in any relationship, while others are unique to polyamorous relationships. Because of the added complexity due to multiple possibilities for triangulation, a higher level of functioning is needed for the polyamorous family to remain functional and stable. A good discussion of these skills can be found in Easton and Lidst (1997). An observer can understand the overall level of functioning and where a polyamorous family may need help by focusing on how well or poorly these skills are handled.

Jealousy, Possessiveness, and Envy

It is necessary for each individual to be able to deal with feelings of jealousy, possessiveness, and envy in themselves and others if the polyamorous family is to be functional. The notion of sharing one's partner with another person is an uncommon idea in the Western conception of family. Polyamory requires sharing. Although recognizing that jealousy, possessiveness, and envy are normally and frequently occurring feelings in many relationships, the challenges presented by these feelings are a constant factor in polyamorous families.

Part of the experience of being in a polyamorous relationship is the opportunity to unlearn these often strong reactions and feelings. An added benefit to unlearning these reactions is that an individual removes himself or herself from the victim role and takes more responsibility for his or her life and feelings. How well or poorly these feelings are handled will have a large effect upon family functionality.

Respect for All Other Relationships

For a polyamorous family to be functional, each individual is required to demonstrate respect for all other ongoing relationships. While some relationships are primary and others secondary, all are important and equally valid. The relationships may not necessarily be equal in time, commitment, or emotional intensity, but they are equal in validity. To the degree that this relational validity is understood, accepted, and communicated, the family will be more or less functional.

Ability to Organize and Juggle Time

All individuals in polyamorous relationships need the ability to organize and juggle time. Polyamory requires people sharing their time and the time of others. Lack of organization related to time often results in hurt feelings, which has negative impact on the family's functionality.

Boundaries and Limits

The individuals involved in polyamorous families need the ability to set and respect boundaries and limits. Although this is important in any dyadic relationship, it is especially important in polyamorous relationships. Polyamory, by definition, involves multiple relationships, and multiple relationships require that the individuals know what the rules, boundaries, and limits of each relationship are. How well or poorly boundaries and limits are handled will affect the functionality of the family. Part of this is each individual having a clear understanding of the level of commitment of each person in each relationship. The levels of commitment vary.

Ability to Have Appropriate Relationships with As Many in the System As Possible

Not all relationships within a polyamorous family are sexual. The more individuals who are not sexual with each other who can have civil, if not warm relations, the more likely it is that the family will remain stable. The more interconnected individuals are, the more likely it is that the family will functionally survive the death or departure of any individual from the family.

Communication and Assertion of One's Needs

The ability to clearly communicate becomes more crucial with the larger number of people involved. A subset of communication—the ability of individuals to assert their needs, including sexual needs—becomes critical. Without clear communication and assertion of one's needs, it is almost inevitable that the person lacking those skills will be unhappy with the polyamorous arrangement, and the entire family will suffer as a result.

Honesty

Although honesty is on most people's list of qualities they want in a mate, it is even more important in polyamorous families. Since polyamorous individuals are having sexual contacts with more than one person, the opportunities to rationalize lying or keeping secrets are ever present. Honesty, however, does not mean telling one's partner everything that is going on with another partner. Each dyad needs to decide upon the level of privacy in that dyadic relationship and to communicate that to all others to whom it is relevant.

Honoring Commitments

Because individuals in polyamorous families have multiple relationships, all are aware if commitments are not being honored with them but are being honored with others. Lack of honoring commitments will lead to triangulation and possibly jealousy, both of which will make the family less functional.

A Sense of One's Own Needs

To a large degree, polyamory is about individuals acknowledging their own needs and creating relationships that honor those needs. To the extent that an individual is out of touch with his or her own needs, that person may agree to commitments that are inappropriate for him or her, and the result will impair the functionality of the family. This may include an individual mistakenly agreeing to be in a relationship with a partner who practices polyamory.

Nonjudgmental Attitude

Many people see monogamy in moral terms—it is the right way to have a relationship. Some individuals pursue polyamorous relationships not merely because they have an interest in nonmonogamy but because their interests extend to other areas that this society has a moral attitude toward, such as homosexuality, bisexuality, and kinky sexual practices such as sadomasochism. To the extent that all the individuals in a polyamorous family are or are not judgmental, the functionality of the system will be affected.

BENEFITS OF POLYAMOROUS RELATIONSHIPS

Some benefits of polyamory are economic. More than two adults living together gain the benefits of economy of size. Chores related to upkeep of a household and child supervision can be shared. Polyamorous adults have often worked out internalized negative feelings regarding human sexuality and present a sex-positive attitude toward children. Breaking the pattern of a two-adult household sets the stage for greater acceptance of diversity, both sexual and gender related.

However, a specific benefit exists for same-sex couples in polyamorous relationships. Both gay men and lesbian women tend to form highly enmeshed dyadic relationships (Green, Bettinger, & Zacks, 1996). They attempt to be all things to each other—friends, lovers, and economic partners. My clinical experience has shown me that the majority of problems gay men have in dyadic relationships results from being too highly enmeshed.

A polyamorous family takes pressure off individuals from having to meet all the needs of the other. That extends far beyond the sexual needs to practical and emotional needs. For instance, a gay man who wants a stable partner but who also wants to have excitement in his life may not be able to get that from interactions with the same person. Polyamory frees up each partner from having to meet all the needs of the other.

UNDERSTANDING FAMILIES

To understand how families function, one needs to be able to describe and assess the family. I find three concepts helpful in this regard. The first is *family systems* (Fogarty, 1976; Guerin, 1978; Gurman & Kniskern, 1981; Leveton, 1984). The second is the *growth model* (Bettinger, 2001; Luthman, 1974), and the third is the *Enneagram* (Palmer, 1995; Riso & Hudson, 1999). Together they make it possible to coherently conceptualize and describe families and how they function.

Conceiving the family as a system allows us to examine the interactional patterns created by an individual as he or she interacts with the other people in his or her life. Within the field of family systems, the approach I find most helpful is termed the *intergenerational* or *transgenerational* approach and is based on the pioneering work of several scholars (Boszormenyi-Nagy & Spark, 1973; Bowen, 1976, 1978; Framo, 1992; Stierlin, 1977; Whitaker, 1976). This approach has continued to be developed by many others.

The intergenerational or transgenerational approach allows us to see individual and family behavior and functioning as the combined result of three forces. One is the individual's intrapsychic makeup, particularly in terms of differentiation of self versus fusion (Bowen, 1976). Second is the transgenerational messages and legacies of the individual's family of origin. The third factor is the societal cultural values and the affect of those values on the individuals. Especially important are those values regarding economic class, race, ethnicity, gender, sexual orientation, and gender identification. These three factors affect the newly created family systems, each of which has their own rules, roles, and expectations. The level of functioning of those individuals and that family are affected by all three. The polyamorous families created by gay men are affected by these forces, as are all other families.

The growth model allows us a way of assessing how an individual or family is functioning, including polyamorous gay male families. The growth model postulates that both individuals and families function along a continuum from low to high functioning and that individuals and families want to grow and increase their level of functioning. Often, individuals and families develop rigid behavioral patterns making change/growth difficult. Many of these patterns (symptoms) have secondary gains, making them difficult to give up. The growth model allows the user to understand where along the continuum a person or family actually is.

The growth model is not the dominant model in the mental health profession—the medical model is. The *Diagnostic and Statistical Manual of Mental Disorders* (American Psychiatric Association, 1994), considered by many to be the ultimate resource of the American mental health professions, is based on the medical model. In this model, if symptoms rise to a certain level, the individual is considered to have a mental illness and is given a diagnosis.

The Enneagram is one of many personality topologies. It is based on the growth model. The Enneagram postulates nine personality types and many subtypes. I choose to use the Enneagram to describe individuals for several reasons. It is, I believe, the most highly developed growth-model-oriented theory of personality. It uses terminology that non-mental-health professionals can understand. Most people can correctly determine their own type and subtypes. While different writers use slightly different terms to label the various personality types, they are closely related. I believe the best overall description of the Enneagram is by Riso and Hudson (1999). Palmer (1995) describes the likely interactional patterns between the Enneagram personality types when those individuals either work together or are in an intimate relationship. Another good description of the likely interactional patterns between intimate partners can be found on Riso and Hudson's Web site at www.enneagraminstitute.com.

When these concepts are applied to polyamorous families, they enable us to describe and assess the level of functionality of a polyamorous family and possibly to point to areas where the family needs help. This begins with looking at the level of functioning of each individual. From there, a series of dyadic, triadic, and sometimes quadratic relationships form—all of which have their own level of functionality. These groupings interact with other individuals, dyads, triads, and so on, which results in a system where functioning can be assessed either as a whole or by looking at parts of the system. Implicit is the notion that a rise or fall in the level of functioning of any individual, dyad, triad, and so on will correspondingly affect the overall level of functioning of the entire family system.

UNDERSTANDING A POLYAMOROUS GAY MALE FAMILY

The following is a hypothetical description of a stable, high-functioning, gay male polyamorous family that is an example of both the primary/secondary and the multiprimary individual model (see Figure 8.1). What appears on first glance to be three separate households—two gay male couples and a single (gay?) father with two teenage boys—is actually seven people involved in a complex polyamorous family that also extends beyond these people to eventually include others who may be thought of as part of an extended polyamorous family.

One way to begin to understand this family is to start by thinking of Victor as the center of a genogram with three lines heading outward from Victor in three directions, indicating three relationships. One line represents Victor (age fifty-five years) and James (age fifty-four years) who have been primary partners for forteen years and live together. A second line represents Victor and Alan (age fifty years). Alan is Victor's second primary partner. Alan and his ex-wife live separately and coparent two teenage boys, Peter (age sixteen years)

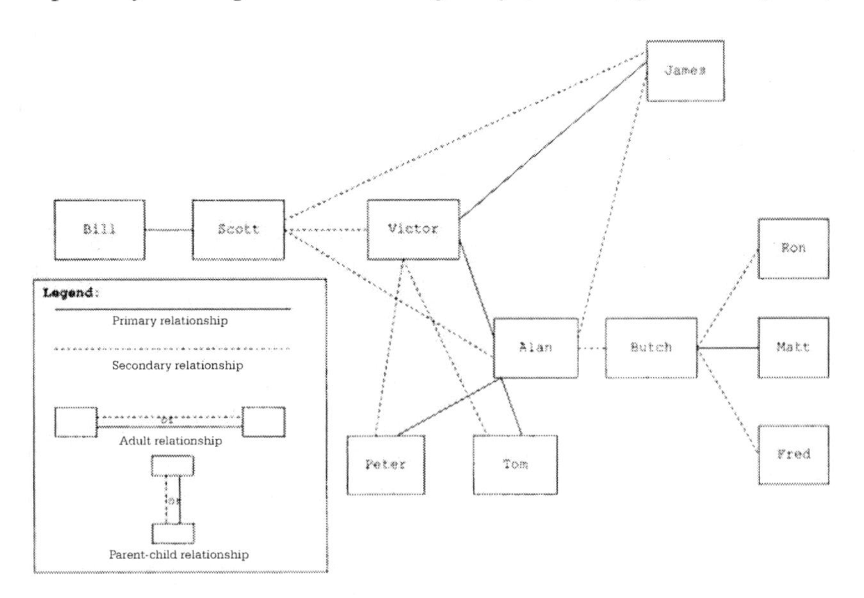

FIGURE 8.1. Genogram of a hypothetical gay male polyamorous family.

and Tom (age thirteen years) who sleep in the home of each parent half of the time. Victor and Alan have been in a relationship for five years. The relationship began casually, developed into a secondary relationship, and is now a primary relationship for both, even though they do not live together. The third line connects Victor and Scott (age fifty-eight years). They have a secondary relationship. Scott lives with Bill (age fifty-seven years), and they have been primary partners for seventeen years. Thus, Victor has two primary partners (James and Alan) and a secondary partner (Scott, who has a primary partner, Bill).

The three on the outside of the genogram where Victor is in the center are all connected by lines to one another, indicating a sexual/romantic/intimate relationship, though of differing intensities. Scott and Alan have developed a strong secondary relationship over the past three years that always involves the presence of Victor. This forms a triad of Victor, Alan, and Scott. Both Scott and Alan have a limited sexual relationship with James that always involves the presence of Victor. This results in a functioning intimate quadrant of Victor, James, Alan, and Scott. Victor, James, and Scott form another triad, as does Victor, James, and Alan. These triads and the quadrant interact as a unit both privately and publicly. Bill is the only one of the five adults who has only one romantic relationship (Scott). Bill has a social relationship with Victor, James, and Alan that always involves the presence of his primary partner, Scott. Each of the remaining four adults form dyads of varying intensity and commitment with the three other adults in the system. Quite important, too, is that Victor has a limited stepparent relationship with Alan's two children. The four often take part in recreational and holiday activities together.

This is the core of the polyamorous family to be discussed. Drawing the line at this point is arbitrary. Alan also has a secondary relationship of five years with Butch. Butch and Matt are primary partners, and Butch also has several other secondary partners of long standing. Coincidently, Scott has a limited, long-standing social relationship with Butch and Matt unrelated to Alan but related to a mutually shared hobby.

To understand the how and why of this family's functioning, I will begin by describing the personality of each individual and the resulting interactional patterns using the Enneagram terminology and concepts of Riso and Hudson (1999) and the dyadic interactional concepts of Palmer (1995). When combined with family systems concepts, this results in an understanding of why this polyamorous gay male family is stable and highly functioning.

The overriding themes of this family are intense gay male sexuality and authenticity. The adults and the children are encouraged to embrace their eccentricities. The first meetings of all the adult dyads were intensely sexual. Much of the early motivation for continuing to see each other was sexual. Frequent and intense sexuality continue to be a major theme, but these relationships have developed into full relationships involving the authentic self of each individual.

Victor is an Enneagram type 7 (the Enthusiast) with a 6 wing subtype (the Entertainer). His greatest desire is to be happy and feel pleasure; his worst fear is to be bored and trapped in pain. He never felt bad about being gay, since it was always the source of pleasurable feelings. Victor has little shame about who he is or ever has been. Expressing his sexuality has been a major theme in his life. Victor has said "I would rather play than anything," and to Victor, play means sex.

He is versatile, energetic, spontaneous, fun loving, passionate, and takes joy in existence. When focused, he is productive and playful. When overloaded, he becomes scattered, insecure, and withdrawn. He is attracted to men who he perceives are more grounded, focused, masculine, and stable than he is. He is a large man but is also quiet, shy, polite, and inner-directed. He is exceedingly honest. Asked directly for his opinion, he will give it truthfully with no consideration for how the listener will feel about him after hearing his opinion. He has always assumed it was the responsibility of the listener to deal with his opinion. He is fiercely independent and is the leader of his life. He does, however, freely give to others on both a personal and professional level. Creativity has always been important to him. In his late twenties, he founded and nursed a gay arts organization that recently had its twenty-fifth anniversary as a local institution. He is content now to work as an administrator for a nonprofit organization and to concentrate on his personal life. Because of his multiple relationships, he believes the decade of his fifties has been the happiest decade of his life.

James is an Enneagram type 8 (the Challenger) with a 7 wing subtype (the Independent). He is tall and imposing and likes to challenge himself and others to be better than they are. His greatest desire is to determine the course of his own life and to deal with both the external and internal forces that make that difficult to do. His greatest fear, correspondingly, is of being controlled by others. If he had to make a choice, he would rather be feared than loved. He is inner-directed.

For a number of years, James has been concentrating more on the intellectual than the sexual, though he attracts considerable attention from gay men wanting to be sexual with him. He is now studying the classic philosophers of ancient Rome and is putting his ideas into a Web site and news group where he interacts with and challenges others. He wants to have an impact on the world. He is in a service profession where he can choose his assignments, and he chooses assignments where he can have verbal interactions related to his studies and ideas with other intellectuals. He is social and outgoing and exudes self-confidence. One of his weaknesses is that he is attracted to the idea that he can outthink almost anyone. When overwhelmed, he retreats into trying to understand more and does not always understand he is accomplishing less. He has a difficult time admitting when he is wrong.

Alan is an Enneagram type 3 (the Achiever) with a 4 wing subtype (the Professional). Everything Alan does, he does intensely and well. He takes great enjoyment from the process. Much of his identity and self-esteem come from his accomplishments. He has successfully run his own business for many years and has been able to support in a middle-class lifestyle—both in his household and the household of his former wife, with whom he now has a strained relationship. He is a great father dedicated to spending as much time as possible with his sons in activities of their choosing. He is painfully aware that his sons, ages thirteen and sixteen, will soon be young adults, and he wants to maximize this opportunity to actively parent them. Between work, the time he spends with his children, and his relationships with Victor and Butch, he is always on the go. He underestimates how long things will take to accomplish and his need for rest.

Alan has an almost unshakable belief in himself that he can attain that which he wants to achieve. When he cannot achieve, he withdraws and becomes uncommunicative. He is a both a quiet and a private man who is not used to sharing his feelings with others. When he does share he is authentic to the core, having little shame about who he is. He has grown considerably in his ability to personally share and communicate with Victor and others during the past five years but is still challenged in that area. For many years as a heterosexually married man, Alan repressed his gay sexuality. He is now at the other end of the continuum.

Scott is an Enneagram type 2 (the Helper) with a 3 wing subtype (the Host). Sex and love are inextricably tied for Scott. He has been sexual with large number of men in his lifetime. He is someone who cannot begin to have sex with another man, even with a stranger, without immediately starting to have feelings of love and connection with that man. Love is the central focus of his life.

He is an intimacy junkie, going into withdrawal and acting out when he believes intimacy is being withheld from him. His nature is altruistic, and he freely gives to others and enjoys helping, but when he believes his love is not being properly returned he tends to become some combination of controlling, manipulative, proud, and/or self-righteous and creates interpersonal drama in the process. Deep down his giving to others is attached to an assumed quid pro quo that is not always the case with the people he is choosing to help.

Bill is an Enneagram type 6 (the Loyalist) with a 5 wing subtype (the Defender). He has had a lifelong issue with chronic mild to moderate depression. Many aspects of his life are dedicated to finding security and support because being totally on his own and having little or no outside support is his greatest fear. He demonstrates the traits of consistency, loyalty, and dedication in virtually all areas of his life. He is detail-oriented and only rarely overlooks anything he has committed himself to completing. Despite a high level of achievement, deep down he has little self-confidence that he can achieve without the help of others. To others, he appears to be the consummate reliable person who never lets anyone down.

He is a purist, a true believer, and will unremittingly defend what he considers to be right and proper. His personal code of conduct is quite high, and he is harsher on himself for slips than he is on others, of whom he is more forgiving. When overwhelmed, he retreats into depression and has a difficult time telling others about his problems. He believes he should be able to take care of them himself. His libido has become almost nonexistent. Depression, the medication he takes to treat it, age, and HIV are all possible explanations for this lack of desire.

All the adults in this family are HIV positive and have been so for many years. They are among long-term survivors of the AIDS epidemic.

Peter, sixteen, is Alan's oldest son. He has always tried to please people, as he cares how others see him. It is likely that he is an Enneagram type 2 (the Helper). Though small for his age, he is, like his father, physically tough and enjoys intense, physically demanding activities. He dresses in a modified Goth style that is popular with some of his peers. He is outgoing. He and his father are similar in their approach to life. Aside from his schoolwork, he is studying a creative art.

Tom, thirteen, is Alan's youngest son. From the time he was young, he appears not to have cared what others seemed to think about him. He is introverted, a loner, and inner-directed. When he accompanies Alan and Peter, as they take part in physically demanding activities, he goes about pursuing tasks that have interest to him, seemingly oblivious to the activities going on around him. In this regard he is more similar to Victor, Alan's primary partner. Both Victor and Tom are inner-directed and somewhat shy. Victor immediately felt a closeness to Tom upon first meeting and saw Tom as similar to himself. Victor validates to Tom that Tom's way of being in the world is okay. It is not clear what Tom's Enneagram type is, and he could be one of several different types, with a possibility he is a type 4 (the Individualist).

Victor's partner, Joe, died of AIDS in 1986. Joe was oriented to monogamy but as he became more ill his ability to be sexual diminished. Victor wanted to be sexual with others, but Joe objected. They unsuccessfully tried ménage à trois and couples counseling to deal with this. When Joe died, Victor went on a sex-and-drug binge that lasted three years. Victor thought he, too, was going to die soon.

Several years later, Victor briefly met James, and they reconnected a year later. James' partner had also died of AIDS. James came for a limited visit and never left. He agreed to stay on the condition that Victor give up using drugs, and Victor complied. They were intensely sexual in the beginning.

By nine years into the relationship, James was concentrating more on his intellectual than his sexual side, and Victor was ready for a regular sexual partner when a mutual friend introduced him to Alan. Victor, being relationship oriented, soon knew he wanted a relationship with Alan and also knew Alan was not ready for a relationship. He saw in Alan the appealing sexual qualities he associates with the archetypal male. To Alan, Victor was an interesting, exciting, tough, and highly sexual gay man who knew how to have intense fun. Alan told Victor he was interested in seeing him again but wanted to make it clear he was in no way open for a relationship for two reasons. First, his priority was raising his children. Second, the experience with his former wife had soured him regarding relationships. Victor and Alan continued to regularly see each other and slowly develop their relationship and sexuality.

Several months after beginning to see Victor, Alan began seeing Butch. Alan's concern for Victor regarding this resulted in his encouraging Victor to also have another sex partner. Two years later, Victor met Scott in a gay bar. Scott was leaving and Victor was arriving, but they talked for a few minutes and exchanged e-mail addresses. In the bar, Victor told Scott of his two relationships, and Scott told Victor about his having a long-term partner. This conversation was appealing to both. They made a sex date for later that week and chatted online for a few days before they got together, learning more about each other.

Scott's long-term partner, Bill, had lost his libido. They had been monogamous for the first eleven years of their relationship. Scott was ready for a regular sex partner and when they met he told Victor he was open to having a sex buddy. Several days after Scott and Victor were first sexual, Scott, Victor, Alan, and James were sexual together.

Scott's introduction into the system immediately changed the balance in terms of intimacy. Love, relationships, and sexuality are the dominant themes in Scott's conversations. This had a significant effect on the relationship between Victor and Alan. Alan began to open up and talk about his feelings. For the first time, he told Victor that he loved him. He also began referring to Victor as his partner. Both Alan and Victor attributed some of this to Scott.

Within this system, each adult (with the exception of Bill) is getting different needs fulfilled by three other adults. Included are the needs for sexuality, intimacy, intensity, sociality, stability, and excitement. This becomes clearer when one looks at the dyadic interactional patterns.

Several dynamics are important in the relationship between Victor and James. Both are fiercely independent and agree to let the other do pretty much as he wants. They understand that neither likes being told what he should do, and they generally refrain from that. Victor respects James' need to retreat into privacy when stressed, and James respects Victor's need for pleasure and adventure. When James is stressed and retreats into privacy, it sets a good role model for Victor, who becomes scattered when stressed. These periods of quietness serve both of them well.

James acts as Victor's protector. James needs to approve of all of Victor's other relationships or Victor cannot continue with that person. James judges them in terms of their character and behavior. James brings a stability to the partnership.

Victor gets other needs met from Alan. Both Victor and Alan share a positive outlook on life. They are both goal-oriented. In their pursuit of these goals both overlook developing problems, which tend to come back and bite them. They share their vast amounts of energy with each other. With Victor's emphasis on having fun and Alan's emphasis on looking good through achieving, they achieve fun times together. This is one of the dynamics that draws them together.

Victor's description of his relationship with Alan is that "Alan is the great love of my life." Victor's moods are very much affected by what is happening in Alan's life. If Alan is having financial trouble or if he is not seeing Victor often, Victor finds himself overwhelmed by feelings of fear and concern and becomes scattered, emotionally shuts down, and withdraws. At these times, he is unavailable to Scott. Scott then generally moves in for more contact until he becomes aware of what is happening, and then lets go.

Victor and Scott are also a fun couple. Scott is a giver, likes to fix people, and sees in Victor an opportunity for both enjoyment and helping. Victor is amazed at how many things Scott does well and admires him. He especially admires how outgoing and assertive Scott is socially and sexually. Both are highly sexual, though it has a different meaning for each. For Victor, the sex relates to pleasure; for Scott it is a validation of being loved. Deep down, Scott feels unlovable, and Victor's willingness to be sexual with Scott has a healing quality for him. Scott's masculinity helps heal Victor, who has some effeminate traits that this society invalidates.

The other significant primary relationship is Scott and Bill. This is a relationship where Scott supplies the intimacy and Bill supplies the safety. Scott depends on Bill to provide a steady and stable home life. Bill's loyalty is especially important to Scott because of Scott's feelings of being unlovable. While Scott intellectually understands that Bill's lack of libido may be related to either depression, medication, HIV, or age, he also reacts emotionally by feeling rejected. Having a stable sexual relationship with Victor validates this part of Scott, making it easier for Scott to accept Bill's love and lack of libido.

The family interacts mostly in terms of dyads and triads and the quadrant of Victor, James, Alan, and Scott. About twice a year all seven individuals—the five adults and the two children—interact as a whole. When Scott and Bill had an anniversary party, all seven were present. All seven went to the local theater company to see a mutual friend perform. This past year on Gay Pride Day, they all met up at one point. This was the first time the children had attended a gay-related event. The children are aware that Victor is their father's partner but the complexities of the relationships with the others have never been discussed. Last Mother's Day Tom sent Victor an electronic greeting card.

This is a stable system despite the many opportunities for chaos for a few reasons. All five adults were raised in intact families. None of their parents separated or divorced. These families were stable and fairly free of chaos. None of the parents were substance abusers or had any other discernable compulsive disorders. They grew up in predictable environments. Their parents modeled responsible behavior.

This probably indicates that most of the parents in the previous generation and the five adults in this polyamorous family fit Bowen's (1976) *Profile of Moderate to Good Differentiation of Self.* The individuals in this range have an intellectual system that can and does override the emotional system much of the time. Bowen believed that couples had similar levels of differentiation or else one would not be able to put up the other. By extension, the same is probably true in polyamory; someone functioning at a lower level of differentiation would not be accepted into the system.

This results in a polyamorous family fairly free of conflicts and drama. The adults are dependable, responsible, and honest people. Although drama and triangulation does occasionally occur, they are short-lived. The individuals recompensate fairly quickly, using their intellectual system to reassert authority over the emotional system. Issues are discussed and apologies are generally made and accepted.

Culturally the adults are quite similar. All the ancestors of the adults came from either Ireland, Scotland, Belgium, Germany, or Poland. Alan was adopted at birth and is uncertain of his biological heritage but was culturally raised in this Northern European tradition.

Another common factor is that all of these men are HIV positive. All are long-term survivors and are healthy by HIV standards. They have all lost numerous friends and loved ones to AIDS, and that continues. They indicate that they have learned from those experiences.

This family also acknowledges that another reason this works is because they are all in their fifties. All have had more troubled relationships in their younger years and have learned from those experiences.

Within this system, each individual has explicit permission to be who they are on both a sexual and total person level. Quirkiness is prized. They challenge one another to be authentic. Being fairly well-differentiated people helps them to accept themselves and the others for who they are. They get off on being different, including having unintentionally created this polyamorous family. They have a found a formula that works for now.

AREAS FOR FUTURE RESEARCH

A number of areas are ripe for future research. Perhaps most important is the need for anthropological studies of gay male mating patterns. We need to know what actually exists that a neutral observer, beginning without preconceived notions, would observe. This would form the basis of future studies of a more specific nature.

Once we have a clearer understanding of gay male mating patterns, one important question would be how frequently does polyamory occur? To answer this it will be necessary to have a better definition of polyamory in order to understand which sexual contacts would be considered polyamory and which would not.

Future research should include examining how bisexuality fits with polyamory. Some of this will involve getting past labels and looking at the sexual and romantic mating patterns of men or women and seeing what is actually occurring. Future research might also look at what qualitative differences can be perceived in systems where men are being sexual only with other men as compared to systems where some of the men are also being sexual with women.

Specific to the models of polyamory discussed earlier in this chapter, we need a more exact definition of what constitutes a primary relationship and what constitutes a secondary relationship. The emphasis here would be on better understanding of the secondary relationship. I believe future researchers will probably need to redefine secondary relationships into secondary and tertiary relationships and describe and define each. The role and effect of anonymous sex should also be included. Scales might also developed to help in understanding the nuances of these relationships. Secondary relationships, as I have defined them, run a wide range that can be narrowed for better understanding.

CONCLUSION

We are now living in a time when the family structures created by gay men are being seriously examined. Some gay men have created family models that are different from the Western heterosexual model of the family. This includes stable polyamorous families composed of more than two gay men. All other members of our society can learn much from these families.

REFERENCES

American Psychiatric Association. (1994). *Diagnostic and statistical manual of mental disorders* (4th ed.). Washington, DC: Author.

Anapol, D. (1997). *Polyamory: The new love without limits*. San Rafael, CA: Intinet Resource Center.

Bell, A., & Weinberg, M. (1978). *Homosexualities: A study of diversities among men and women.* New York: Simon and Schuster.

Bettinger, M. (2001). *It's your hour: A guide to queer affirmative psychotherapy.* Los Angeles: Alyson.

Blumstein, P., & Schwartz, P. (1983). American couples: Money, work and sex. New York: William Morrow & Company.

Boszormenyi-Nagy, I., & Spark, G. M. (1973). *Invisible loyalties: Reciprocity in intergenerational family therapy*. Hagerstown, PA: Harper & Row.

Bowen, M. (1976). Theory in the practice of psychotherapy. In P. J. Guerin (Ed.), *Family therapy* (pp. 42-90). New York: Gardner Press.

Bowen, M. (1978). *Family therapy in clinical practice*. New York: James Aaronson.

Coleman, E., & Rosser, B. (1996). Gay and bisexual male sexuality. In R. Cabaj & T. Stein (Eds.), *Textbook of homosexuality and mental health* (pp. 707-721). Washington, DC: American Psychiatric Press, Inc.

Easton, D., & Lidst, C. (1997). *The ethical slut*. San Francisco: Greenery Press.

Fogarty, T. F. (1976). Systems concepts and the dimensions of self. In P. J. Guerin (Ed.), *Family therapy* (pp. 144-153). New York: Gardner Press.

Framo, J. L. (1992). *Family-of-origin therapy: An intergenerational approach.* New York: Brunner/Mazel.

Green, R-J., Bettinger, M., & Zacks, E. (1996). Are lesbian couples fused and gay male couples disengaged? Questioning gender straightjackets. In J. Laird & R-J. Green (Eds.), *Lesbians and gays in couples and families: A handbook for therapists* (pp. 185-230). San Francisco: Jossey-Bass.

Guerin, P. J. (1978). *Family therapy: Theory and practice.* New York: Gardner Press.

Gurman, A. S., & Kniskern, D. P. (Eds.). (1981). *Handbook of family therapy* (Vol. 1). New York: Bruner/Mazel.

Labriola, K. (1999). Models of open relationships. In M. Munson & J. Stelbourn (Eds.), *The lesbian polyamory reader* (pp. 217-225). Binghamton, NY: Harrington Park Press.

Leveton, E. (1984). *Adolescent crisis: Family counseling approaches.* New York: Springer Publishing Company.

Luthman, S. G. (1974). *The dynamic family.* Palo Alto, CA: Science and Behavior Books.

McWhirter, D., & Mattison, A. (1984). *The male couple.* Englewood Cliffs, NJ: Prentice-Hall.

Minuchin, S. (1974). *Families and family therapy.* Cambridge, MA: Harvard University Press.

Munson, M., & Stelbourn, J. (Eds.). (1999). *The lesbian polyamory reader.* Binghamton, NY: Harrington Park Press.

Palmer, H. (1995). *The Enneagram in love and work: Understanding your intimate and business relationships.* New York: HarperCollins.

Riso, D., & Hudson, H. (1999). *The wisdom of the Enneagram: The complete guide to the psychological and spiritual growth for the nine personality types.* New York: Bantam Books.

Saghir, M., & Robins, E. (1973). *Male and female homosexuality: A comprehensive investigation.* Baltimore: Williams & Wilkins.

Stierlin, H. (1977). *Psychoanalysis and family therapy: Selected papers.* New York: Jason Aronson.

Weitzman, G. (1999). What psychology professionals should know about polyamory. Paper presented at the meeting of the 8th Annual Diversity Conference, Retrieved from http://www.polyamory.org/~joe/polypaper.htm.

Whitaker, C. (1976). The hindrance of theory in clinical work. In P. J. Guerin (Ed.), *Family therapy* (pp. 154-164). New York: Gardner Press.

Chapter 9

Coming Out As "We 3": Using Personal Ethnography and the Case Study to Assess Relational Identity and Parental Support of Gay Male, Three-Partner Relationships

Eric Aoki

BACKGROUND

Using an academic letter format, I use a blended-methodological approach of personal ethnography and qualitative case study to assess the three-partner, gay male relationship and the role of parental support. In working to understand better the relational "We 3," I first provide an account of my relational experience with two other men. I discuss the process of our coming together and then make a methodological turn to provide insights from both e-mail and face-to-face interviews with one set of parents who have supported their gay son in his three-partner relationship. As I, personally, have not had an in-depth conversation with my own parents regarding this issue, I use the parental case study to bridge an academic conversation regarding the negotiation of what might be termed a second or relational coming-out process with parents. Finally, I discuss how insights from the first, personal coming-out process provided the parents with tools to keep the conversation going and to support their son's relational coming out as a "We 3."

doi:10.1300/5792_10

THE ACADEMIC LETTER

4 January 2004
Dear Kathy,[1]

As the year comes to a close, I am reflecting on the past seven years of living life out of the dreadful closet. I keep thinking about my family, my life partner(s), and how I have come to know this place, a place of presence, in negotiating my self with others in my life and in society at large. I have been thinking about the power of communication, particularly self-disclosure, to help others understand or at least be asked to recognize the lesser-known and discussed facets of the human condition—in this case, the condition of being politically and socially marginalized in representation and voice or existing as one of many individuals who cannot always identify with the heteronormative and traditional flow of social life and practices. I have been thinking through this academic letter[2] for several months now—six to be exact—but only now did I know that I would write this letter to you.

I wanted to come out to you *yet again,* but differently, in this academic letter. I want to move beyond coming out as an individual who is gay, for that *process* has already been christened for my life, to discuss issues relating to coming out relationally as a gay man in a three-partner, relational connection.[3] The content of what I have to share and work through in theory, methodology, voice, and communicative practice is something that I knew you, as my undergraduate and master's professor in communication studies (1986-1992), would provide support for; I also knew you would provide a safe zone for speaking and thinking about issues of gay identity when communicating our interpersonal selves (not without your own critical questions and reflection, of course). Mostly, I knew you would simply allow me to be open with who I am, in a letter of this sort, particularly if I did it with academic elegance, critical thought, and an imperative to advance knowledge of the human condition and the diversity of our communication practices. In the process of coming out relationally, in this letter I want to also provide a glimpse of what it may be like to negotiate diversity within diversity. I want to share what I learned from a set of parents who have negotiated this relational situation with their son and his two partners. I know the safety that I remember was and still is the case in your undergraduate classrooms and graduate seminar. So, in this letter, I assess another type of coming out, a relational coming out with *three* partners, not the more typical *two* partners of coupled life.

I read in *Genre* magazine that this type of relational arrangement can be referred to as a "We 3" (Towle, 2002, p. 34). Towle (2002) asserts, "While the typical outsider believes a three-way relationship is based around sex (the more the merrier), it's typically based on the same factors as any successful two-person relationship—trust, common interests, physical attraction, the desire to share a life with a partner and, most of all, love" (p. 35). It is the topic of "We 3" and the element of support from parents that I want to discuss in this letter.

In two previous academic letters,[4] I spoke, first, of coming out to my students in the academic classroom and, second, of negotiating the interpersonal and intercultural dimensions of an HIV sero-discordant relational connection. In the second letter, more specifically, I addressed at some level a relational connection with two men of my life, Trevor[5] and Ryan. In this letter to you, I want to clarify more strongly that in looking back (after Trevor passed away) I felt *more in the closet than not* with regard to my relational connection with these two fine men of my life. Reflecting on those earlier relational years, in negotiating being gay, being in an international and interstate long-distance relational life, negotiating Trevor's HIV-positive status, and being naive about how to proceed with the complexity of all of these cultural factors of my life, I did not know how to negotiate or communicate best, much less at all, the circumstances of my relational life with both Trevor and Ryan. Particularly, *I* was not comfortable with disclosing that I was romantically linked with two men in my life, even if all three of us were living out love quite well in our relational arrangement.

In this letter to you, Kathy, I hope to relieve a bit of my conscience, my heart, and some of my thoughts on negotiating a "We 3" relational connection. I no longer exist in this model of relational life, but I know that I have learned about diversity and acceptance in some substantially new ways from having been a part of a romantic life with Trevor and Ryan simultaneously. Hence, for this letter of learning and life sharing, I will be using a blended-methodological approach of personal ethnography (Crawford, 1996) and a qualitative case study of one set of parents who have provided support for their son and his two partners living in a "We 3" for over five years. I hope to locate a productive methodological intersection for laying foundation and insights into this underdeveloped and often unaddressed topic of study.

With regard to the value of learning from and attending to a mode of personal ethnography, Crawford (1996) explains:

> The ethnographer may be more of a copyist of personal impressions than a chronicler of cultural events. If the ethnographer has any expertise, it is the expertise that comes from subjective experience and implicit knowledge. As an ethnographer, I am an expert about what only I verify—a state of affairs subject to emotional vulnerabilities, intellectual instabilities, and academic suspicion [or skepticism] . . . Thought of in these terms, taking the ethnographic turn, living and writing the ethnographic life, is essentially a self-report of personal experiences. Ethnography, then, becomes autoethnographic because the ethnographer is unavoidably in the ethnography one way or another, manifest in the text, however subtly or obviously. (p. 158)

For me, the topic that I address in this letter to you is a topic that I have lived. As a traditionally trained ethnographer who is flexible on the traditional-critical continuum of fieldwork practices and philosophical underpinnings, I explore some methodological and philosophical aspects of Crawford's (1996) defined personal ethnography while also extending my exploration with a qualitative case study of one set of parents[6] who have provided support to their son and his two partners.

I have not had an in-depth conversation with my own parents, so I was interested in seeking an outside parental perspective on this topic as well. In conducting qualitative e-mail and face-to-face interviews with one set of parents who support their son's relational connection, I believe I open the door to another level of insights on a relational arrangement that I came to know, unexpectedly yet firsthand, in my own life. When Crawford (1996) speaks of "living and writing the ethnographic life" (p. 158) and addresses a perspective of cautions or problems of "go[ing] into the field" (p. 163), I realized that, in some ways, I was already up to my knees in the muddied field. For me, the immediacy of being already at least partially in the field gave me a sense of the experiential confidence of knowingness while it simultaneously burdened me with the concern of being too entrenched and overwhelmed in this field. I needed a sounding board, so to speak. I needed to stop asking in my own head the *what-ifs* of disclosing my relational situation. However, I was not ready to live pragmatically or ethnographically in experience with my own parents. So, when a set of parents became available to me for reflection and inquiry on this topic, I knew it would provide a fortunate opportunity to help make sense of the field in which I stood. Perhaps in employing aspects of personal ethnography and experiential voice I can work toward an academic conversation with the voices of the parental case study to help qualitatively thicken the story that I share with you. Hence, in this letter, I share both personal insights regarding a "We 3" relational connection and the knowledge learned from parents who actively support their son and his two relational partners.

Again, this topic of research on multiple-partner, romantic relations is one that has not found much research space in the academy. Overwhelmingly, relational research has focused on the couple, and more often the married, heterosexual couple. In critical response to Sullivan's (1995) *Virtually Normal: An Argument About Homosexuality,* Warner (1999), in moving beyond a unified stance to support mainstreaming gay identity through marriage, criticizes:

> In the name of love, Sullivan would obliterate not just queer theory, with its conferences and articles—that goes without saying—but the world-making project of queer life. . . . But with no politics, no public, no history of activism or resistance, no inclination to deviate from the norm, and no form of collective life distinct in any way from that of "society." What we have left to "affirm and celebrate" turns out to be *couples* and those who are "manfully struggling" (perhaps with a whiff of bondage here) to be in a couple. (p. 139, emphasis original)

I point to Warner's argument here, not to argue and align, specifically, with any movement away from the rights of equity wrapped up in fighting for same-sex marriage or to argue against the notion of the couple, for I advocate on behalf of same-sex marriage with those who desire it, and I celebrate couples every day in my life. Rather, I use Warner's position to emphasize the challenge in making and finding social space for relational connections that live *outside* the construction of the relational couple, where the normalizing and grounding of two has the potential to breed social assumptions and stereotypes, cultural stigmatization, exclusion in social policy and media representation, and judgment about the morality of living lives.

Finally, Kathy, it was in your research methodology seminar that I learned the following practice, which I share with students in my interpersonal and cultural communication classrooms as well as work to include in my own research agenda. The practice is the following: *There is value in conducting research and learning about marginalized and underrepresented identities, whether culturally or personally inspired for research, even if those identities make up a small percentage of our human conditions and practices.* For, in the study of cultural differences, we might better understand and also learn something more about ourselves and others with whom we communicate, share, and negotiate cultured space and life.

Personally, I did not ever expect to be in a relational connection with someone who would pass away from HIV/AIDS complications, nor did I ever expect that I would, simultaneously, be involved with two wonderful men prior to this loss. Those circumstances, in my case, simply evolved with the happenings of life and love. Although the HIV/AIDS issue had its own set of personal, relational, and social negotiations—more than I can share with you here in this letter—the relational negotiation of the "We 3" presented its own set of challenges. Back then, I used to think, with nervousness, about the following questions: How, in everyday conversation, does one find the discursive space to disclose, casually, that he has *two* men as romantic partners? More specifically, when friends, family, and acquaintances asked me about Trevor (i.e., the first and publicly known partner), how could I get out of the trap of responding to that couple-oriented question and not feel the shame of keeping the truth about Ryan in the closet, so to speak? I even thought through (a bit differently yet all over again) the following question: Although my mom, dad, and family supported me when I came out as gay, would they support me in a three-partner relational connection or would that be simply too much for anyone to ask of his parents? The doubts crept back in, and along with the nondisclosed fact of Trevor's HIV-positive status,[7] I, hence "We 3," decided to not disclose with my parents (and society at large) this truth. For more years than I am proud of or happy about, I, once again, found myself in a "different closet" to negotiate (or rather retreat into) with regard to sexual orientation and love.

With regard to negotiating the closet, Jandt and Darsey (1981) assert that coming out should have two criteria:

> First, it should enable self-acceptance; it should help a person identify in a positive way with what she or he is. This does not mean that coming out should be a course in homosexual chauvinism; gay is good, but it is not necessarily inherently any better . . . [and second] the concepts used in homosexual literature should liberate and allow the individual to define himself or herself in terms that encourage the exploration of his or her potential. (p. 25)

At the time, I was not certain I was prepared to accept this relational facet of my life, much less negotiate with others what this meant. In addition, I was coming up empty in my search for signs in either gay or mainstream literature that the relational identity I lived was anything that people would understand, much less take seriously. So, over and over again, the closet won the battle. I was not ready to come out. In silencing this aspect of my life, it was easier at times for me to negotiate that I had an open relational connection with Trevor, for I assumed (and soon, correctly, found out) that people viewed my "open" relational connection with Trevor as the *more typical* story of the commitment-phobic partner (me) or the sexually liberal couple (us), two views that socially we do, oddly enough, know how to make assumptions about, apply to, and negotiate regarding relational life generally and/or with regard to gay culture, specifically. It was only a matter of time, however, before I could no longer tolerate the effects of being in the relational closet, for in my coming out as a gay man, quite publicly, I knew all too well the liberations and privileges (despite its own set of challenges) of being out. Slowly but surely, albeit cautiously, in my disclosure and framing, I, with a couple of my closest friends (not family), slipped into conversations that Ryan and Trevor had known each other and that I was in love with both men, intimate with both men, and occasionally spending time on holiday with both men. Given our careers and long-distance homes in different cities, this was not the case very often. When it did happen and I shared these facts, however, I always felt as if I was living with an integrity that all three of us deserved in our lives.

As I think back to how this relational connection with Trevor and Ryan developed, I know that two variables carried influence. First, although Trevor asked me to be honorable with his heart, his emotions, and to care for his life, he did not require a defined commitment of the typical and traditional couple type; nor did he need monogamy with me as an expression of my love for him, particularly since we lived at a distance and we both knew that his sexual desire and interest decreased as his HIV complications increased. Second, Trevor encouraged me to find an intimate life with another individual, someone that he too could love, respect, and trust, for he believed that I was way too young (i.e., thirties) to be absent a life of relational adventure, companionship, intimacy, and sex in its fullest spectrum (see Aoki, 2004). So, over time, Ryan, a prior relational partner, and I became reacquainted. Several years earlier, Ryan and I had parted amicably in the months prior to Trevor and I connecting and establishing a life together—at a distance, but together.

When Ryan and I parted ways, he was still negotiating his life in the closet and I was coming out full force. Not even our strong attraction to each other could weather the storm of negotiating different sides of the closet door. Though remaining friends in our separation, Ryan and I always held onto our love for each other. Trevor knew this, Ryan knew this, and I knew this. So, when my life with Trevor evolved to the point previously related, Trevor and I knew that we wanted to talk with Ryan. So, we did. In our series of life chats, Ryan saw how much Trevor and I loved each other. In addition, Ryan began to feel the love I still held for him and the love that Trevor developed for him, first through me and then through the beautiful interactions with one another. As Ringer (2001) asserts in "Constituting Nonmonogamies,"

> [T]here is a set of beliefs that sees sex as not something necessarily reserved only for one partner but as an important need, one that should be met through people who play an important role in one's life. These beliefs would not view one-time sexual episodes as a means of fulfilling one's sexual needs. Rather, these needs would be met by men who become significant others in addition to the primary relationship and fulfill one's sexual needs over time, thus enlarging the concept of relationship from two to more people. (p. 146)

Ryan not only became an important person to me intimately, but he received both Trevor's and my love. It is fair to say that we did not really see our love as defined by strictly nonmonagamous sexual needs but rather relational and love needs as well. Over time, Ryan became a part of our love, and we a part of his.

Although our emotional and romantic bonds were differently constructed, Trevor, Ryan, and I evolved into an intimate relational connection where, even at a distance from one another (London, California, and Colorado, respectively), we prioritized our schedules as best we could and lived our lives as three men sharing love and life. At some level, the distances involved allowed us the privilege of not having to explain the complicated details of our lives together. With Trevor's family and friends in London being the only set of individuals who really knew of our relational arrangement, negotiating the details of our "We 3" was in some ways simplified and manageable.

This obfuscation, however, meant that we lived with the self-erosion of esteem that results from being closeted while nonetheless being out-and-proud as gay men (the irony of it all). Personally, I had reached a point of being confident, secure, and privileged enough to be out about my individual identity (e.g., "I am gay") but not my relational identity (e.g., "Please don't ask me additional questions that will put me in a position to have to lie to *myself* and you about my relational life with two men"). The fear, shame, and exclusion of even considering that three is a possibility for any real relationship always seemed to get in the way of disclosing this fact. Perhaps at times this complication of denial was my/our own doing, but is not this the power of the closet, to keep individuals silent because one really never knows what the response or implications might be? In retrospect, having lived my choices of the past, it is difficult for me to see anymore why I allowed myself to live for others' opinions and not for the relational integrity of what Trevor, Ryan, and I were so fortunate to have had. This is a difficult realization, come to at a point that seems, in these days since Trevor has passed on, a bit too late.

So, Kathy, I suppose this is where the motivation to share, reflect on, and learn even more about "We 3's" or the like comes from in my newfound voice. When, for instance, was the last time you saw a multiple-partner, relational connection represented (in a positive and healthy manner) on television, gay or straight? How about talked about in everyday life? Some folks I have gotten to know through the years tell me that they know people who are in relational connections of this type or who practice a slightly different arrangement of relational connections—many of the stories I hear are of polyamorous, heterosexual relations or open relational arrangements, be these straight or gay. Often, however, when any of these relational arrangements are mentioned, it is much too easy to attach stereotypical assumptions regarding deviance, noncommitment issues, or judgment on grounds of morality. Add gay to the mix and a whole new door has been opened with regard to judgments of sexual promiscuity and perversion, while another closet door slams shut in the move toward progress with relational and sexual liberation. If you think about my shared story, we entered our relational connection not to have loose and meaningless relations but rather to enhance the depth and quality of our shared lives in love. We entered our relational connection to foster our lives, our life situations, and our love for one another.

However, the power of two, relationally, is a mighty strong force—at least as it has been disciplined and socialized through global institutions and policy. In our relational life, where Trevor, Ryan, and I became a part of one another's lives through both circumstance and choice, we,[8] of course, wanted cultural acceptance, but I believe we understood that cultural disclosure, acknowledgement, understanding, and recognition as a "We 3" would have to come first. My guess is that many people will *believe* and *feel* that this way of life is asking for too much, socially and culturally, or is too different a break from how people in society typically do love. Again, my perspective has never been to eradicate the notion of the *couple*. I simply want to raise the view that two does not always provide the relational comfort or needs imperative to *doing* love. Although Trevor's passing altered the *living* status, not memory, of our "We 3," and although Ryan and I are connected presently as two men loving with an open[9] relational connection, the questions and concerns of our life as a "We 3" remain ever present. So, now, I thought, is the time to go (re)searching outside of my own life.

As happenstance goes, I became friends with two amazing individuals[10] who are parents to a son who has lived a long-term and engaged life with his two relational partners. Perhaps through the parents' disclosures, their stories, I might locate planes of understanding and paths toward social acknowledgement, negotiation, and recognition for this relational life situation. Perhaps I might even find some insights for my life.

The two parents, William and Arleen, were socialized into traditional yet quite different family systems in the United States. Although William came from an intact parental household, Arleen grew up in a family of divorce where "little of this lifestyle [of divorce] was typical at the time." William reminisces, however,

> In my adolescent years when I was initially socialized to think about romantic relational life, I used my parents as models, and their model was reinforced in media. Man was with woman; they enjoyed each other's company; they ultimately made a commitment to each other; and then married. But you didn't have to make a commitment right away.

In addition, thirty years after a heartbreaking experience with a high school girlfriend who devastated his life on the evening of prom and into the near future, William found himself selecting with a good friend nostalgic songs for a music anthology, a series of over 300 songs from 1955 to 1972. While thinking of these songs, William reflects on the quite exclusive centering of heterosexuality and the opposite-sex couple as *the* model for relationships. He notes,

> As I have reflected on my adolescence through my song selection, I have characterized myself as a romantic—most of my songs are songs of relationships. And considering my family and friendship socialization, they were boy/girl relationships. There was never any discussion that I can ever remember of other relationships. By the same token, among my guy friends, there was never any mention of relationships other than boy/girl relationships.

Arleen states that she and William have "been married thirty-five years and this relational life is not what [she] experienced as part of [her] early family life." She notes her experience and socialization as such:

> Growing up, my family life was early parental divorce, grandmother lived with us, working mother who dated a fair amount and enjoyed a good time and eventually was married and divorced several times. Although never stated, I think I saw opposite-sex relationships as having little romance, a means to an end and entertainment. [My] friends' family life appeared to be outwardly happy parents; dad worked and mom was a homemaker. All dating experiences, movies, proms, burgers, parties, were heterosexual. I guess my thoughts about future romantic, relational

> life included heterosexual, long-term commitment (as opposed to my mother's marriages/divorces), happy family, stereotypic fifties, sixties, but I also don't remember there being much of a conscious thought process. My earliest memory of homosexual was in college when my mother described the local floral shop owner as "gay."

Arleen also notes how over the thirty-five years, and regardless of her early family experience with divorce, she has appreciated her relational life with her partner. In addition, William notes, "In graduate school I met Arleen. What a great match! And I still get nostalgic over our music." Over time, life has brought forth joys and challenges as these two individuals have enjoyed their life together.

So, with these two individuals coming primarily from heterosexual and mostly traditional coupling experiences, and even with the less typical (at the time) divorce family experience, how do two parents begin to negotiate and ultimately support their gay son? In addition, after his disclosure of sexual orientation, how do parents come to support him and his not one, but two partners?

On the matter of their son's sexual orientation, Arleen notes, "During high school, our son announced that he was gay. He felt he had known for a long time but now it was time for his parents to know. I met some of his early partners." With regard to coming out as gay, Arleen says that she cried. "Tears were the outward response based on fears of societal judgment for our son and HIV." As for William, his response was initially more fearfully angry and directive. William notes:

> I remember my first words: "What can I do to change that?" That question has plagued me for years. I had two students come out to me because they could not come out to their parents before that. I respected the students and continue to communicate with them and call them my friends today. But when my son came out I said, "What can I do to change that?" You know what makes that even more problematic when I reflect on it? My older son, who I think is socialized as close as one can be to me without cloning, upon learning of his brother's sexual preference, said, "No matter. I love you." After the initial shock and remorse for my first words, I don't believe I ever had problems with his being gay *per se*. Rather, I worried (and to some extent I

> think I still do) about his well-being. What are the implications? Can he be okay? Will he be a victim of violence?

Interestingly enough, despite my own reservations and fears of sharing my "We 3" relational life with my own parents, William and Arleen remind me that perhaps the relational coming-out process (coming out again but differently) does not have to be the problematic conflict that I believe it to be. I know different parents will respond differently, but in my mind, I mostly saw the "We 3" as being too much for my parents to handle and accept (even though knowing that my parents accept me as a gay man), so I once again retreated to the relational closet regarding this part of my life. Perhaps for some parents, skills and insights learned in the first coming-out process of sexual orientation can be carried forward into the disclosure of a relational "We 3." With regard to William's negotiation of his son and his two partners, he states:

> [My son] had been in the City by the Bay for two or three years. He liked it. For the first couple of years, he fluked upon a great house, a friend of a friend, where he rented a room, about a mile from where he worked. Arleen and I fell in love with San Francisco and visited him regularly. Then the guy who owned the house sold it. [Our son] sought out lodging. He found it in a less-than-great area of the city. After a couple of murders, the most recent of which came on the front steps of his apartment complex, [he] decided he needed a new environment. He committed to a new apartment, but the new apartment landlord stiffed him and said at the last moment that he couldn't move in without additional money. [Our son] balked . . . [he] was going to be left on the street. By some miracle quirk of fate, [he] was taken in by [two men], friends of friends, apparently. They gave him a room for the time being. In my mind, they saved his life for the time being. And before I knew it, they apparently became partners. I cannot honestly remember when or how I learned of them being partners. It just seemed to evolve.

Towle (2002) states, "Most successful three-way relationships begin with a stable couple who decide to bring a third person into the mix" (p. 35). In this case, it appears that over time, William and Arleen's son became a relational part of an already intact relational unit of two. With this foundation set, William holds the view that the two men who became his son's partners "saved" his son's life; from this experience, he holds a positive assessment of their lives coming together. Arleen also notes, "Response to announcement of [our son's] present relationship was calm, accepting, and glad to have my suspicions confirmed. My concerns in a three-partner relationship were centered around one partner being an outsider or partners pitting one against another. That can be a concern in any threesome relationship and not particular to our son's relationship." With their mostly favorable responses to their son's "We 3" relational life, disclosure concerns seem to center on negotiating their son's sexual orientation prior to the perceived concern with the difficulty of negotiating his "We 3" relational life. Arleen, for example, states:

> Initially I had great fears of our son telling his two grandmothers he was gay. The only surviving family members are two grandmothers, brothers, and one aunt. Guess I considered them rooted in old values; homosexual lifestyle had never been a discussion item in either family home, and I wasn't too sure of their acceptance. However, without any discussion or forewarning, our son came out to both grandmothers and they have been very accepting. Brother's reaction to son's coming out was a nonchalant—"oh yeah." With friends and colleagues, I don't necessarily bring up the subject but by the same token I wouldn't avoid it. Nearly all of my close friends and people I've worked with for some time know our son is gay and are aware of his multiple partners. All have been outwardly accepting and understanding.

William continues to center the issue of primarily negotiating his son's being "gay" but also addresses the perceived challenges of multiple partners. He notes,

> I want people to like me; I want people to like my family. My challenge, even worry, is that upon learning of my son being gay, others will judge him, me, and my whole family, not by who we are but rather by the stereotypes that go along with labels. Being gay and having a relationship with two other guys makes my son's labels even more difficult to try to understand, and thus more easily shunned or despised.

William continues:

> [That] having been said, I am surprised at how quickly and openly our immediate family and friends accepted both our son's being gay and his being in a "three" partnership. My mother, mother-in-law, and sister are all conservative, and my father's influence on my mother and sister would have suggested some intense resistance to the entirety of the situation. Outwardly, that has never happened, and considering that our families are very close, I believe inwardly the resistance even has been minimal. . . . Because of the challenge or worry noted . . . , I, at least, have been cautious in sharing our son's sexual preference and relationship with friends. However, as we have shared more and more, our friends have embraced more and more. I sometimes sense that they see him exploring relationships as simply an extension of his exploring life—which he has done since he was in diapers. He has always pushed the envelope, taken risks, and done things a "little differently."

The viewpoints put forth by both Arleen and William suggest that the issue of being gay is perhaps the primary and more central concern to address when disclosing their son's life to others. The relational status of three partners, however, has the potential to add concerns when negotiating their son's relational life, although not being, necessarily, a more difficult negotiation. As William so poignantly states,

> With other relatives in other parts of the country and with distant friends, the topic of relationships just has not come up a lot. I have never lied about [our son's] relationships, but I guess I am negotiating in that I don't bring it up, either. As noted, I have worried that others would think the worst of me as well as [him] because of my son being gay. And, I think that remains a selfish concern. But it is that concern that more often haunted me than any concern about how people would think of a "three" relationship.

With this statement having been made, I went back to William and asked him whether dealing with the first coming out (sexual orientation) provided skills for the second coming out (the "We 3"). He told me that it was not so much skills as insights. When I asked him to elaborate, he brought up some issues that he had shared with me earlier.

William told me that after hearing several stories from some of his son's friends who came out to their parents and experienced bad to tragic outcomes, and after having one of those friends tell William that he liked hanging out with him and Arleen because of their acceptance, that these "insights" helped him understand that he never wanted to be the type of parent who would disregard or disown his own son. Having gained this insight makes it easier for William to want to negotiate his son's relational life, even if this means having to negotiate two partners. As William made clear to me, "I don't fully understand, but I respect them for who they are individually and as a partnership, and I respect their choices. And particularly as it involves my own son, I love him."

Arleen provides the broader potential for parental acceptance among multiple parents. In one of her stories, she states,

> Another year on one of our California wine trips, the first partner's parents joined us, and the boys rented a limo so we could all ride together. We had a fun day sipping wine, stayed in a local motel, ate breakfast together, etc. In retrospect, I think the boys were incredibly nervous about the parents getting together. But over the years, we've become good friends and have occasionally gotten together without the boys. Only recently have we met [his] second partner's mom and she too is a delightful person . . . It's nice to have all the three set of parents' acceptance, and I truly believe we're all very comfortable with one another—the boys and parents. I am a parent of two sons, one homosexual with two other partners, not married legally or by societal standards; one married and divorced legally and by societal standards. Relationships with sons, their partners, present or divorced, and partner's families are very much the same with both boys.

Whether it is trying to figure out how to house their son and his two partners in a bed that is large enough for all three of them when they visit their home or negotiating their son's identity and relational life with family and friends, neither Arleen nor William ever sugarcoat the fact that understanding their son and his relational partners has been or continues to be easy or without challenge. They do, however, consistently demonstrate what working toward understanding, love, and support means for their role as parents in their son's life.

William shares a story of being in Paris with Arleen and their son. He mentions how they had to wait for two hours to get seated in a restaurant. Once seated, however, he tells the story as such:

> A bottle of wine and a magnificent dinner grew into conversations about relationships and the future and the past. [Our son] talked of both his joys and tensions in his relationships with the guys. As noted earlier, Arleen and I knew of the relationship, as the information had sort of evolved through that year, but this was the first time that we openly and extensively discussed his and all of our relationships. I don't think we had gotten seated in the restaurant until near ten. I know we didn't leave until about one. I loved the lingering and the conversing and the sharing. I saw the love and joy and tension in his eyes and heard it in his voice. I suspect he perceived the same from me, and Arleen. He wanted us to understand, and at the same time to know of his uncertainty of where the relationship might go and how long it might go and what the implications might be. It is near five years later now. The guys wear each other's rings to signify their relationship. They have broken a lot of barriers since then. [We] have talked seriously on numerous occasions since then. But, I don't know that we have broken as many barriers nor shared as much in any single conversation as we did that evening.

As I reflect on William's story, I am reminded how often you, Kathy, while seated in your class, reminded me about the power and importance of conversation. I remember learning that the power of conversation does not guarantee an easy ride, but it does provide us with a means to negotiate our lives, and our identities, with others. Through this blended-methodological, academic conversation of personal ethnography and qualitative case study with William and Arleen, I have been reminded that parents can sometimes be our strongest advocates.

I know, however, more generally, that although we cannot always know how our parents will respond, if they have already accepted our lives as gay individuals, they may have the necessary insights to further understand our lives in a "We 3." I know that there is no guarantee, but prior to thinking through this topic on my own, and in the process of writing this letter to share what I learned from William and

Arleen, I can see multiple views of response rather than just the one I feared.

Perhaps in future studies, researchers might continue to explore the following questions in more detail: When learning of a son's or daughter's relationship in a "We 3" or a model outside of the traditional couple, what communication skills do parents use to provide support? What insights from the personal coming-out process do parents carry forward into the negotiation of their son's/daughter's relational coming out as a "We 3"? How might parents open conversational spaces for their gay son or daughter to potentially disclose the status of his or her relational life beyond that of the traditional couple? Finally, for individuals who do not have particularly supportive parents regarding one's gay identity, what are the implications for disclosing a relational life that does not uphold the status of the traditional couple?

As I think through the privilege I start with in having parents who accept me as their gay son, I now *feel* that my conversation with my parents has the potential to play out much like the situation with William and Arleen. I know there is no guarantee, but in writing this letter to you, I have enabled my ability to see beyond the power of the closet, be it personal or relational. I want to work toward Tierney's (1997) notion of using the power and site of the academy to explore queer topics such as the one I have shared with you in this letter. I find myself, presently, in a position within the academy to extend research questions beyond that of the large magnum of studies dedicated to investigating the traditional couple.

As I noted at the onset of this letter, I did not ever imagine that I would at some point in my life find myself in a "We 3." From William and Arleen I learned that they, too, had not necessarily had a life of socialized training that prepared them for the personal and relational discussions that they have ultimately had with their son. Perhaps if in some small way we begin to talk about these life issues in our classes and in our homes, and perhaps if we share this academic letter with others, we might, together, open new spaces for insights toward negotiating a diverse humanity, a humanity that acknowledges and respects diverse lives. Finally, in speaking specifically of the diversely cultured life that I feel privileged to have lived thus far, despite the personal and sociocultural challenges that have been a part of it, I hope this letter provides, in some small way, a means to reflect on and embrace what living a life filled with love, compassion, integrity, and support can be.

With Respect,
Eric

P.S. Thanks for reading. Should you want to check out some of the books I mentioned or get further clarification on items noted in this letter, what follows are the Endnotes and References.

NOTES

1. Dr. Kathy (Katherine) Adams is a colleague, friend, and professor/mentor of mine. Her classes played an imperative role in my development, both academically and personally. Over a decade since spending time in her classes, she continues to provide a positive influence to my career and life. Kathy is presently the Chair of the Department of Communication Studies at California State University, Fresno.

2. This is the third (of four planned) academic letters that I have written for publication. This academic letter follows, for example, the style and format of the first letter that I wrote for a chapter titled "Making space in the classroom for my gay identity: A letter I've been wanting to write" in *Teaching diversity: Challenges and complexities, identities and integrity* (Aoki, 2003). As used in the first and second essays (see also Aoki, 2004), I believe the letter format can be shared with family, friends, colleagues, professionals, and students and in an *accessible* and *practical* way invite conversations on the complex issue of sexual orientation/identity, interpersonal and cultural relations, and the politics of everyday life. When dealing with stigmatized cultural identities, I believe that both accessibility and practicality is its own type of advocacy for enhanced conversation and understanding.

3. I use the term *relational connection* because I was not and have not been married or unionized with either of my romantic partners. A friend of mine gifted me this alternative terminology when speaking of my relational life; nonetheless, I recognize that word choice for advancing or attending to political policy requires a more mainstream negotiation of language use, e.g., gay relationship and civil union partners.

4. As with those two previous academic letters, Kent Ono's (1997) "A Letter/Essay I've Been Longing to Write in My Personal/Academic Voice" had a profound influence on my conceptualization and understanding of voice and in how I wanted to *use* as a scholar my voice(s) in the paths of cultural advocacy and understanding. Again, I owe a debt of gratitude to Professor Ono for providing an alternative methodology for my academic writing. Finally, with the format of this essay, I have taken some liberty with APA guidelines for aesthetic presentation of the academic letter.

5. I have changed the names of individuals in this essay, including those of the two parents of the case study, for reasons of confidentiality. Although the lives, including my own, which are noted in this letter are/were "out" in many contexts, I realize that we still live in stigmatized times with regard to diversity, particularly with

regard to being gay and in negotiating the lives of our children who are gay. Hence, the names used are pseudonyms, with the exception of my own name, Eric.

6. This one set of parents is whom I gained access to for this project.

7. Trevor and I decided to keep confidential the details of his health from my parents, for he looked healthy, and we cared not to add further worry to their lives. Since his parents were well aware of his health status, Trevor and I planned to tell my parents at some opportune time when we could both sit down and *explain at length* the implications with them. That moment never materialized.

8. I use "we" here, not to speak for my late and present partners, but rather to communicate our commonly known and shared perspective of cultural advocacy.

9. I use "open" here to communicate being open to dating or seeing others, but still connected to each other. I also use "open" to mean that we communicate our relational connections honestly with each other and with relational others with whom we date, see, and/or have sex with.

10. The individuals noted are the interlocutors or participants of the parental case study used for this academic letter. Appropriate protocol was followed to achieve clearance from the Regulatory Compliance Office of Human Subjects on the Colorado State University campus.

REFERENCES

Aoki, E. (2003). Making space in the classroom for my gay identity: A letter I've been wanting to write. In B. Timpson, S. Canetto, E. Borrayo, & R. Yang (Eds.), *Teaching diversity: Challenges and complexities, identities and integrity* (pp. 91-101). Madison, WI: Atwood Publishing.

Aoki, E. (2004). An interpersonal and intercultural embrace: A letter of reflection on my gay male relational connections. *Journal of Couple & Relationship Therapy, 3*(2/3), 111-122.

Crawford, L. (1996). Personal ethnography. *Communication Monographs, 63,* 158-170.

Jandt, F. E., & Darsey, J. (1981). Coming out as a communicative process. In J. W. Chesebro (Ed.), *Gayspeak: Gay male & lesbian communication* (pp. 12-27). New York: The Pilgrim Press.

Ono, K. A. (1997). A letter/essay I've been longing to write in my personal/academic voice. *Western Journal of Communication, 6*(1), 114-125.

Ringer, R. J. (2001). Communicating our relationships: Constituting nonmonogamies. In M. Bernstein & R. Reimann (Eds.), *Queer families, queer politics: Challenging culture and the state* (pp. 137-151). New York: Columbia University Press.

Sullivan, A. (1995). *Virtually normal: An argument about homosexuality.* New York: Alfred A. Knopf, Inc.

Tierney, W. G. (1997). *Academic outlaws: Queer theory and cultural studies in the academy.* Thousand Oaks, CA: SAGE Publications.

Towle, A. (2002, January). We 3. *Genre,* pp. 33-35.

Warner, M. (1999). *The trouble with normal: Sex, politics, and the ethics of queer life.* New York: The Free Press.

Chapter 10

Same-Sex Marriage and Legalized Relationships: I Do, or Do I?

Esther D. Rothblum

On January, 7, 2004, *USA Today* (Bayles, 2004, p. 1) quoted Bob Doyle, who had been with his partner Greg Parks for twenty-seven years and recently had a civil union in Vermont: "It solidified our relationship with ourselves, our peers and our families. . . . There is more acceptance because we are a legal entity."

On August 31, 2003, *The New York Times* contained the following interview in its article "Now free to marry, Canada's gays say, 'Do I?'" (Kraus, 2003, p. 1): "Ambiguity is a good word for the feeling among gays about marriage," said Mitchel Raphael, editor in chief of *Fab,* a popular gay magazine in Toronto. "I'd be for marriage if I thought gay people would challenge and change the institution and not buy into the traditional meaning of 'til death do us part' and monogamy forever. We should be Oscar Wildes and not like everyone else watching the play."

As these two quotes illustrate, same-sex legalized relationships, including marriage, are not without controversy even in lesbian and gay male communities. This chapter will describe the legal status of same-sex relationships, including marriage, in the United States and other countries, and present some theories that are for and against

---

This article was written while the author was on sabbatical leave at the Lesbian Health Research Center of the University of California at San Francisco, the Women's Leadership Institute at Mills College, and the Beatrice M. Bain Center for Research on Women at the University of California at Berkeley.The author gratefully acknowledges the help of Kees Waaldijk, Senior Lecturer in Law at the Universiteit Leiden in the Netherlands, who networked me into many of the European authors cited in this article.

doi:10.1300/5792_11

same-sex legalized relationships. It will review the very sparse literature on legalized same-sex relationships and provide some suggestions for future research.

HETEROSEXUAL MARRIAGE AS A MODEL FOR SAME-SEX MARRIAGE?

In their book *The Case for Marriage: Why Married People Are Happier, Healthier, and Better Off Financially* (2000), Waite and Gallagher make the following statement:

> Marriage is not only a private vow, it is a public act, a contract, taken in full public view, enforceable by law and in the equally powerful court of public opinion. When you marry, the public commitment you make changes the way you think about yourself and your beloved; it changes the way you act and think about the future; and it changes how other people and other institutions treat you as well. (p. 17)

To what extent can the same statement be made about same-sex marriages?

The same-sex marriage debate is gaining ground at a time when heterosexual marriages are declining in frequency. U.S. Census data indicate that 5.5 million Americans were living together and not married in 2000, compared with 1.1 million in 1970 (Eskridge, 2001). In the 2000 Census, more Americans were living alone than those who were married, nearly half of single mothers had never been married, and the rate of middle-aged adults who had never married had doubled since 1970 (Eskridge, 2001). More than half of all marriages ultimately end in divorce.

Eskridge (2001) points out that lesbians and gay men used to get heterosexually married in order to avoid detection of their sexual orientation. Now that same-sex couples can be more open about their sexual orientation, the rate of lesbians and gay men marrying someone of the opposite sex in order to "pass" has greatly declined. Nevertheless, many lesbians and gay men were heterosexually married in the past. According to 1990 U.S. Census data, 19 percent of gay or bisexual men in same-sex couples and 31 percent of lesbians or bisexual women in same-sex couples had been heterosexually married in the past (Cahill, Ellen, & Tobias, 2002). Almost 40 percent of same-sex couples who had civil unions in Vermont consist of at least one partner who was heterosexually married in the past (Bayles, 2004).

SAME-SEX MARRIAGE

In 1989, Denmark became the first nation in the world to legalize lesbian and gay male relationships (Soland, 1998). Since then, Belgium, Canada, and the Netherlands have legalized same-sex marriage, and other nations have legal registration for same-sex partnerships (France, Germany, Hungary, Iceland, Israel, Norway, Portugal, South Africa, Sweden) (Eskridge, 2001). Legal recognition of same-sex relationships is currently being debated in countries all over the world (see Wintemute & Andenaes, 2001, for most comprehensive review of international status). Just recently, Dutch and Belgium same-sex married couples won the right to be recognized as married in all countries of the European Union (Arie, 2003).

The United States of America has no federal legislation for same-sex relationships. This fact never ceases to surprise members of the general public, who hear so much about "gay marriage" in the media and in religious institutions that they have long assumed such legislation already exists. As of this writing, only three states have or will have some form of legal recognition of same-sex relationships. In Vermont, Act 91: an act relating to civil unions, took effect on July 1, 2000. This law stated that a same-sex civil union is the equivalent of marriage. In California, same-sex couples were given most of the rights of married couples beginning on January 1, 2005, and the Massachusetts Supreme Court ruled on November 18, 2003, that lesbians and gay men have a right to marriage, giving the legislature 180 days to amend the marriage law. In all cases, this legislation is legal only in those three states, and only at the statewide level.

Lumping together legal rights offered by various countries and regions can be misleading. For example, same-sex couples in Belgium can get legally married, but this does not include legal coparenting status. Denmark has had registered partnerships for same-sex couples since 1989, but these partners could not adopt each other's children until 1999 (Lund-Andersen, 2001). In contrast, eight U.S. states and the District of Columbia currently permit a child to have two legal mothers or two fathers (Eskridge, 2001). Australia has widespread legal recognition of unmarried heterosexual relationships, putting them on a par with heterosexual marriages. Thus, in Australia, lesbian and gay male couples are unlikely to advocate for marriage but instead for similar legal protection as that available to heterosexual couples (Millbank & Morgan, 2001). In France, both same-sex and heterosexual couples can have civil unions ("pacte civil de solidarite" or pacs). For heterosexuals who can also choose marriage, pacs represent a less formal union; for lesbians and gay men it is the only option. Borrillo (2001) has thus described the pacs as "midway" between marriage and cohabitation for same-sex couples.

As soon as the first legal referendum took place for same-sex marriage, many U.S. states introduced legislation prohibiting recognition of same-sex marriage from other states. As of this writing, thirty-seven U.S. states have such legislation. Because the U.S. Constitution indicates that the laws of one state, including marriage, should be recognized by other states, the Defense of Marriage Act was signed into law in 1996, which states that no U.S. state is required to honor same-sex marriages from other states. Furthermore, opponents of same-sex marriage are currently advocating for a constitutional amendment banning same-sex marriage.

In the past few years, the U.S. public has become increasingly tolerant of lesbians and gay men. Polls indicate that the majority of Americans know someone who is gay or lesbian and support gay rights (Bumiller, 2003). Gay characters are appearing in television situation comedies and reality shows. Yet when it comes to marriage, the public opposes legalizing same-sex marriage by a strong margin. A July 2003 opinion survey indicated that 59 percent of Americans opposed allowing gays and lesbians to marry compared with 32 percent who were in favor (Lochhead, 2003). When asked about support of "legal agreements giving many of the same rights as marriage," 51 percent were opposed and 41 percent in favor (Lochhead, 2003). A multitude of factors accounts for this opposition. Yep, Lovaas, & Elia (2003) state that the debate in the mainstream media has consisted of "historical, philosophical, religious, moral, political, legal, personal, and emotional grounds" (p. 46).

DO LESBIANS AND GAY MEN WANT TO MARRY?

With all the debate in the mainstream media about gay marriage, many people are unaware that same-sex marriage is by no means the universal ideal in lesbian and gay male communities. Yep and colleagues (2003) have presented a model of two competing sexual ideologies in the United States. The *assimilationist* position argues that all people have the right to get married and that marriage results in stable relationships. In contrast, the *radical* position asserts that marriage is an oppressive institution and that same-sex relationships should be unique and freely chosen, not mimicking heterosexual norms.

In their international compendium of same-sex partnerships, Wintemute and Andenaes (2001) refer to a *liberal* versus *progressive* stance in favor of same-sex marriage. The liberal argument posits that same-sex marriage presents no threat to society, and same-sex couples should be able to enjoy the same benefits as heterosexual couples. The progressive position states that "the sameness argument marginalizes most queer people" (p. 117) and sanctioning marriage undermines and hides other ways of relating. Interestingly, they also present a model for taking an antimarriage position. The *traditional position* states that same-sex marriage would normalize and legitimize lesbian and gay relationships and thus undermine heterosexual marriage. The *progressive position* asserts that same-sex marriage would denigrate lesbians and gay men who are not coupled and bring the state into same-sex partnerships.

Legal experts specializing in same-sex partnerships are similarly divided along these lines. Mary Bonauto, an attorney who played a major role in the Vermont civil union legislation (Moats, 2004), has differentiated wanting same-sex marriage from its legal availability. She wrote: "Whether or not an individual chooses to participate in the institution is a different issue from having the choice—as a free and equal citizen—to marry the person of his or her choice" (Bonauto, 2001, p. 177). Conversely, Nitya Duclos (1991) cautions same-sex couples to consider the negative as well as the positive ramifications of marriage. She points out that heterosexual marriage disadvantages women, so same-sex marriage, too, should be examined separately for each gender. Legal recognition also means that same-sex relationships will be regulated by law and that the "effort of making out a case for 'sameness' has costs both for those who try to fit the mold and for those who clearly cannot" (p. 50).

Gender Differences Among Same-Sex Couples in Legalized Relationships

Due to the very nature of their definition as "same-sex" legal relationships, national registries keep data of the number of female versus male couples. Thus, one of the few facts known about legal same-sex partnerships is the ratio of men to women. Waaldijk (2001) has provided the numbers of same-sex partnerships in Denmark, Norway, Sweden, Iceland, and the Netherlands for each year since the legislation began. In all of these countries men predominated, usually in a ratio of three to one. Early data on Canada (October 22, 2002, http://www.gaydemographics.org) indicate slightly more male than female couples getting married in the first few months of the legislation. Lesbians predominate in all Canadian provinces except Quebec, Ontario, and British Columbia, but the large urban areas in these provinces (Montreal, Toronto, and Vancouver, respectively) account for more men. In Vermont, twice as many women as men have had civil unions (Solomon, Rothblum & Balsam, 2004).

What could account for this difference in gender ratios between Europe and the United States (the data on Canada are very preliminary)? Although it is impossible to know the actual number of lesbians and gay men in any society, most surveys (e.g., Laumann, Gagnon, Michael, & Michaels, 1994) find more gay men than lesbians. Thus, one could argue that the ratio of gay men to lesbians who have legalized relationships in European countries more accurately reflects the gender ratio. Secondly, Soland (1998) theorized that fewer lesbians than gay men took advantage of the Danish registered partnership legislation because same-sex partners could not adopt children, including children of their partner (this restriction was lifted in Denmark in 1999 but still exists for same-sex marriage in Belgium). A third argument is that two men in a couple on average would have higher incomes than two women. Thus, gay men may benefit more from the financial aspects of legalized relationships, such as inheritance (all the European countries with same-sex legalized relationships have national health care coverage, so this is not an issue). Finally, Soland (1998) suggests that more lesbians questioned the notion of marriage as socially conservative. It is possible that radical politics among lesbians are more prevalent in Scandinavian and northern European nations than in North America as a whole.

What about the preponderance of women in same-sex legalized couples in the United States? Currently in the United States, only civil unions in Vermont have the same legal rights as marriage in Vermont, and only at the statewide level. The pending California and Massachusetts laws, too, will affect couples only in those states and for statewide benefits only. Thus, in contrast to Europe and Canada, same-sex legalized relationships in the United States are primarily a symbolic act, and it is possible that women are socialized to value the symbolism of marriage more than men. Most benefits of marriage are at the federal level (e.g., inheritance, retirement, Social Security, sponsoring a partner from another country for U.S. immigration, filing joint income tax) (Cahill et al., 2002), and thus men, whose higher incomes may have more to gain from legal marriage, are not interested. As gay historian John D'Emilio stated (in Bayles, 2004, p. 2): "There hasn't been a rush for civil unions because there isn't much advantage to it."

OTHER DATA ON LEGALIZED SAME-SEX RELATIONSHIPS

Other than gender, surprisingly little information is available about same-sex couples in legal relationships. Scherf (1999) published a report on male/male, female/female, and male/female couples who had legal registered partnerships in the Netherlands. This legislation began in 1998 (i.e., before same-sex marriage was legal in the Netherlands). Based on data provided by municipalities, registered partnerships were most frequent in the largest urban areas. This ratio was due to the higher percentage of same-sex couples, especially men, who registered in larger urban areas (male/female couples were more evenly distributed across municipalities). Couples in registered partnerships were considerably older (early forties on average) than those who got married (age thirty for men and twenty-eight for women on average). This may have been due to the "catching up" nature of couples who had not been able to take advantage of this legislation before (Scherf, 1999, p. 16).

Letters were sent to 222 municipalities with over 20,000 residents, asking them to send a letter to all registered partners in their district (Scherf, 1999). Of these municipalities, 141 replied and sent out a total of 1,575 forms to registered partners. A total of 510 couples replied, of which 480 agreed to a telephone interview. The research team limited their interviews to 51 male/male, female/female, and male/female couples, respectively.

Sixty percent of interviewees reported that they did not have a religion, compared with 40 percent in the Dutch population. Interviewees were also more highly educated and more likely to have dual-earner incomes than the Dutch population as a whole. Thirty percent of male/female registered couples had children, compared with 24 percent of female/female and 20 percent of male/male couples. Asked whether their decision to register the partnership was emotional or financial, male/male couples were evenly divided. Female/ female couples were more likely (61 percent) to indicate emotional rather than financial (35 percent) reasons, whereas male/female couples more often reported financial (72 percent) over emotional (18 percent) reasons (Scherf, 1999).

Our research (Solomon et al., 2004; Solomon, Rothblum, & Balsam, 2003) focused on same-sex couples who had civil unions in Vermont during the first year of this legislation (2,475 civil unions took place during the period from July 1, 2000, to June 30, 2001). Based on information on the civil union certificates (which are public information), only 21 percent of the couples were from Vermont, two-thirds of couples were female, and 10 percent of individuals were members of ethnic minority groups. We sent a letter to each couple, congratulating them on their civil union and asking them if they were willing to participate in a research project that focused on "demographic information, your relationship, your connection to your family of origin, and social supports available to you in your community." We also asked civil union couples if they would provide us with contact information of a heterosexual married sibling and his or her spouse, and also a gay or lesbian couple in their friendship circle who had not had a civil union. We received reply forms from 947 couples indicating willingness to participate in the study.

We had funding to send out questionnaires to 400 civil union couples, as well as 400 lesbian and gay couples not in civil unions and 400 married heterosexual couples. Of the 400 sets of questionnaires sent out, we received back at least one questionnaire from 388 (97 percent) "families" of couples (this ranged from receiving questionnaires from both members of all three types of couples to only one questionnaire from all six possible respondents), including 659 out of 800 questionnaires (82 percent) from lesbians or gay men who had a civil union, 466 (58 percent) from lesbians or gay men not in civil unions, and 413 (52 percent) from married heterosexuals.

Lesbians in both types of couples (those in civil unions and those not in civil unions) had higher levels of education, were less religious, were less likely to have children, and had been in their current relationship for a shorter duration than heterosexual married women. Lesbians were more likely to share housework and child care, whereas heterosexual married women did more of these tasks than their partners. Heterosexual married women perceived more support from and had more contact with their families of origin than did lesbians. Lesbians in civil unions were more "out" about their sexual orientation than those not in civil unions and were also, to some extent, closer to their families of origin.

Gay men in both types of couples were less religious, more likely to live in large cities, had relationships of shorter duration, and were less likely to have children than heterosexual married men. Gay men were more likely to share some household tasks, whereas heterosexual married men did less of these than their partners. Gay men perceived more social support from friends and to some extent had less contact with their families of origin than heterosexual married men. Gay men in civil unions had more contact with their families of origin, were more likely to have mutual friends with their partner, were less likely to have considered ending their relationship, were more likely to have children, and more often had joint checking and savings accounts compared with gay men not in civil unions (Solomon et al., 2004).

Both of these studies were conducted when the new legislation (registered partnerships in the Netherlands and civil unions in Vermont) had just ended its first year. Much more research is needed to examine factors that affect same-sex couples in legalized relationships over time.

FUTURE DIRECTIONS

The countries and U.S. states covered in this article represent only the tip of the iceberg. Many other countries and U.S. states have some legislation protecting the rights of unmarried couples, including same-sex couples (see Wintemute & Andenaes, 2001, for a review). Lesbian and gay organizations of countries on every continent are working toward legal rights for same-sex couples. Furthermore, as same-sex couples in legal relationships travel and live around the world, countries will need to deal with the reality of such relationships.

At the same time, the increasing salience of legalized same-sex couples raises political issues even within LGBT communities. How representative are same-sex couples in legal relationships of lesbian and gay male couples in general? Should LGBT communities be advocating for institutions such as marriage? How can we question such laws without coming across as reactionary?

Finally, endless room remains open for research on legalized same-sex couples. Given that same-sex partnerships and marriages need to register with state or national government registries, this is an ideal avenue to gather data on a whole population. Most available research on same-sex couples has focused on small, volunteer, convenience samples. In addition, same-sex marriages can be compared with heterosexual marriages, and little research has been done in the LGBT arena with good heterosexual comparison data. It is also important to compare same-sex couples in *legalized* relationships with lesbians and gay men in coupled relationships who have chosen *not* to legalize their relationship. This may yield some data to explain the gender differences in legalized same-sex relationships, as well as understanding some of the ideological reasons why lesbians and gay men do or do not legalize their relationships. Finally, public data also permit examination of who terminates a legal relationship.

In addition to these methodological suggestions, many content areas can be explored among same-sex couples in legalized relationships. Who chooses to become legally united and why? What factors contribute to relationship quality and to relationship termination versus longevity? How does outness affect same-sex couples in legal relationships, and are there discrepancies in each partner's level of outness? What is the role of children in couples' decisions to legalize their relationship? How can same-sex couples serve as a model of equality for heterosexual couples?

REFERENCES

Arie, S. (2003, September 25). Gay marriages to get European passports. *The Guardian,* Retrieved from http://www.buzzle.com/editorials/text9-25-2004-45838.asp.

Bayles, F. (2004, January 7). Vermont's gay civil unions mostly affairs of the heart: Law didn't spur legal battles or an "invasion." *USA Today*, pp. B1-B2.

Bonauto, M. L. (2001). The freedom to marry for same-sex couples in the United States of America. In R. Wintemute & M. Andenaes (Eds.), *Legal recognition of same-sex partnerships: A study of national, European and international law* (pp. 177-210). Oxford, UK: Hart Publishing.

Borrillo, D. (2001). The "Pacte Civil de Solidarite" in France: Midway between marriage and cohabitation. In R. Wintemute & M. Andenaes (Eds.), *Legal recognition of same-sex partnerships: A study of national, European and international law* (pp. 475-492). Oxford, UK: Hart Publishing.

Bumiller, E. (2003, August 10). Cold feet: Why America has gay marriage jitters. *The New York Times,* Section 4, p. 1.

Cahill, S., Ellen, M., & Tobias, S. (2002). *Family policy: Issues affecting gay, lesbian, bisexual and transgender families.* New York: The National Gay and Lesbian Task Force Policy Institute.

Duclos, N. (1991, Summer). Some complicating thoughts on same-sex marriage. *Law and Sexuality, 1,* 31-61.

Eskridge, W. N. (2001). *Equality practice: Civil unions and the future of gay rights.* New York: Routledge.

Kraus, C. (2003, August 31). Now free to marry, Canada's gays say, "Do I?" *The New York Times,* pp. B1, B6.

Laumann, E. O., Gagnon, J. H., Michael, R. T., & Michaels, S. (1994). *The social organization of sexuality: Sexual practices in the United States.* Chicago: University of Chicago Press.

Lochhead, C. (2003, November 19). Massachusetts court allows gay marriage. *San Francisco Chronicle,* pp. A15, A22.

Lund-Andersen, I. (2001). The Danish Registered Partnership Act, 1989: Has the act meant a change in attitudes? In R. Wintemute & M. Andenaes (Eds.), *Legal recognition of same-sex partnerships: A study of national, European and international law* (pp. 417-426). Oxford, UK: Hart Publishing.

Millbank, J., & Morgan, W. (2001). Let them eat cake and ice cream: Wanting something "more" from the relationship recognition menu. In R. Wintemute & M. Andenaes (Eds.), *Legal recognition of same-sex partnerships: A study of national, European and international law* (pp. 295-316). Oxford, UK: Hart Publishing.

Moats, D. (2004). *Civil wars: A battle for gay marriage.* New York: Harcourt, Inc.

Scherf, Y. (1999). *Registered partnership in the Netherlands: A quick scan.* Amsterdam: the Netherlands. Report by the Ministry of Justice, Scientific Research and Documentation Centre (WODC).

Soland, B. (1998, Spring). A queer nation? The passage of the gay and lesbian partnership legislation in Denmark, 1989. *Social Politics,* pp. 48-69.

Solomon, S. E., Rothblum, E. D., & Balsam, K. F. (2003). Money, housework, sex, and conflict: Same-sex couples in civil unions, those not in civil unions, and heterosexual married siblings. Unpublished manuscript, University of Vermont, Burlington, VT.

Solomon, S. E., Rothblum, E. D., & Balsam, K. F. (2004). Pioneers in partnership: Lesbian and gay male couples in civil unions compared with those not in civil unions, and married heterosexual siblings. *Journal of Family Psychology, 18,* 275-286.

Waaldijk, K. (2001). Small change: How the road to same-sex marriage got paved in the Netherlands. In R. Wintemute & M. Andenaes (Eds.), *Legal recognition of same-sex partnerships: A study of national, European and international law* (pp. 437-464). Oxford, UK: Hart Publishing.

Waite, L. J., & Gallagher, M. (2000). *The case for marriage: Why married people are happier, healthier, and better off financially.* New York: Broadway Books.

Wintemute, R., & Andenaes, M. (2001). *Legal recognition of same-sex partnerships: A study of national, European and international law.* Oxford, UK: Hart Publishing.

Yep, G. A., Lovaas, K. E., & Elia, J. P. (2003). A critical appraisal of assimilationist and radical ideologies underlying same-sex marriage in LGBT communities in the United States. *Journal of Homosexuality, 45*(1), 45-64.

Chapter 11

Same-Sex Marriage: The Difficult Road Ahead

Vincent J. Samar

"Certainly our decision today marks a significant change in the definition of marriage as it has been inherited from the common law, and understood by many societies for centuries." With those words, the Massachusetts Supreme Court, in *Goodrich v. Department of Public Health,* 440 Mass. 309, 798 N.E. 2d 941 (2003), went down in history as the first state supreme court to find that its state's ban on same-sex marriage violated its state's constitutional requirement to afford due process. It was also the third such court to find that such bans deny fair and equal treatment to all their citizens.

Previously, the supreme courts of Hawaii in *Baehr v. Lewin,* 74 Haw. 530, 852 P. 2d 44 (Haw. 1993) (since reversed by state constitutional amendment) and Vermont, in *Baker v. Vermont,* 170 Vt. 194, 744 A. 2d 864 (Vt. 1999), under the Vermont Common Benefits Clause, had held that such bans fail to afford equal *legal* benefits to those who seek to live in committed same-sex relationships compared to their opposite-sex counterparts. The Vermont decision has since been codified into that state's law with a new statute conferring all the legal benefits and responsibilities of marriage under the legal imprimatur of "civil unions." Similar to the Vermont decision, the Massachusetts Supreme Court stayed for 180 days the likely effect of its holding, in order to provide the state legislature a chance to take appropriate action before the lower (trial) court ordered the issuance of marriage licenses. The Massachusetts decision is in several important ways different, however, from the Vermont ruling.

First, although the Massachusetts decision recites a very long list of legal benefits and responsibilities associated with marriage (especially

doi:10.1300/5792_12

but not exclusively as these relate to children), the court was also very clear in recognizing the intangible benefits of marriage: "Civil marriage is at once a deeply personal commitment to another human being and a highly public celebration of the ideals of mutuality, companionship, intimacy, fidelity, and family" (440 Mass. At 322, 798 N.E. 2d at 954). Such language may signal what a future court response will be if the state's legislature tries to respond to this court's ruling by adopting a Vermont-styled civil union approach. For in both its tone and content the language of the decision suggests that what is needed is marriage; nothing else should suffice. In the court's words,

> Marriage is a vital social institution. The exclusive commitment of two individuals to each other nurtures love and mutual support; it brings stability to our society. For those who choose to marry and for their children, marriage provides an abundance of legal, financial, and social benefits. It also imposes weighty legal, financial and social obligations. (440 Mass. At 312, 798 N.E. 2d at 948)

Implicit in the court's language is also the very personal way in which marriage can exhibit for the couples involved deep commitments to each other's aspirations and their individual capacities to bring those aspirations to fulfillment.

Second, this was the first state supreme court to find, under its state constitution, that bans against same-sex marriage violate *both* its due process and equal protection clauses:

> Barred access to the protections, benefits and civil obligations of marriage, a person who enters into an intimate, exclusive union with another of the same sex is arbitrarily deprived of membership in one of our community's most rewarding and cherished institutions. That exclusion is incompatible with the constitutional principles of respect for individual autonomy and equality under law. (440 Mass. At 313, 798 N.E. 2d at 949)

The earlier decisions had all followed more strictly a state-equal-protection (or close cousin to equal protection in the case of Vermont's equal benefits) type approach.

Third, the fact that the court engaged a rational basis review of the statute makes its holding that such bans violate the state's constitution all the stronger. Normally, rational basis review is a far easier standard for a statute to meet in order to be found constitutional, since it requires only an impartial lawmaker to logically believe that the classification serves a legitimate governmental purpose, which justifies it in the face of the harm done to the disadvantaged group. A court, in performing a rational basis review, would normally be satisfied if the statute were a reasonable exercise of the state's police power to achieve a legitimate interest. There would be no need for any higher degree of scrutiny of the governmental purpose as would be the case if the court went further to find that lesbians and gay men, as a group, have endured a long history of social discrimination, which embodies a gross unfairness, for which they are politically powerless to change. That higher standard is usually the one that makes the government's job in getting its statute to pass constitutional muster almost impossible. Nevertheless, the court, even though relying on the lower standard, was unable to agree with the government's rationale for restricting marriage to only opposite-sex couples. That rationale was to promote procreation, provide a more optimal setting for child rearing, and preserve scarce state and private financial resources. The court found that none of these arguments justified the government's restriction. Under Massachusetts law, marriage was not limited to only those who procreate or promise to procreate. Moreover, same-sex couples were already raising children well, and Massachusetts law prohibited discrimination in child custody cases based on sexual orientation. Finally, state and private aid to families is usually based on need and not on whether a couple comingles its funds.

What the court did find was that civil marriage is a creation of the state through its police power and that in matters implicating marriage, family, and the upbringing of children due process and equal protection overlap. In this regard, because opposite-sex marriage was already recognized as a fundamental right by both the state and federal constitutions, unless an important reason existed for separating the liberty interest of gays and lesbians from those of other people, a position already renounced by the U.S. Supreme Court's recent decision in *Lawrence v. Texas,* 539 U.S. 558 (2003) (holding unconstitutional state laws prohibiting adult consensual homosexual sodomy), when it came to marriage there was no basis to treat the interest of same-sex couples any differently from the interests of opposite-sex couples.

What happens next? I would like to suggest a hypothetical scenario for how the future might look, assuming that the Massachusetts decision is not overturned by adoption of a state constitutional amendment. The scenario I have in mind begins with a couple, James and Howard, who currently reside and work in Boston and have lived there together for fifteen years. Recently, Howard was offered a new job with the city of Chicago, which he plans to take, in part because the city grants domestic partnership benefits. James is employed in a private-sector job, which will allow him to relocate to their Chicago loop office; however, this job provides no spousal benefits for the domestic partners of same-sex couples. Jim and Howard also have custody of their two children, one by a surrogate-mother arrangement with Howard as the natural father and the other as the natural child of James, whom Howard was allowed to second-parent adopt after James's ex-wife abandoned the child. After the Supreme Court of Massachusetts rendered its decision, the state legislature amended its marriage act to allow same-sex marriage. Having always wanted to marry because of the social recognition and the benefits that accompany marriage, prior to their leaving Boston James and Howard got married before a justice of the peace, with the marriage being properly recorded in the county records. On arriving in Chicago, however, the couple finds that the city would no longer provide health care benefits for its same-sex coupled employees. Apparently, a right-wing group had challenged the local ordinance that allowed the city to use taxpayer money to fund the benefits on the ground that this was a violation of the home-rule law. Under that law, the city can operate as a government, but it cannot do more for its employees than the state of Illinois can do, and the state of Illinois has adopted a marriage statute that prohibits "a marriage between two individuals of the same sex" (750 ILCS 5/212[4] [2004]). Further, the statute defines marriage as "a legal relationship between one man and one woman." Concerned with what this could mean for their future life together, James and Howard sue along with seven other similarly situated couples, under the full faith and credit clause of the federal constitution, to have their marriage recognized so that they can obtain the same benefits from Howard's employer as their opposite-sex counterparts. The city defends, saying that the full faith and credit provision of the U.S. Constitution allows the Congress to set out how it will be applied, and that the Congress via the Defense of Marriage Act ("DOMA"), 28 USC

§ 1738C (2004) (originally passed in 1996), has decided nc quire states to recognize same-sex marriages performed in states. Determined to fight for what they believe and citing U.S. preme Court cases that have held miscegenation statutes to be unconstitutional and marriage to be a fundamental right, the couples claim that DOMA is itself unconstitutional, as a violation of the *federal* equal protection clause. What happens next will depend on how the federal courts, and ultimately the U.S. Supreme Court, probably six years down the line, interpret these laws. If the courts follow the miscegenation precedent given that the Supreme Court in *Lawrence* has recognized a liberty interest in same-sex relationships under the due process clause, the result will likely be that same-sex marriage will be allowed throughout the United States.

However, those who oppose same-sex marriage also can read the writing on the wall. They will see the same scenario and try to reelect a sympathetic president to pack the courts with judges who will steer away from this outcome. Alternatively, they will try hard to obtain passage by two- thirds of the Congress and three-quarters of the states of a federal constitutional amendment barring same-sex marriage and making marriage strictly an institution between one man and one woman nationally. If the latter happens, federal law will have written into it a specific provision designed for no other purpose than to discriminate against a single class of people. The next few years should be decisive in seeing how all this plays out. This is what gives me pause that the road ahead is clear but also full of pitfalls.

PART III: CLINICAL ISSUES IN GLBT FAMILY STUDIES

Chapter 12

Sex, Drugs, Rock 'n' Roll . . . and Children: Redefining Male Couples in the Twenty-First Century

David E. Greenan
Gil Tunnell

We live in changing times. Year 2003 was a banner year for raising the consciousness of all Americans regarding homosexuality. The U.S. Supreme Court striking down sodomy laws as unconstitutional, the Episcopal Church consecrating a gay bishop, Canada legalizing same-sex marriages, and the Massachusetts State Supreme Court protecting equal rights for same-sex couples were all profound societal events. While these events have created crises for conservative political forces now vowing to fight such radical changes to the status quo, the changes have created both crisis and opportunity for same-sex couples. Many gay couples welcome the increased social recognition and greater legal rights, but others—accustomed to living a secretive, double life straddling the minority gay culture and mainstream culture—are made anxious by societal phenomena that heighten their visibility and potentially provoke discrimination. Some couples are content to remain coupled within the gay counterculture without the trappings of marriage, which they consider a heterosexual institution they wish for no part of (Belluck, 2003). Many male couples are pondering the question: If we could legally marry in the United States, would we? Are we ready to make a legal and potentially lifelong commitment to one man? Recently in a therapy session with a same-sex couple considering having a commitment ceremony, one of the men said candidly, "It's the 'forsaking all others' vow that bothers me."

doi:10.1300/5792_13

Simultaneously with same-sex couples receiving greater visibility, same-sex couples are parenting more frequently and more visibly (Usborne, 2003). Having children of their own was unthinkable to gay male couples only a decade ago. Again, the possibility of gaining benefits heretofore denied them creates both opportunity and crisis for many male couples as they struggle over the issue of whether to have children.

Inevitably, as more men settle into domestic partnerships and raise children, we experience the universal problems of maintaining intimate relationships as well as issues idiosyncratic to gay male couples (Greenan & Tunnell, 2003). The absence of norms and rituals for gay couples, the diffuse boundaries of gay male couples, the lack of negotiating skills that many men have in dealing with other men, and, with the possible exception of Massachusetts, the nonexistence of laws in the United States granting legal rights to same-sex couples all contribute to undermining the ability of couples to experience stable relationships (Greenan & Tunnell, 2003). Increasingly, we see male couples and their families seeking out the services of family therapists to stabilize their relationships. In many ways these families look similar to those in the majority culture, but some issues are idiosyncratic to being gay and in a same-sex relationship.

A SYSTEMIC PERSPECTIVE

Regardless of the presenting problem or sexual orientation of a couple, families and couples generally present for treatment with an identified patient. The message to the therapist, implicitly if not overtly stated by one of the adult members of the family, is for the therapist "to fix the scoundrel and all will be well in our household." The task for the family therapist is to help the family to identify what behaviors collectively maintain the presenting problem and explore with them how to activate the resources to solve their *mutual* problem. While acknowledging their presenting problem, the family therapist's role is to help the family system discover what complementary behaviors maintain the symptom and keep the symptom bearer as the identified patient. Once the therapist has identified the narrow interactional behaviors that keep the family stuck in rigid, predictable patterns, the focus of structural systemic therapy shifts. The final stage of treatment is for the therapist to help the family create an environ conducive for them to experiment with novel, more adaptive, and potentially more fulfilling behaviors.

The structural therapist's philosophy is driven by a nonpathological, health-driven belief system that within the family there exist dormant but accessible resources to resolve their problems (Minuchin, 1974; Minuchin & Fishman, 1981; Minuchin & Nichols, 1993; Minuchin, Lee, & Simon, 1996). In working with same-sex families, we have discovered that the interactions the queer family has with larger, often marginalizing systems (i.e., families of origin, schools, religious and governmental systems) must be addressed in treatment for it to be effective. Further, as paradoxical as it may seem, the behavioral norms within the gay community also undermine same-sex couples (e.g., nonmonogamy, recreational drug usage). Both sets of outside forces, from the mainstream culture and the gay community, can work to destabilize male couples and must be integrated into a successful couple therapy (Greenan & Tunnell, 2003).

Male couples and their families present therapists with two particular challenges: (1) male couples have few role models to guide us in constructing our relationships, and (2) gay men, like straight men in general, are prone to be conflict-avoidant in their intimate relationships and often have a knee-jerk response to either withdraw or separate when the inevitable first signs of disagreement occur. These two features of male couples alone make for an inherent instability, yet it is important for the therapist to understand that the reasons for this intrinsic instability are primarily contextual, relational, and societal, not due to either individual character pathology or the nature of homosexuality. The therapist must be mindful of the destabilizing effects of larger systems in order to help the couple become more secure and more functional. Same-sex couples in the United States are embedded within larger religious, civil, and social systems that marginalize and discriminate against them. Perhaps no other type of dyadic relationship faces as much societal discrimination (Tunnell & Greenan, 2004). The therapist must help gay couples rediscover their collective resources and inherent resiliency to survive under such conditions.

Gay men, long before they become coupled, have had much experience in surviving hostile environments. Gay boys grow up in family and social environments unreceptive to their being gay. In few other family configurations do parents not typically share the child's minority status. Moreover, parents are often unaware or in denial that the child is coping with a "terrible" secret. Regardless of when a male discovers he is attracted to other males—which can be as early as age three or as late as sixty (see Savin-Williams, 1998)—and his degree of comfort with that discovery, all homosexuals experience the need, at least initially, to keep the information secret. Many gay boys develop a false self, a portrayal of their identity that is acceptable to those people to whom he is most strongly attached, in order to maintain the relationships he is so dependent on (Greenan & Tunnell, 2003). Many gay boys develop this ability to pass as heterosexual and masculine by feigning interest in girls and adopting culturally condoned masculine behaviors and pursuits. The consequences of doing otherwise can be harsh and traumatic. Children, especially boys, police one another to enforce gender norms. Some gay boys remain true to their real selves and are either unable or refuse to develop a false social identity. Those boys who cannot pass are often taunted mercilessly by family and peers, who call them sissy, faggot, and queer and sometimes physically beat them. For this latter group of children, being gay is particularly traumatic because they have no one to which they can turn. They often feel abandoned by their attachment figures and significant others—even though the parents may not realize what is going on and might actually offer support if they did—at a time when they desperately need love and reassurance. The child's shame about being gay, as well as the shame he anticipates from his parents, keeps him emotionally isolated. Despite his real dependency on the parents, he cannot afford to seek their help. As his financial and emotional dependency on his parents lessens in late adolescence or early adulthood, the young gay male can better afford to take the risk of coming out. However, the years of being emotionally autonomous and self-sufficient and functioning independently of genuine social support do not magically disappear after he comes out and looks for a romantic partner. For many adult gay males, conditioned by earlier traumatic experiences, forming an intimate bond with a partner on whom one can emotionally trust can be daunting.

CASE ILLUSTRATION: MARK AND FRED

The following case illustrates these factors as they affect a samesex-couple. Our model of treatment in working with male couples (Greenan & Tunnell, 2003) is adapted from structural family therapy

(Minuchin, 1974; Minuchin & Fishman, 1981) and for training purposes can be described in three stages—joining, enactments, and unbalancing.

Joining: Creating an Alliance As the Therapist Takes a History of the System

In this early stage of treatment, when the therapist and family are getting to know one another, the therapist has several specific tasks to accomplish. The first one is to determine what issues have brought the family into treatment. In the case of Fred and Mark,* it was Fred who called the therapist to make the initial appointment. When the therapist asked in the first session, "How can this process be useful? What brings you here?" Fred blasted Mark. Fred, a compact Latino lawyer in his late thirties, dressed in Armani, launched into an articulate, well-organized, verbal assault against his partner, Mark. He told the therapist that he was fed up with the relationship, specifically Mark's self-centeredness, and he was ready to sever their ties. Fred's face appeared white with anger as he continued the list of the insurmountable difficulties he had with Mark. His primary complaint was that he had already lost his privacy and autonomy, and now, with Mark's subletting a separate apartment, he feared he was in danger of losing his connection with Mark. All in all, he did not see much point in continuing their relationship.

According to Fred, Mark was consumed by his two teenage daughters, whom he recently had begun to coparent with his former wife. "It's blatantly clear to me that you prioritize your children over our relationship. Your children run your life. You never set limits. Furthermore," he added, "raising Mark's children was never part of the bargain nor why I fell in love with him in the first place." The final straw had been Mark's subleasing an apartment. He ended his case with, "I have no desire to be 'a breeder.'"

Mark, a large, handsome opera singer of northern European descent, also in his late thirties, retaliated in a voice so loud the therapist flinched for fear that other therapists in the suite would be alarmed. Mark was highly emotional but much less articulate than his partner as he attempted to defend himself. He yelled that Fred was only interested in parties and going out to the clubs high on X (ecstasy). "I'm

*All names given in cases are pseudonyms.

fed up with that scene. Furthermore," he shouted, "you act like you're still single." He went on to say that he had leased his own apartment so that his kids could have a home where they could visit him. Before Mark could pause for a breath in his tirade, Fred rejoined that he actually was glad that Mark had sublet an apartment; he would now be able to sleep in peace knowing that Mark's daughters were not going to drop in at any moment.

Ten minutes into the first session, the therapist felt overwhelmed and knew he needed to pay attention to these feelings. Structural family therapy privileges the behaviors and feelings of both the therapist and family as they happen in the "here and now" of the session. The belief is that the interactions occurring in the session are a microcosm of the family's relationship outside the therapist's office. The therapist then uses the feelings generated, or behaviors observed in the family to intervene therapeutically. In this situation, the therapist chose to share his feelings with the couple in order to join with them empathically and also to offer a perspective that gave them some hope toward changing their experience. The therapist said, "You're trying to do so many things at once—become a couple, coparent children. You must feel overwhelmed." Then, as both men nodded their heads, he continued, "No wonder separate apartments feel like a solution! Let's see if you can separate some of these issues into more manageable chunks."

The first order of business with a highly volatile and impulsive couple such as Fred and Mark is for the therapist to take control of the session and create emotional safety in the room. One way a therapist can do this is by creating structure and using his hierarchical position to slow down the couple. With highly volatile couples such as this one, the therapist chose to address each man individually. By becoming central and proximal to the family, other than physically separating the couple, the therapist is able to lower the emotional intensity of the session.

The therapist said, "I hear you both are overwhelmed and hurt. Mark, it seems like the only solution to coparenting your daughters is to distance yourself from Fred. Perhaps you don't see how threatened Fred is by your new role?"

Turning to Fred, the therapist said, "And Fred, your response to Mark as a parent appears to be driving him away from you. You talk to him as if you're cross-examining him in court! We will return to these patterns, but right now, turn your chairs toward me and talk to me. I need to get to know more about you as a couple. Have there been some good times? How long have you been a couple? How did you meet? What was your courtship like?"

These questions, though simple, are complex in their intent. The therapist's intervention is communicating many things to the family: I'm in charge here and I would not tolerate abusive behavior; I acknowledge you as a family in crisis, but I want to know the other aspects of your relationship. The therapist is not only interested in the couple's inability to solve problems; he is equally interested in their strengths. The focus of the session shifted to the type of foundation on which they had they built their relationship.

Many gay couples jump into a committed relationship without the benefits of getting to know each other through courting rituals that young adults in the majority culture engage in at an early age. When the inevitable disagreements occur, gay couples often have neither the history nor the relational skills honed and supported by developmental processes during adolescence to endure the inevitable challenges to any relationship (Greenan & Tunnell, 2003).

Structuring the early stages of treatment helps the family feel safe and conveys to them that the therapist has some sense of where the therapy might be going. Simultaneously, the therapist is able to begin to explore the dormant strengths (Genijovich, 1994) a couple has as he or she ascertains where they are in their life cycle (Carter & McGoldrick, 1989). Are they in the early stages of becoming a couple and struggling to create an identity of a "we," or are they in a later stage and coping with the stresses of expanding their system to include children? Fred and Mark appeared to be struggling with at least two stages in the life cycle of their family simultaneously, a stressful situation for any couple. The therapist continued to remain central and focused on the early stages of their relationship. Fred and Mark had met two years ago and, without the benefit of any courtship, they had instantly fallen in love with each other. They had met at a backers audition for a new opera in which Mark was performing. Fred, as the composer's attorney, had attended the performance. Fred and Mark were immediately attracted to each other and started to date secretly. Fred reported that he was out professionally and to his biological family, while Mark said he remained closeted for professional reasons and for fear that his wife would not grant him the rights to coparent his daughters.

Mark told the therapist he had been in the midst of an acrimonious divorce when he met Fred. His wife had been suing him for sole custody of their two children. Fred, using his legal knowledge, had been helpful in advising Mark about his legal rights. Mark's face softened as he told the therapist how helpful Fred had been with the fears he had that he would lose the right to parent his daughters. Fred had also calmed Mark as he reassured him that legally his wife could not withhold his right to parent his daughters based exclusively upon his being gay.

Mark and Fred concurred, for the first time in the session, that the first year and a half of their relationship had been a honeymoon. Fred had a large circle of gay and straight friends whom he had introduced to Mark. Mark tentatively began to go out to clubs with Fred. Fueled by ecstasy and crystal meth (methamphetamine), he told the therapist how for the first time in his life he felt free to be himself. The therapist decided not to challenge the couple for the moment on their use of recreational drugs. He wondered to himself, though, how much these feelings of happiness might not be exclusively a result of falling in love but the effects of the chemicals they were taking. However, he made the decision it was too soon to enter that realm of their relationship, as he was still in the process of joining with them.

We view recreational drugs as destructive to individuals and very destabilizing to families. Their use is often reflective of intimacy needs not being met in the couple system. One possibility is that the therapy would need to address how the couple could learn to comfort each other without the use of drugs. The therapist made a mental note to explore the drug usage later.

The men reported initially having a sexually passionate relationship that was in sharp contrast to the absence of any sexual pleasure in their relationship today. Within three months of meeting, Mark had given up his own apartment and moved in with Fred, a process that more or less unfolded without much discussion in terms of what it meant. Did living together mean that they now viewed themselves as a couple? What type of commitment were they making to each other? Had Fred's apartment become "their" apartment, or was Mark only a temporary guest? Because they were enjoying each other so much—going to the theater and other cultural events together when Mark was not performing; having great sex; lingering over long, romantic dinners; and biking together on weekends—the men had been content to let the relationship grow and develop in its own time without addressing any of their differences. Focusing on an obvious strength, the therapist reflected back how many similar interests they had from which they derived mutual pleasure.

As the couple began to warm up to the therapist and share with him the positive details of their life together, they began talking about the drugs they took. They enjoyed clubbing on the weekends and routinely took X before going out dancing with a group of friends. Occasionally, they would also use crystal meth to enhance their sexual life. They seemed to have little insight into the long-term, deleterious effects of either drug or the addictive qualities of crystal meth. The therapist chose at this point to highlight how destabilizing these drugs can be for many couples' relationships as he explored how often they used these drugs. He ended by wondering aloud if the drugs could be contributing to their problems. Neither man was particularly defensive about their drug use, but Mark pondered the therapist's idea that drugs made their situation worse. He volunteered that the drugs made him feel depressed for several days after he used them. The therapist attempted to make a transition by asking, "When did you start feeling less like a couple?"

Mark, staying with the topic of drugs, said he thought their troubles began when he wanted to stop using X and going to clubs. Fred cut him off in midsentence with, "No! Our troubles began six months ago when the court awarded you joint custody of the kids!" Fred told a story of how the balloon had popped on their relationship once Mark's daughters started visiting him at "Fred's home." Fred said he was accustomed to living alone. Not only had his home become a revolving door, his place was a mess because the teenagers never picked up after themselves. Furthermore, Fred complained, the older of the two went to a school near their apartment and would frequently stop by after school—unannounced. "I often work at home and I resent the interruption. And [as Mark tried to protest], we can't sleep together now that the girls are in our lives several days a week." He ended his litany of complaints by saying, "When I fell in love with Mark, I didn't bargain for children!" Mark, taking advantage of an opening as Fred paused for a breath, yelled, "What would you like me to do? They're my children, for god's sake!"

The two men glared at each other and turned to the therapist in frustration. The therapist resisted the couple's pull to rescue them. He simply reflected the dynamic of their interactional patterns, or enactments, in the session: "It seems very difficult for either of you to hear the other. Neither of you leave space for the other to think or respond thoughtfully. I feel like I'm on the front lines of a war. While your task seems to be how can you feel generous enough to put the other's needs before your own, it seems like you're caught in a never-ending tug-of-war."

These presenting problems are not unusual, and the dynamics of the couple are not out of the ordinary for a first session. What makes the case exceptional is the additional stresses placed on them as a same-sex couple struggling with too much "relational ambiguity" (Green & Mitchell, 2002). The therapist had at this point observed many enactments that illustrated the dynamics of their relationship. He chose to focus on the tensions they were experiencing regarding becoming a couple, separating from the single life of a large-city gay culture that normalized the use of drugs and casual sex as rights of passage for many gay men. The therapist believed the couple, without the benefit of a courtship, had built their house on stilts in shifting sands. As evidenced by Fred's earlier reference to "my" apartment, the therapist wondered aloud if they had ever created a home that belonged to them as a couple.

Equally difficult, as the couple struggled to create an identity, they were trying to become a blended family, integrating Mark's children into their relationship. Struggling to expand from two to four, it was not clear to the therapist that they had ever constructed an identity as a couple that prioritized the "we" needs over each man's individual "I" needs. There was a noticeable absence of "we" language in their discourse. All couples struggle with this transition—one that often looks like a power struggle over which tribal culture will dominate. For this gay male couple, the struggle appeared to be compounded by Mark's being in the closet and the additional deleterious effects of a majority cultural bias that questions whether gay men can be good parents. They had no support system of other parents, gay or straight, who were struggling with similar issues and who could resonate with them. The first order of business was to address that they were two men trying to make a family as they continued to live parallel and separate lives.

In the developmental life cycle of gay men, presenting a false self socially in early life has the effect of keeping the individual separate and isolated from others. Behaviorally adaptive for that stage because it provides the gay boy some modicum of safety from others who might harm him, many gay men come to depend entirely on themselves because relying on others for emotional support can be very risky. Most males in Western culture, regardless of sexual orientation, are socialized to be emotionally autonomous, stoic, and independent. Gay males are not only not immune to this social conditioning of gender roles but they are often forced to become even more autonomous, stoic, and independent out of fear of being rejected by their attachment figures if they reveal their more authentic selves (Greenan & Tunnell, 2003). Thus, gay males as they go through adolescence and early adulthood are deprived of basic negotiating skills with romantic partners—skills that straight boys have the opportunity to acquire through adolescent dating rituals. Later, when gay men develop coupled relationships, conflict within the couple can be extremely threatening: Just when they feel they have found their soul mate and life seems better than ever, they may be particularly averse to rocking the boat for fear of losing the relationship. In fact, this fear of being abandoned if he reveals more of his authentic self to his partner is very similar to a gay boy's initial fear of abandonment if his parents were to find out he was gay.

Enactments: A Map for the Therapist

Structural family therapy occurs in three overlapping but conceptually distinct stages: joining, enactment and unbalancing. As we join with the family and discover their presenting problem, we simultaneously begin to think about what complementary behaviors maintain the family's presenting problem. Complementary behaviors become clear to the therapist as he or she observes the couple in "enactments," having them talk directly to each other, instead of the therapist, about some issue. Families present therapists with overwhelming amounts of information. The therapist must focus on one aspect of the relationship in order to be effective and for the couple to experience some relief. Fred and Mark's therapist could have intervened at many levels of their relationship, focusing on the family life cycle and tasks associated with each stage of their life cycle.

As the therapist joins with the family, he or she begins to map their dynamics so that he or she can identify a theme. The therapist identifies "the theme" by observing enactments—interactions in the session—and reframing the family's problem within the context of their circular, complementary interactions. In this early phase of treatment, the therapist also needs to look through many lenses to contextualize the observed behaviors (i.e., the effects of gender socialization, culture, socioeconomics, race, ethnicity, religion, and sexual orientation on the couple) so as to not pathologize their behavior.

Based upon his observations, the therapist developed a hypothesis of a theme for Fred and Mark: Two men living parallel lives in search of becoming a couple. Through observing their enactments as they talked about their issues, he began to help the couple identify the complementary behaviors of their system which resulted in circular patterns (Minuchin et al., 1996; Nichols & Minuchin, 1999) that precluded their being able to solve problems. By identifying this theme, the therapist was able to focus the couple on specific behaviors that illustrated the theme. One pattern became immediately obvious: as Fred attacked Mark, Mark attempted to counter and then he withdrew. The therapist was now in a position to reframe their presenting problem. Mark's parenting was not the primary problem, but rather the couple was caught in a distancer/pursuer dynamic without seeing how their particular behaviors precluded closeness.

In order to slow down Fred and Mark's knee-jerk response to attack and then shut down, the therapist continued to share with them his conceptualization of their theme, "You are two men in search of a home." The theme restated their problem as not existing within an individual and simultaneously offered them hope of a resolution.

The couple had met and begun dating at an early stage in Mark's gay identity development (Cass, 1979). Mark was professionally and personally closeted. His struggle, though appropriate for his stage of gay identity, was in sharp contrast to the stage in which Fred was. Fred was not just out of the closet in both his personal and professional lives, he was an active participant in the night life enjoyed by many single gay men. Initially this difference in stages of their gay identity had attracted both men to each other as Fred took the lead in introducing Mark to gay life and his friends. The problem was that Fred had introduced Mark to a life of *single* gay men focused on the club scene. Early on in their dating, Mark had been thrilled to discover this facet of gay life in the big city and enjoyed seeing Fred being so carefree at the clubs. He described Fred as very romantic and affectionate. The therapist wondered aloud what Mark could do that might encourage Fred to show that side of himself outside of the clubs and without drugs. Both men look stymied by this question and the possibility that a solution to their crisis of how to become a "we" might exist within their relationship.

Fred was surprised to hear Mark say how much he loved seeing the playful side that Fred showed when he was on drugs. This time the therapist challenged Mark, "Have you ever been successful in bringing out the playful side of Fred without drugs? Do you know what you do that makes him so serious and angry? Fred treats you like you're his adversary, not someone he enjoys playing with."

In this early stage of treatment, the therapist had chosen his words carefully. He wanted to convey to the couple the idea that they had created a system that was integrally woven together. If Fred could not relax and be playful, Mark was doing something that inhibited Fred's spontaneity. The therapist believed that Mark might activate the fun-loving parts of Fred. The therapist's message was simple: "You no longer are individuals. You have created a relationship more complex than either of you, and, within that system, you have the resources to make your lives more satisfying—or more miserable." The therapist worked for several sessions with the couple to identify the complementary behaviors that maintained their distancer-pursuer system.

Unbalancing: New Ways of Being a Couple

As therapy progressed, it became clear that the couple had also co-constructed a relationship in which Mark was possessor of the more vulnerable emotions. Mark would express these softer, tender feelings in ways that made Fred squirm. At the beginning of one session, Fred shared with the therapist that he had spent the week with his mother, who had been diagnosed with a potentially terminal illness. He had chosen to go to Puerto Rico alone, leaving Mark at home. As Fred talked, Mark began to cry. Fred continued to talk about his mother without affect, helplessly but stoically observing Mark's tears. The therapist queried Fred, "How is it that it is Mark who expresses the sadness over your mother's diagnosis?"

Fred responded that he had a headache. He did not know what to do other than to be strong. As a Latino man, he explained that he was expected to be present as a resource for his sisters, and now for Mark. "I can't fall apart, too." The therapist wondered if Fred's headache might not be the result having to be "the sturdy oak," so he asked him, "Do you ever get to lean on Mark and let him support you?" Mark responded for Fred, "Fred is uncomfortable expressing feelings." The therapist said, "If he's uncomfortable expressing his feelings, maybe it's something you are doing to him. Fred's mother is dying. See if you can help him."

Here the therapist unbalanced the two men's preferred style of relating by encouraging new behaviors. First, he was relentless in rejecting individualistic, internal explanations for behavior within the couple. In systemic thinking, individual behavior is *always* in response to an interpersonal context. The therapist then focused on the inequity that existed between the two men in the expression of emotions as he encouraged the men to explore new behaviors.

As Mark expressed less personal emotion, he was able to become more relational and encourage Fred to talk more about his mother's illness. Although initially resistant to owning the ways he silenced Mark, as he began to listen more, Fred slowly began to express more of his own sadness. Fred told Mark about his trauma of growing up in a first-generation Latino family in a predominantly northern European neighborhood, where he had been marginalized due to the darkness of his skin. He had quickly learned to pass as straight so as to not further incur the scorn of his peers.

Fred's parents had moved from Puerto Rico when he was a small child so that he and his sisters could have better educational opportunities. Both of his parents worked two jobs so that their children could go to parochial schools. Fred, the first in his family to go to college, had graduated with honors from an ivy-league school. Although he came out to his family in college, his sexual orientation was never fully acknowledged in his family; Fred's gayness was a topic never again mentioned or discussed. In his current living situation, Fred's parents accepted Mark as "Fred's roommate," not as Fred's potential life partner. Thus, although ostensibly Fred was more "out" than Mark, Fred had not fully integrated his gay identity into his life.

This couple demonstrates the therapeutic necessity of working within the context of multiple systems when doing family therapy with gay men. Fred explained that it was unthinkable in his conservative Latino Catholic family for him to be open about his male partner. Although the therapist respected the cultural differences (Green, Bettinger, & Zacks, 1996), he also reflected that Fred's decision not to be more open with his family deprived the couple of family support. The couple was struggling with the limited way they had defined their relationship *and* they lacked support from other major social systems. The homophobia of the majority culture that organized Mark to feel so unentitled to parent his children and inhibited Fred in being more out to his parents, as well as Fred's being subjected to rigid gender stereotyping as a Latino man reared in a family where only women had the latitude to express vulnerable emotions, were all factors that undermined the couple's stability.

The therapist began to work at multisystemic levels with the couple as he simultaneously maintained focus on their struggle to create an identity as a couple. The couple began to create a more equitable relationship in which Mark could be the caretaker as Fred struggled with his mother's deteriorating health. The therapist also encouraged the couple to explore resources within the gay community that might support and stabilize their relationship.

Both men were raised Catholic and were spiritual but neither had been to any church in years. "Is that something you miss?" the therapist inquired. Both men concurred that with the approaching Easter holy days, they would like to go to services. The therapist knew of a Jesuit parish in a gay-friendly part of the city that welcomed lesbian and gay people and had a large number of gay couples with children in its congregation. Attending services, Mark discovered another resource, a group for gay dads at the local lesbian, gay, bisexual, and transgendered community center.

Once the couple was stabilized and Fred agreed to Mark's desire to discontinue recreational drugs, the therapist began to work with them regarding parenting issues and the lack of boundaries that existed with Mark's children. Mark related to Fred his fear that he would be a bad father and how that fear held him hostage, keeping him from setting limits with the girls. Fred was able to make some suggestions, such as the couple would have alternate weekends alone. On weekends when Mark had the children, Fred either did activities by himself or occasionally began to join them on outings. As the girls got to know Fred better, Fred found that he enjoyed them more. Mark continued to live in a separate apartment. However, when his children were not visiting, he slept over at Fred's apartment. The couple's relationship became more stable, and they experienced greater satisfaction, with an increased capacity for tolerating differences. For the first time in their relationship, they experienced an ability to compromise without either men fearing a loss of power.

In one turning-point session, the couple came in once again in their old fight/flight mode—Fred analytical, attacking Mark, and Mark defensive, bouncing off the walls with emotions. The therapist asked each man to speak, one at a time. As each addressed the other, the source of their stress became clear. They were trying to make plans for an upcoming spring vacation, when Mark's children would be out of school. Fred wanted the couple to go to the Caribbean alone, and Mark wanted to take his children. Fred said, "No way am I going on vacation with your children. You spend every other weekend with them! It's time we had a vacation." Mark's face got red as he took up a combative stance, "You're asking me not to see my kids. I promised them a vacation trip."

Initially addressing the couple's system, the therapist asked how once again they had got themselves into an either/or stance that allowed no room for problem solving. "You're in a tug-of-war and each of you is pulling on the rope! Where's the 'we' in this stance?" "Mark, do you know what have you done to make Fred feel so excluded?" Without waiting for a response, he turned to Fred. "Do you expect that Mark should absolve himself of his parental responsibilities? You're putting him and your relationship in a no-win position." Fred shook his head as the therapist continued. "Why is it that Mark thinks you want him to neglect his children? The way you're talking to him now doesn't seem to be working. Perhaps your language serves you well in your work as an attorney, but in here your language seems to put him on the defensive. Try talking to him using some other language, one that's less lawyerly."

Fred spoke to Mark, initially in his lawyerly manner but eventually using a less combative voice, about how much he had been looking forward to this vacation as time together. At first Mark looked at him skeptically but slowly he began to hear Fred's new language—words that spoke of love for Mark and a desire to be more intimate both sexually and emotionally with him. Fred spoke more like a partner about how much he missed being close with him since Mark started to coparent his children and how stressful it was for him to see Mark torn apart by the acrimonious relationship he had with his former wife.

Hearing this new language, a language of "we," Mark became less defensive. He too wanted time alone but he felt so guilty going off without the girls. In a compromise, he suggested that perhaps they could go away as a couple for a long weekend and then he could take the children skiing upstate for a few days. Fred quickly agreed to the compromise. Although they had not solved the fundamental issue of how they were going to deal in the long term with Mark's adolescents, they experienced the ability to problem solve parenting issues as a couple.

During this period of time, the couple reported less use of recreational drugs *and* expressed a desire to have a closed relationship. The therapist realized he had totally lost focus on that part of their relationship. During the initial intake session, the couple had hesitated when the therapist had inquired whether they had an open or closed relationship. They seemed to have some version of a "don't ask, don't tell" policy. Their loose agreement appeared to be that when they were apart for career reasons, either man had permission to have outside sex, but not when they were together. At the time, the therapist had thought to himself that neither man seemed comfortable with the rules, nor was he sure that it served them well in their struggle to become a couple. However, with parenting issues in the forefront of their problems as a couple, the therapist had never returned to this boundary issue.

Although intellectually open relationships can have great appeal and often represent a rejection of the majority culture by gay men, the lack of boundaries can threaten a couple's ability to create an identity (Greenan, 2003). Open boundaries around sex exacerbate the problem same-sex couples have of relational ambiguity (Green & Mitchell, 2002). Open boundaries can also contribute to a couple's avoidance of conflict as they turn to other resources to get their needs met. Of the two men, the therapist had thought that Fred might revolt at this potential loss of freedom. However, Fred had concurred with Mark that he also wanted a closed relationship. It was obvious to the therapist that this was a discussion the men had had on their own and both seemed relieved.

A WORK IN PROGRESS

Fred and Mark still had many issues. What was Fred's role to be when they were with the children? Could the biological parents create a nonadversarial language, setting aside their differences and hurts to coparent their children? Could Mark explain to his children the true nature of his relationship with Fred, that they were a committed couple though a nontraditional one? Family therapy would need to expand to include this other family system that was bumping up against and interacting with the couple's system. Mark's children were not going to be on their own for a few more years and, even then, the therapist anticipated that Mark would want them to be part of his life. The couple and the biological parents needed a forum where they could negotiate these complex issues. Coming out to the adolescent girls potentially could decrease everyone's anxiety and allow for more fluidity between the two systems.

The next order of business in the therapy was for Mark to invite his former wife in for a coparenting session without Fred's presence. If the parents could reach an understanding of the importance for Mark to acknowledge his relationship with Fred, setting limits with the girls might become easier. Fred would also potentially feel less threatened as Mark took up his father role with more confidence. Negotiating the division of time regarding the girls' spring break had given them confidence that they had the skills to become a stronger couple.

CONCLUSION

Fred and Mark experienced some of the stresses all ex-spouses face in struggling with issues of blended families. Increasing numbers of gay male couples are having children on their own, through either surrogate mothers or adoption. Although families led by same-sex couples are in many ways like majority families—attending PTA, taking the kids to little league and soccer games, and arranging play dates, these families face particular stresses from the mainstream culture and their families of origin until greater acceptance occurs. Gay-affirmative and gay-knowledgable family therapists will be in greater demand in the twenty-first-century. Identifying resources, normalizing developmental stages, and creating a safe environ for gay families to negotiate intimate relationships will become much more the norm in family therapy. Therapists need to be trained to work systemically with these issues. Very few family training institutes exist and still fewer provide education that focuses on the unique issues of same-sex families. Peer supervision groups are a necessity for therapists engaging in this work, as even the most senior therapist can become inducted into the family's dynamics. Support groups and other resources need to be created for same-sex families to address the isolation that minority families experience.

As this case illustrates, coparenting children in blended families is stressful for both the biological and the nonbiological parent of the new couple. The newly created couple must collaborate carefully to decide how they will divide labor and responsibilities in this instant family, and the role of the nonbiological parent must be carefully negotiated. Such tasks are relatively new for gay male couples. Although male couples have long existed, they were largely invisible in society until the AIDS epidemic. While male couples are gradually becoming accustomed to public visibility as same-sex couples, new challenges await as they face pressures to have or not have children.

Even the initial decision regarding whether to have children is often fraught with conflict, with one man often more eager and the other more reluctant. Many gay men have simply assumed in developing their gay identity that they would never have children. For some gay men, it is a relief not to be obligated in any way to parent children, while others have longed for the chance. If a couple decides on a family of their own, parenting challenges the strength of the most secure, stable couple as they wrestle with whose parenting style will prevail. For male couples already struggling to define what it means to be a minority couple as they straddle the norms of both the mainstream culture and the gay community, the tasks of being a minority family, as well as parenting itself, can seem overwhelming.

Like many male couples, Fred and Mark were conflict avoidant. Despite the power struggle that they enacted in the therapist's office, Mark's flight to leasing another apartment highlighted the couple's relational dynamic of never learning how to compromise and take turns in letting the other lead. Even more problematic was the lifestyle they had led in the early stages of their courtship. While stimulating and sexually charged, it had postponed consolidating their identity as a couple.

The phenomena of recreational drugs and clubbing has great appeal for many gay men because the environ enhanced by drugs creates an instant sense of community amongst a population that has been isolated. The dual phenomena of heterosexism and homophobia, as well as the massive loss in a community devastated by the AIDS epidemic, have created unique challenges for gay men who desire close relationships with other men. Furthermore, for a population that typically has not had the adolescent experience of dating and courtship, the drugs that accompany the club lifestyle ease the social stress that many feel regarding dating rituals. Drugs that specifically target social discomfort and heighten sexual drive are a potent aphrodisiac for thousands of gay men. However, drugs such as crystal meth are highly addictive and correlate with both hypersexuality and unsafe sex. Not only is this scene dangerous for single gay men, it is an anathema to gay men creating stable families in the twenty-first-century and markedly increases the relational ambiguity of the couple. Mark and Fred successfully traversed this slippery path as they redefined the nature of their relationship.

REFERENCES

Belluck, P. (2003, November 26). "Gays respond: 'I do,' 'I might' and 'I won't.'" *The New York Times,* p. A1.

Carter, B., & McGoldrick, M. (1989). *The changing family life cycle: A framework for family therapy* (2nd ed.). Boston: Allyn & Bacon.

Cass, V.E. (1979). Homosexual identity formation: A theoretical model. *Journal of Homosexuality, 4,* 219-235.

Genijovich, E. (1994). *The impossible blended family* (Videotape). Boston: Family Studies, Inc.

Green, R.-J., Bettinger, M., & Zacks, E. (1996). Are lesbian couples fused and gay male couples disengaged? Questioning gender straight jackets. In J. Laird & R.-J. Green (Eds.), *Lesbians and gays in couples and families: A handbook for therapists* (pp. 185-230). San Francisco: Jossey-Bass.

Green, R.-J., & Mitchell, V. (2002). Gay and lesbian couples in therapy: Homophobia, relational ambiguity, and social support. In A.S. Gurman & N.S. Jacobson (Eds.), *Clinical handbook of couple therapy* (3rd ed., pp. 546-568). New York: Guilford Press.

Greenan, D.E. (2003, May/June). Open relationships and gay couples. *Psychotherapy Networker,* pp. 35-40.

Greenan, D.E., & Tunnell, G. (2003). *Couple therapy with gay men.* New York: Guilford Press.

Minuchin, S. (1974). *Families and family therapy.* Cambridge, MA: Harvard University Press.

Minuchin, S., & Fishman, C. (1981). *Family therapy techniques.* Cambridge, MA: Harvard University Press.

Minuchin, S., Lee, W.Y., & Simon, G. (1996). *Mastering family therapy: Journeys of growth and transformation.* New York: Wiley.

Minuchin, S., & Nichols, M. (1993). *Family healing: Tales of hope and renewal from family therapy.* New York: Free Press.

Nichols, M., & Minuchin, S. (1999). Short-term structural family therapy with couples. In J.M. Donovan (Ed.), *Short-term couple therapy.* New York: Guilford Press.

Savin-Williams, R.C. (1998). *"And then I became gay:" Young men's stories.* New York: Routledge.

Tunnell, G., & Greenan, D. E. (2004). Clinical issues in gay male couples. *Journal of Couple and Relationship Therapy, 3*(2/3), 13-26.

Usborne, D. (2003, November 3). Gay baby boom: How kids are shaking up gay life in the city. *New York Magazine,* pp. 3-6.

Chapter 13

Achieving Competent Family Practice with Same-Sex Parents: Some Promising Directions

Jacky Coates
Richard Sullivan

It is an irony of unintended consequence that in recognizing the legality of same-sex marriages or civil unions three Canadian provinces have effectively ascribed same-sex couples a status akin to that of mid-twentieth-century Catholics. They can get married but they cannot get divorced. In Canada, marriage is defined within provincial statutes, but the *Divorce Act* falls within the jurisdiction of the federal government and this act has not yet been amended to acknowledge recent changes in British Columbia, Ontario, and Quebec. The federal Liberal government has signaled its intent to amend the *Divorce Act* at some point over the next few years, but in the interim it faces a federal election in which most politicians would prefer not to campaign on this potentially divisive issue. The safest strategy for avoiding the pitfalls of controversy has been to refer the question of same-sex marriage to the Canadian Supreme Court for an opinion on whether the denial of same-sex marriage abrogates the equality rights of sexual-minority citizens under the Canadian Charter of Rights and Freedoms. The court has tended to a more liberal interpretation of the charter and in doing so enables the federal government to point to legal inevitability as the impetus for the recognition of same-sex unions and their legal dissolution.

Given their present inability to divorce except perhaps by moving to a jurisdiction where their union is not recognized anyway, same-sex couples would do well to afford themselves of every opportunity

doi:10.1300/5792_14

to enhance their prospects for marital success. This might well involve recourse to marital and family therapy. It is here that we encounter another of the unintended consequences of change. For marriage and family practice professionals, the recognition of same-sex marriage raises the question of competency requirements for practice. Most family practice professions, including psychology, social work, and nursing, are already guided by codes of ethics requiring respect for diversity. Official ascription of marital status, however, may increase the onus on professions with a recognized family practice specialization to increase their competency requirements for practice with sexual-minority families. This chapter explores some of the requirements for ethical practice with same-sex parents and then reviews some of the theoretical trajectories that hold promise for adapting existing family practice frameworks to promote competent practice with families headed by same-sex parents.

THE REQUIREMENTS OF ETHICAL PRACTICE

Ethically competent practice requires more than respect for diversity and a commitment to perform equally well with different families. Gregory Janson (2002) has argued that knowledge, skills, and experience are prerequisites for competent practice and that these are not generally achieved with respect to sexual-minority families through the educational programs of the disciplines most commonly providing family counseling (psychology, medicine, and social work). Although the codes of ethics of these professions may express value convictions that oblige adherents to practice in such a way as to affirm human dignity in diversity, these convictions alone will not necessarily produce competent practice. The key to competent practice with same-sex parents does not rest so much with specific therapeutic techniques, according to Janson (2002), but rather with "clinical competence in individual therapy with GLBT clients, adequate supervised experience, and thorough knowledge of the sociocultural, clinical, legal and ethical issues that pertain to sexual minorities" (p. 329). A further challenge for regulatory and standard-setting authorities within these professions is to respond to statutory changes in definitions of marriage and the family by requiring and facilitating continuing education to achieve the knowledge, skills, and experience necessary for competent practice.

Raising children in the context of a same-sex relationship can involve a number of variables that are distinct from raising children in heterosexual families. Creating and maintaining healthy and functional family relationships in same-sex parenting couples, therefore, involves a complex set of challenges and requires a unique perspective on ways they can be addressed. As Janson (2002) suggests, there may be no one approach to competent practice with sexual minority families, but some may lend themselves more readily to the integration of perspectives useful to an understanding of their experience.

Contemporary debates about the legal recognition of same-sex marriages stand as an example of social regulation at the boundary between the family and the state. Up to now, the denial of social recognition has complicated the development of family role structures for same-sex parents. Family systems theory, with its emphasis on differentiated roles and distinct boundaries, may hold some promise for exploring the experience of same-sex parents. We will argue, however, that family systems theory alone is not sufficient to address the impact of heterosexism and homophobia on parenting in a same-sex relationship. Any intervention that knowingly stops short of addressing the source of family problems is arguably questionable, both in terms of ethics and competence. Hence, we also explore complementary constructs from structural social work, ecological systems theory, and queer theory to illuminate the challenges in family role differentiation unique to same-sex parents.

FAMILY SYSTEMS THEORY: ROLE DIFFERENTIATION IN SAME-SEX PARENTS

Deriving from the work of Salvador Minuchin (1974) with later adaptations by Carl Broderick (1993) and others, family systems theory attends to the ways families are affected by and respond to their social environments in adapting their roles and internal systems to the requirements of their own survival and the changing needs of their members. It takes as its starting point the transactional patterns that regulate family members' behavior. These patterns become fixed over time and the extent to which they are rigidly fixed or adaptively flexible is a primary concern of family systems theory. These patterned behaviors ultimately serve as guides or rules for what constitutes acceptable communicative or behavioral exchanges between family members. These rules are of two types: *generic*—the normative patterns that typify a culture at a particular point in time (e.g., that parents usually have a higher order of authority in family resource management than do children); and the *idiosyncratic* modifications of generic constraints within a particular family (e.g., the complementarities that evolve between couples). These idiosyncratic role complementarities are what distinguish two people as a couple and as a parental subsystem within the family system.

These idiosyncrasies typically express both accommodation to cultural conventions and individual tendencies, as when a feminist forms an economically egalitarian partnership with a man who just happens to be handy around the house. The mistake that many beginning therapists make in working with gay and lesbian couples is to expect these complementarities to evolve along traditional gender lines. In other words, they look for a butch and a femme. This may be more an artifact of history and mythology than reality. You may still see it among older couples whose ideas of role complementarity were formed before they had any alternative role models within the gay and lesbian community. This is equally true for heterosexual couples, insofar as older people are more apt to conform to traditional gender roles. Most couples today operate at similar levels of conventionality along the continuum of gender-role expression. The complementarity is apt to be more complex than in heterosexual couples and also more fluid, in part because it is not reinforced by social conventions. The more conventionally feminine partner in a lesbian relationship may also be the household mechanic and carpenter, and the more conventionally masculine partner in a male dyad may be the more nurturant member of the household and may also more often accede to his partner's preferences in most areas of decision making. It is also important not to make any assumptions about their sexual roles based on their social presentation.

The flip side of this lack of traditional norms for same-sex couples is the absence of any social recognition of their partnerships or any reinforcement for their role adaptations as couples and as families. This is what Fiona Nelson (1996) described as the social vacuum in which the nongestating mother in a lesbian household has to try to achieve recognition of her maternal role in a social context that provides her with no archetypes. Sullivan and Baques (1999) provide the case example of the male couple who adopted their son in the United States and had to face a Canadian immigration officer who took it upon himself to uphold tradition by refusing to recognize them as parents. This may also characterize the couple's extended families, some of whom may recognize the couple's child as their kin without recognizing their relative's partner as a parent. This is reinforced by provincial and federal legislation that recognizes only one of the parents as a biological or adoptive parent. The consequence is that the child is in legal limbo if the recognized parent dies or is incapacitated because the other parent has no recognized custody rights. Similarly if that person dies intestate (without a will), the child has no claim on the estate even if he or she has been parented by that person throughout his or her life. This makes it all the more important to advise same-sex parents to have carefully detailed wills expressing their wishes for custody and inheritance. It also makes it important in the assessment phase for the therapist to assess the degree of role recognition that they have achieved with their respective families of origin and their families of choice within the gay and lesbian community prior to becoming parents.

Defining Family Boundaries in the Context of Heterosexism

For all couples, it is important to achieve clear boundaries as a couple within their extended families. Not to do so before they have children is apt to cause problems in their adjustment to parenting. A family system is comprised of subsystems, such as parental and sibling subsystems. In order for a family to function optimally, it is important that roles and expectations be clearly delineated for each subsystem. Over time, these expectations become systematized as normative rules defining who within the family participates in each of its subsystems, how, when, and with whom. In effect, these expectations set the boundaries between subsystems of the family and between the family and its social context. When boundaries between subsystems are not clear, two pathological extremes are possible: an *enmeshed* family or a *disengaged* family (Jones, 1980).

Because boundaries differentiate the family system by expressing specific expectations for members and because members learn particular interpersonal skills through participation in a subsystem, it is important that each subsystem operate without undue interference. A parental subsystem, for example, must operate without interference by in-laws and children. Clarity of boundaries provides a barometer of family functioning. In the disengaged family, a relative absence of structure, order, or authority is apparent; ties between family members are weak or nonexistent. The enmeshed family, by contrast, is characterized by a high resonance and interlocking between parts such that members intrude on one another's roles and may be rigidly defended against any one member's adaptive transactions with external systems.

Among gay and lesbian families, as with other minorities who perceive their families to be operating in an ambivalent or hostile social environment, a greater risk of enmeshment exists, which will become more apparent when developing children begin to try to assert some measure of autonomy in seeking a life beyond the family. Disengagement is a greater risk where extended family and community have not recognized the sexual minority parent as legitimate. Some same-sex parents compound the problem in seeking to create a new postheterosexist family reality that does not recognize archetypes such as mother and father, and hence they encourage their children to call them by their first names. Although their intent may be admirable, the eschewal of clear parenting roles may be a mistake, particularly in families that have not achieved clear boundaries and a strong family identity. We do not yet live in a postheterosexist world, and families seeking to achieve clear boundaries and a strong family identity for their children are best advised to adopt or create nomenclature that distinguish family membership. Defining the parental dyad also guards against enmeshment or triangulation in a family where historical or institutional factors may already incline the child to an alliance with one parent over the other, as when one parent comes to the partnership with a child from a prior union or when the couple adapts to perceived heterosexism in the school system by designating only one parent for duty at parent-teacher meetings.

Either enmeshment or disengagement ultimately expresses itself in symptoms that may bring a family to a therapist for assistance. These symptoms are often borne by one person whose behavior expresses the problems within the family. Nonetheless, family systems theory emphasizes the wholeness of the family as an entity and focuses analysis not on individual members but on the workings of the family as a whole. The primary focus of this approach is the organizational structure the family has developed to carry out its functions of nurturing, supporting, and socializing family members. Problems generally arise in relation to the boundaries and alignments between the subsystems to which families delegate various tasks and responsibilities. This delegation process can be either implicit or explicit (Leslie, 1988). Minuchin defines boundaries as "rules defining who participates and how" (Leslie, 1988, p. 57). These rules apply to the family's relationship with the outside world and also to the relationships between subsystems of the family. The affective dimension of these relationships is captured in the concept of alignment, which refers to the emotional or psychological connections among family members. Although families are expected to contain close emotional connections between members, some alignments within families can be dysfunctional, as when triangulation or an intergenerational coalition occurs.

Murray Bowen's concepts of differentiation of self and triangulation are also relevant to therapies deriving from family systems theory, although Bowen disassociates his theory from those of other family systems theorists (Bowen, 1978). Bowen's concept of the differentiation of self distinguishes people in terms of their degree of fusion or differentiation between emotional and intellectual functioning. Simply put, it distinguishes among those whose affective relational styles are either predominantly reactive or reasoned. It is related to the degree of emotional separation that people achieve from their families of origin (Kerr, 1988). According to Bowen, the most undifferentiated people "are totally relationship oriented," are dominated by feelings rather than intellect, and "inherit a major portion of the world's serious health, financial and social problems" (Bowen, 1978, p. 367). Those with higher levels of differentiation have a more solid sense of self, are more psychologically healthy, and experience fewer problems in living. A relationship between more highly differentiated individuals "is a functioning partnership [in which] the spouses can enjoy the full range of emotional intimacy without either being deselfed by the other" (Bowen, 1978, p. 370).

In essence, family systems theory views family dysfunction as having to do with the structures developed by a family in order to carry out its functions. The clinical therapist working from this perspective will work first to observe and analyze the structures of a family to determine where problems are located and then will begin, through a variety of therapeutic techniques, to attempt to change problematic structures in order to relieve the dysfunctions. The therapist determines the therapeutic goals from the observations of the family structure and the resulting determination of the changes that need to occur (Leslie, 1988).

Interventions

In family systems therapy, the tasks involved in addressing problems include joining and accommodation, with three subprocesses of the latter including techniques of maintenance, tracking, and mimesis. Maintenance refers to providing support and reinforcement for family structures. Tracking involves following the content of the family's communication and behavior while encouraging them to continue. Mimesis involves accommodating oneself to the family's style and affective range. Only when joining has been successful can restructuring begin, because restructuring involves more confrontation than would be advisable were the family already not engaged with their therapist.

Susan Jones (1980) provides a succinct summary of Minuchin's (1974) work on the areas necessary to consider in an assessment of family functioning. Such assessment must first include an analysis of the family structure in terms of its transactional patterns as well as an evaluation of the flexibility of the family system and its ability to adapt and restructure itself in response to changes in circumstance. An assessment also includes attention to the family system's resonance or sensitivity to individual members' actions and a determination of where the family system would be located on the continuum of enmeshment and disengagement. The therapist must also consider the family's life context and its sources of support and stress. The family's developmental stage must also be determined, along with the ways in which the system performs the tasks appropriate to that stage. Finally, the therapist examines the ways in which the symptoms of the identified patient within the family are used to maintain the family's preferred transactional patterns (Jones, 1980).

It is Minuchin's dimension of the assessment of the family's life context that is particularly important with minority families. If a family experiences its community context to be hostile or nonengaging, any tendency toward fusion or enmeshment may be amplified. Similarly, disengagement with its community may limit a family's resources for problem solving. Attention to the domains beyond a family's immediate boundaries is scant in most traditional family therapies. A synthesis of family systems therapy and structural social work, however, may hold promise for work with families headed by same-sex parents.

STRUCTURAL SOCIAL WORK

Structural social work was introduced into Canadian social work education in the 1970s, and it has been elaborated by Robert Mullaly (1997). *Structural* in this context refers to the social construction of disadvantage in the functioning of social institutions, whereby the distribution of the social good is determined along lines of class, gender, race, sexual orientation, disability, and so on. The very term *structural* is intended to cue social workers that their practice should focus on the structures of society and not solely on individuals and families (Mullaly, 1997).

The structural approach does not prioritize different forms of oppression (for example, racism, classism, heterosexism, and so on) into a hierarchical ordering of most to least fundamental, but rather considers forms of oppression to intersect with one another. As a result, a total system of oppression can be seen to be operating as different forms of oppression interact with one another in various contexts. The structural approach to social work is also notable in that it works both with social institutions and as a "generalist model of practice requiring knowledge and skills for working with individuals, families, groups, and communities, always making the connection between the person and the political" (Mullaly, 1997, p. 105).

This approach does not contradict the theory and methods of family systems therapy but rather expands that practice to include both the elevation of awareness among family members whose experience is affected by various forms of oppression and intervention at the level of social structures. The politicization of awareness can itself be a liberating practice insofar as it can remove self-blame for problems associated with transactions across family boundaries. It can also identify the points of intersection between individual and family experiences and problematic social structures. This is consistent with family systems therapy's attention to transactions across systems boundaries.

Examples of such work at the boundaries of family experience and social structures include the work of advocacy groups such as Action Canada for Population and Development (ACPD) and the Planned Parenthood Federation of Canada (PPFC), who have made an influential submission to the House of Commons Committee on the Rights of the Child. Together ACPD and PPFC reported to the Commons in September 2003 urging that Canada's compliance with the United Nations Convention on the Rights of the Child requires the solemnization of same-sex marriages. The failure to do so submits the children of these unions to continuing stigma and the risk of discontinuity in their family lives if the biological or adoptive parent dies and that person's next of kin asserts legal rights that the parent without legal rights or recognition does not possess. In other words, these children stand in continuing risk of loss if only one parent has legal recognition. This legal limbo also potentially deprives them of inheritance rights and any other federal or provincial benefits in respect of the nonbiological parent if that parent dies intestate. These examples may seem extreme, but they illustrate some of the structural dimensions by which same-sex parents and their children are disadvantaged.

These illustrations demonstrate the continuing institutional disrespect that reinforces the marginalization of sexual-minority families. Family practitioners who are aware of these factors can work with families to develop an understanding of the social sources of their distress and empower them to engage in collective efforts at remediation. A family systems therapist working from a dual perspective that integrates the tenets of structural social work can also help the family identify the ways in which their social location affects their internal structure and organization. If one parent is rendered invisible and inconsequential to the social systems his or her children are engaged in, for example, it is almost inevitable that the other parent will be charged with more responsibility for mediating the children's interaction with those systems. This effectively renders the one parent powerless and introduces an imbalance in their parenting roles. This imbalance does not go unnoticed by their children. Similarly, if their extended family and community fail to recognize the boundary around the parental dyad, they are more apt to breach that boundary and destabilize the family system. Maintaining the roles and boundaries between family systems and subsystems is very much the work of family systems therapists. From the perspective advanced here, that work is enhanced by efforts to achieve recognition and social equity within the broader social context. Other approaches to family practice are also enhanced through integration of perspectives that enlarge the focus of more traditional therapies.

ECOLOGICAL SYSTEMS PERSPECTIVE

The ecological systems perspective provides a lens through which family practitioners can view individual problems in the broader context in which they are located. This perspective is therefore promising as "a unifying paradigm for social work knowledge and practice" (Allen-Meares & Lane, 1987, p. 515). The ecological systems perspective offers an important alternative to psychodynamic theories that focus on individual psychology as the location for investigation and intervention. As such, ecological systems approaches allow for more emphasis on changing environments as opposed to individuals.

Similar to family systems theory, the ecological systems perspective is a derivative of general systems theory. Central to the ecosystems perspective is the metaphor that humans are connected to their environments through a series of interlocking systems comparable to the ecosystem of the biological sciences. These systems are characterized by their interdependence such that an action in one system reverberates throughout other systems. In this way, individuals are part of their nuclear family system, their extended-family system, the system that is their school or workplace, their neighborhood, church, local community, and so on. The influence between and among these systems is reciprocal, so that individuals affect the systems in which they interact as well as these systems having individuals. Reciprocal adaptation between individuals and their environments is essential for the survival of both. The ecological systems perspective provides a means to investigate a client's situation in its totality. An ecological approach allows a survey of a client's world to determine which systems act as a source of stress and which systems may be a source of support and strength. Problems may be seen as originating in one or more of the systems with which the client interacts rather than as intrinsic to the client as an individual. Interventions can then be directed toward larger systems as well as individual clients and can make use of systems that are helpful to the client. This requires the practitioner to scan a family's context for positive supports as well as problems. For a family that has become disengaged from its community, this may imply the facilitation of connections with other systems (families, organizations, or services) with the potential to affirm the positive aspects of the family's own structure.

The ecological systems perspective is also useful in exploring role differentiation in same-sex parenting couples in that it directs us toward an investigation of the impact of the reciprocal relationships between sexual-minority families and the many social systems with which they interact. It allows us to hypothesize that role differentiation is not simply a negotiation within individual couples but rather one that takes place within the context of their surrounding social environments. The ecological systems perspective recognizes that the broader social context in which same-sex couples parent their children will have a tremendous impact on the way they structure themselves. In turn, the existence and increasing visibility of gay and lesbian families will affect broader social systems and institutions. The ecosystems perspective allows an analysis of role differentiation to examine the complexities of the interrelationship between these families and their environments. We can illustrate this with an example from one of the co-authors' own experience.

> My partner and I take our baby to the hospital emergency department. First we need to speak to a clerk, who enters our information in the computer. She takes the name of the baby and myself, then says, "and the father's name?" I explain that our family has two mothers and no father and give her the name of the other mother. Later, the nurse speaks mostly to me, then turns to my partner and says, almost severely, "And who are you?" My partner indicates that she is the other mother of our child. The nurse lightens immediately. "*Ohhhh,*" she says, "*partners.*" Then she says, "Do you know Mary? Mary and her partner have just had a baby, and they tried for so long. We're just so happy for them."

Clearly, role differentiation is not something gay and lesbian families do only in private or in some sort of cultural vacuum. Like other families, they negotiate with broader social systems every day. Although heterosexual parents may not need to think much about these negotiations, they can become a daily stress for sexual-minority parents. The need to explain their family structure to staff at the hospital or the school compounds the stress that may already be associated with any negotiation with these systems. The response of the broader system, in this case the representatives of the health care system, have an impact on both how parents feel about representing their family publicly and how they feel about their roles in relation to each other as parents. As one of the co-authors has experienced, although hospital and school forms do not include our family composition at this specific intersection of history and geography, we can generally count on not being the first same-sex family that staff have encountered. In Vancouver, British Columbia, both the visibility of other same-sex parents who have come before us and the attempts to sensitize health care workers have an impact on our experience as same-sex parents as we interact with the health care system.

The perspectives of structural social work and ecological systems theory can assist the family practitioner in situating their clients' experience in their own unique social and historical context. In addition, queer theory has emerged in recent years to help us understand the ways in which the experience of gay and lesbian parents may differ from other minority parents.

QUEER THEORY

> When I came out as a lesbian in the mid-1980s, it never occurred to me that I would become a mother. In fact, it did not occur to me for another decade that motherhood was a possibility for me. The identities of *lesbian* and *mother* were mutually exclusive categories, and when I fell in love with a woman, my life was mapped out before me. I had a ready-made identity as a lesbian, and this identity precluded motherhood.

Queer theory has emerged in recent years from the academic discipline of gay and lesbian studies. As with other theory, queer theory developed within a specific social context: the gay and lesbian liberation movement beginning in the late 1960s and early 1970s following the Stonewall riot. The concept of a gay or lesbian identity created the conditions of possibility for the subsequent development of queer theory. The political work done by the gay and lesbian liberation movement has made great strides toward the visibility and acceptability of lesbians and gay men in certain urban areas of North America.

Much of the intellectual groundwork for queer theory was laid by Michel Foucault (1990) in his seminal work, *The History of Sexuality,* which delineates the diffuse nature of contemporary power relations and the ways in which sexuality has become "a principal point of access to individual subjectivity for the exercise of power in the modern age" (Blasius, 1994, p. 65). The meanings attached to sexual behavior have changed throughout history, and the concept of identity flowing from sexuality or sexuality as a way in which a subject would constitute itself is a modern phenomenon. In this way, although homosexual behavior has always existed throughout history and in different contexts, it is only in the modern age, with the exercise of power through medical discourses and the resistance by lesbian and gay activism, that we have come to think of a person as having a gay or lesbian identity.

It is then within a poststructuralist context that queer theory develops. Central to queer theory are a number of interrelated concepts: (1) that sexuality is political; (2) that sexual identity is a social construction; and (3) that the category of *queer* encompasses a variety of nonnormative expressions of sexuality, including lesbian, gay, bisexual, and transgender. Queer theory is by its nature ambiguous and uncertain—chameleonlike—as it deconstructs and destabilizes identity categories that we have come to think of as self-evident. As Annamarie Jagose (1996) writes, "queer is very much a category in the process of formation. It is not simply that queer has yet to solidify and take on a more consistent profile but rather that its definitional indeterminacy—its elasticity—is one of its constituent characteristics" (p. 1).

Arguably, queer theory has emerged as a response to both gay liberation and lesbian feminist ideas and political movements. Gay liberation posits an innate gay identity or the concept of sexual orientation, a binary system wherein an individual is either heterosexual or gay/lesbian and that one's sexual orientation is intrinsic to one's personhood. Lesbian feminism situates lesbianism as a political way of being in the world for women who want to exceed the love of men or live their politics through having intimate relationships with women and not with men (Faderman, 1985). Queer theory moves our thinking beyond binary categories of heterosexual or gay/lesbian identity to think of all sexuality as social construction.

Queer theory is central in a number of ways to an exploration of how lesbians and gay men differentiate their parenting and domestic roles. First, it does not objectify gay and lesbian lives but rather positions the theorist as a queer subject. Queer theory is theory made by queer thinkers about queer existence. Second, queer theory includes a historical perspective in understanding the ways in which sexuality is political and how sexual identities have been formed. Finally, queer theory is constructivist in its views on sexual identity and pluralist in its thinking about what can compose a queer identity. Using queer theory exposes what has been thought to be self-evident about being a gay man or lesbian and allows for a more flexible construction of identity that, we suggest, can encompass parenthood as well as other activities and identities. Queer theory can also provide a window for the examination of roles in queer relationships, a subject that to some extent has been quieted through the politics of lesbian feminism.

WEAVING TOGETHER STRANDS OF THEORY: ROLE DIFFERENTIATION AND QUEER PARENTS

> In having our baby, we probably have spent more time in the lawyer's office than we have in the fertility clinic. It takes a fair bit of work to make sure that our family has legal protection as an entity here in British Columbia. There are donor contracts, wills, custody and guardianship agreements, and adoption proceedings. We want to make sure that our child has the security of a two-parent family and that no one could legitimately challenge my partner's right to parent her should anything happen to me. These are steps that are unique to same-sex family formations. We need to proactively deal with many systems in order to create and protect the structure of our family. We feel a certain degree of comfort at this point in time in Vancouver, British Columbia. We feel much more vulnerable when we travel to other jurisdictions where the systems are less familiar and where heterosexism and homophobia are more socially legitimate.

The Social Context of Same-Sex Families

Historically, both lesbians and gay men have been more likely to conceive children through previous heterosexual unions. Arnup (1999) documents a history of discrimination in Canadian and American courts from the 1970s through the 1990s as lesbian mothers have tried to win custody of their children from heterosexual marriages. Progress in terms of legal recognition for lesbian and gay families has been advancing slowly in some arenas, such as custody battles between heterosexual and gay/lesbian parents, and more quickly in certain respects in specific jurisdictions. The past ten years have seen considerable advancement toward equality rights for lesbians and gay men in British Columbia. Nonbiological parents can now adopt the biological children of their partners in stepparent adoption proceedings. The names of same-sex parents can appear on birth certificates, although the provincial government in British Columbia is appealing this decision. Same-sex marriages are being performed in most Canadian provinces. British Columbia is one of the most progressive jurisdictions for lesbian and gay parents in North America, and still the backlash regarding our increasing social legitimacy remains steadfast.[1]

Ecological systems theory can assist in determining the particular stresses on lesbian and gay families that may contribute to the way in which parents differentiate their roles. Depending on the political and social climate of various jurisdictions, queer families will experience varying degrees of stress from external sources that have the potential to be threatening. Due to these perceived and real external sources of threat, queer families may have varying abilities to be "out" in different spheres of our lives. If we must be closeted in certain arenas (e.g., at work, to our families of origin, in our cultural community or our neighborhood), it becomes difficult to be equally involved parents, since we cannot easily maintain one reality inside our homes and another outside. Thus, one parent may be more primary while the other may have a more secondary and less public role.

Fusion and Differentiation in Lesbian Parenting Couples

Family systems theory can also be useful, along with ecological systems theory, in understanding the ways in which the boundaries of a queer family can be eroded through external social systems as a result of homophobia and heterosexism. In lesbian families, the erosion can occur through extended families, for example, that exclude the nonbiological mother or deny or ignore her parental status. This denial of status for the nonbiological mother may result in her becoming marginalized within the family. Alternatively, Rohrbaugh (1992) suggests another family dynamic that can emerge in lesbian families as a result of coping with these external sources of stress:

> These patterns of boundary invasion lead lesbian partners to cling to each other in an attempt to shut out the rejecting, homophobic world; this coping strategy seeks to develop and protect the sense of stability and permanence that our culture enhances in heterosexual relationships but diminishes in lesbian ones. . . . The social isolation caused by secrecy can contribute to difficulties with boundaries and differentiation. (p. 5)

As a result of drawing inward to buffer against external sources of stress, lesbian couples may tend toward fusion rather than differentiation in their relationships. This can lead to defenses against psychological merger, such as triangulation and coalitions, as well as open conflict and lack of sexual intimacy (McCandish, 1987; Rohrbaugh, 1992).

Problems with fusion and lack of differentiation may lead lesbian couples to seek help from counselors and social service agencies in attempts to preserve their relationships. Queer theory may also be able to provide insights into the tendency for lesbian couples to move into patterns of fusion, since queer theory deconstructs lesbian as an identity and allows for a plurality of ways of being queer. The inclusiveness of various ways of being queer in queer theory, including butch/femme roles as one example, provides models of difference rather than sameness. When lesbian partners are able to freely explore their difference without fear of loss or censure, one could argue that fusion may be less likely to characterize a relationship.

Lesbian feminism has been a key ideology in the lesbian community and a formative part of lesbian culture. A number of ways of being lesbian in lesbian culture have been recognized, often influenced by the intersection of sexual identity and social class. As Jagose (1996) documents, the first lesbian organization in the 1950s in the United States—the Daughters of Bilitis—was exclusionary in terms of class and advocated a type of homogeneous respectability for lesbians. Working-class women and women who identified as butch were not welcome. Lesbian feminism, beginning in the 1970s, arguably advocated a particular homogeneity as well, but in terms of political ideology rather than respectability. Lesbian feminism advanced the idea that lesbianism was less a sexual orientation and more "a way of being in the world that, potentially, includes all women" (Jagose, 1996, p. 47). According to this ideology, "gender, rather than sexuality, is the primary identification category. . . . Consequently women (rather than gay men) are the natural political allies of lesbians" (p. 50). In fact, some lesbian feminists would go so far as to view gay men as part of the patriarchal structure that oppresses women. For example, Marilyn Frye (1983) sees "woman-hating [as] an obvious corollary of man-loving" (p. 136).

Some aspects of feminist thinking and practice have been central to the development of lesbian feminist ideology and potentially may inform the ways in which lesbians structure intimate relationships. The way in which feminist collectives are conceived reflects a particular analysis of task and role division in feminist organizational systems. Janice Ristock (1993) describes feminist collectives as "nonhierarchical, participatory democracies" (p. 220). Ristock (1993) goes on to quote Zofel in defining feminist work:

> There are no hierarchies, knowledge and information is shared (and not used as oppressive instruments of power), responsibilities are rotated and everybody learns and is capable of doing any of the jobs. There should be as little specialization as possible or rather: everywoman is a specialist in all tasks. (p. 220)

Feminism has critiqued the family as a site of women's oppression and in particular the gendered division of labor in the home. When applied to creating an alternative family, then, it stands to reason that some women influenced by feminist thinking will resist the adoption of roles in relation to domestic and parenting tasks in the attempt to equalize tasks and roles.

Similarly for gay men, the conscious or unconscious assumption of homophobic or masculinist ideologies that devalue more traditionally feminine nurturant roles may complicate the evolution of their parenting roles and must be attended to in assessment. The elucidation of internalized homophobia and its effect on role assumptions can benefit from queer and feminist theories.

Interesting definitions of feminist work appear in descriptions of the division of labor in lesbian parenting couples in a variety of empirical studies. For example, Fiona Nelson (1996) reports that lesbian couples who conceived their children by donor insemination tried to divide mothering evenly, with each partner performing the same tasks with equal frequency. Other studies have found that lesbian parenting couples describe being equally involved in parenting and domestic tasks (Chan, Brooks, Raboy, & Patterson, 1998; Vanfraussen, Ponjaert-Kristofferson, & Brewaeys, 2003). Although dividing parenting and household tasks equally does not necessarily mean that parents are not differentiated in their roles, it is suggestive that roles are not easily differentiated and that tension may develop if couples expect their roles to be identical.

Lesbian feminism, of course, is but one component of a complex lesbian culture that also includes elements that may be somewhat antithetical to lesbian feminist discourse. Butch/femme role division would be one aspect of lesbian culture that lesbian feminism might like to disavow. Other women will find the politics of lesbian separatism narrow and essentialist. Also, although some women may identify completely with lesbian feminism and others with butch/femme culture, these are by no means mutually exclusive categories, and arguably both are part of the fabric of lesbian culture and identity. Queer theory is helpful here in that lesbian identity is not unitary, but rather contains contradictions and complexity. Queer theory also encompasses plurality and inclusiveness, allying lesbians with gay men, bisexuals, and transgender people.

The Construction of a Queer Family

Since queer theory deconstructs the identity categories of lesbians and gay men, it also has the potential to deconstruct other categories such as mother, father, and family. As increasing numbers of lesbians and gay men choose to become parents and form families openly rather than in a context of deception (Sullivan & Baques, 1999), a certain freedom is created to invent our families the way we choose. Indeed, as Stephanie Brill (2001) argues, "There is no one face to a queer family. . . our community has the opportunity to totally reinvent what family means to us" (p. 1). As a result, the one characterization that can be made about gay and lesbian families is that they are enormously diverse. Some of the varied family structures may include: families formed through adoption, blended families in which one partner is a stepparent to the other's biological children, families led by couples who have borne children together through donor insemination or surrogacy, and single-parent families.

Further, a sperm donor may be known or anonymous. In situations in which the donor is known, he may or may not play a role in the child's life. Sometimes the donor may play a father role, sometimes an uncle or friend-of-the-family role, or sometimes he is distanced from the family. Sometimes gay men and lesbians form families together and a child may have three or four parents rather than two. Same-sex families also create and find comfort in queer kinship networks or *families of choice* in much the same way as heterosexual families may view extended family. Children may have many significant others in this chosen family and these people may play a much more involved role in their lives than that played by relatives in a more traditional extended family. In this way, the capacity for role differentiation in queer families is immense, and the way in which individual families may define their family boundaries will be diverse. This presents a challenge to any family practitioner who attempts to approach a sexual minority family with a single, normative script for family membership and functioning. Competent practice requires the assessment of the unique and diverse ways queer families may have come to their current construction and the meanings attached to their respective roles.

One distinction that may have varying levels of meaning in different families is the distinction between biological and nonbiological mother. Although a number of studies show biological and nonbiological mothers to be equally involved in parenting their children (Chan et al., 1998; Nelson, 1996; Vanfraussen et al., 2003), doubtless a potential for inequality may need to be addressed in some families. Barbara McCandish (1987) notes the vulnerability of the nonbiological parent in the absence of acknowledgement from legal and social systems. This parent may be entirely dependent on the child's response and her partner's expectations to give her a place in the family. Queer theory reveals the way in which even the category of biological mother can be deconstructed as lesbian couples find ingenious ways for both partners to be biologically connected to their child. Some have achieved conception wherein one partner is the genetic mother and the other is the birth mother. Social and legal systems are left to catch up as lesbian couples create their families in unique ways that call into question traditional family roles and structures.

Clearly the theoretical and clinical terrain in which lesbians and gay men are forming families is shifting. The role differentiation to which family systems theory would have us attend is complex insofar as our families have a unique and variable interrelationship with social and legal systems in specific jurisdictions. As the legal and social terrain also shifts, so do the meanings that are attached to concepts of identity associated with being queer, a father, a mother, or a family. No prototypical structure can be imposed upon queer families as normal or healthy. Rather, a complex body of knowledge from family systems theory, structural social work, ecological systems, and queer theories can be integrated to help understand the specific struggles of queer families in the context of our social environments.

CLINICAL IMPLICATIONS

Social workers and other family practitioners are faced with a complex and shifting landscape when attempting to address role differentiation in families headed by same-sex couples. No one theory is adequate to the task. Family systems theory provides insights into the way in which families organize themselves to fulfill their functions and the ways in which family structure can be dysfunctional. However, family systems theory deals with the operations of the family primarily as a microcosm in isolation from the other social systems of which it is a part. In a sense, family systems therapy treats the family as if it exists unto itself in a sort of historical and cultural vacuum. Family systems theory is also silent on questions of gender and sexuality, perhaps assuming a normative heterosexual family without acknowledging either that the family can operate as a site of oppression for women or that individuals may form alternative types of families in which to meet intimacy needs and raise children. Despite these omissions, family systems theory proposes concepts that can be useful in working with same-sex families if we turn to other theories to provide the context that is lacking in more traditional approaches.

Ecological systems theory is particularly useful to the clinician in assessing the social systems surrounding the queer family to determine which systems are sources of difficulty and which systems are sources of strength and support. The use of ecological systems theory allows the clinician to examine the impact of systemic oppression in the lives of families and to see how these external sources of oppression affect the formation of family structures. As discussed earlier, the closeting of relationships, for example, may lead couples to *marginalize* a nonbiological parent and define roles too rigidly, giving this parent a peripheral role. Alternatively, pressures due to heterosexism and homophobia may lead couples to rigidify the boundaries separating their families from the outside world and turn inward in a defensive dynamic which further isolates the family and creates enmeshment in the couple relationship. An ecosystems approach assists the practitioner to examine the linkages between the family and the systems with which it interacts.

Ecological systems theory has been critiqued for being limited in various ways (Payne, 1997). This article does not engage these limitations but rather uses this theory for what it can contribute as a way of documenting the interfaces between queer families and the many systems with which they must interact. To address the exact character of the systemic oppression faced by queer families, we have turned to structural social work and queer theory.

Queer theory makes use of history to explain how identities came to be constructed through sexuality as heterosexual and as gay or lesbian and focuses attention on the marginalization of some of these identities. Critics of queer theory have concerns that it is has become a scholarly domain "whose interests are textual rather than social" (Jagose, 1996, p. 111) and as such is apolitical. Since queer theory is very much a theory in formation, we would agree with Gary Kinsman (1996) that it is not by definition relegated to an academic context and that its insights can be given "a more social and materialist grounding to make them more relevant to critical historical, social, and political investigations, and to social-movement activism" (p. 14). Critics have also been skeptical of queer as a gender-neutral category and concerned about the possible erasure of lesbian experience because of the allying of women and men in queer theory. Annamarie Jagose (1996) counters this in identifying the distinction between gender and sexuality, which is not incompatible with feminism.

Rather than focus on the potential deficiencies of queer theory, we have chosen to make use of its characteristic flexibility to illuminate the developmental task of role differentiation in queer families. As a theory in formation, we believe that its application to queer families is not internally contradictory and that its synthesis with other approaches to family practice is promising.

Finally, for the practitioner working with queer families that are experiencing various family relationship problems, this article suggests that a thoughtful integration of family systems theory, ecological systems theory, queer theory, and the tenets of structural social work is useful for drawing together what each can contribute. Such an analysis can situate the structures that have developed in an individual family within a broader context of legal and social systems, with an awareness of lesbian and gay history and identity formation. This creative use of theory can help the clinician to interpret the various levels that may need attention when a problem surfaces in relation to role differentiation, boundaries, and alignments in family structure, enabling interventions in broader systems and in the family. The clinician may be able to assist an isolated family to make connections with other queer families in order to broaden its kinship network. The clinician may help bring to awareness the effect that homophobia and heterosexism has had on the structures that have developed within the family. The clinician's own awareness of the options for legal remedies in specific jurisdictions can help create security for same-sex families. This in turn can be helpful in maintaining family boundaries and allowing parents to differentiate with greater comfort in the security of their parental roles. Building into one's clinical practice an awareness of the history of the formation of gay and lesbian identity, of homophobia and heterosexism as forms of oppression, and of legal remedies for same-sex families can help to create a working relationship that is relevant to the needs of queer families. Interventions at various levels, such as encouraging linkages among same-sex families and helping families to access legal protection, may have an indirect effect on changing family structures. Finally, building into one's practice an awareness of the ways in which the public existence of same-sex families has an impact on changing social structures gives queer families a sense of acknowledgement for their strength and competence in the daily work of just being a family.

As we have written elsewhere (Sullivan & Baques, 1999), gay and lesbian parents are not waiting on the resolution of social dissension to get on with the job of raising their children. Therefore, it behooves policy makers to observe the intergenerational covenant and not impede them in the process. It is not unreasonable to expect that legislative changes in the definition of marriage and the family will be interpreted by professional regulatory bodies to require evidence of professional development consistent with those changes. This also imposes an obligation on theorists and practitioners to be creative in formulating and synthesizing approaches that go beyond the limitations of traditional practices in order to affirm the experiences of sexual minority families. Competent practice will require nothing less. In these pages, we hope to have contributed some ideas that will be useful to family practitioners navigating their way through the changing landscape of family life.

NOTE

1. Witness the comments of Larry Spencer, Canadian Alliance MP, who said to reporters that he would support any initiative to put homosexuality back in the Criminal Code and that advancement toward gay and lesbian rights is the product of a well-orchestrated conspiracy (O'Neil, 2003, p. A1). Although Spencer was fired over his remarks, the same article quotes many other Canadian politicians regarding their views on equality rights for gay men and lesbians. It is difficult to imagine another minority group in contemporary Canada being the subject of such debates regarding basic rights.

REFERENCES

Action Canada for Population and Development and Planned Parenthood Federation of Canada. (2003). *Report on Canada's compliance with the convention on the rights of the child in response to Canada's second periodic report to the committee on the rights of the child.* Ottawa, Quebec, Canada: Author.

Allen-Meares, P., & Lane, B. (1987). Grounding social work practice in theory: Ecosystems. *Social Casework, 68,* 515-521.

Arnup, K. (1999). Out in this world: The social and legal context of gay and lesbian families. *Journal of Gay & Lesbian Social Services, 10*(1), 1-25.

Blasius, M. (1994). *Gay and lesbian politics: Sexuality and the emergence of a new ethic.* Philadelphia: Temple University Press.

Bowen, M. (1978). *Family therapy in clinical practice.* New York: Jason Aronson.

Brill, S. A. (2001). *The queer parent's primer: A lesbian and gay families' guide to navigating the straight world.* Oakland, CA: New Harbinger Publications.

Broderick, C. (1993). *Understanding family process: Basics of family systems theory.* Newbury Park, CA: Sage Publications.

Chan, R. W., Brooks, R. C., Raboy, B., & Patterson, C. J. (1998). Division of labor among lesbian and heterosexual parents: Associations with children's adjustment. *Journal of Family Psychology, 12*(3), 402-419.

Faderman, L. (1985). *Surpassing the love of men: Romantic friendship and love between women from the renaissance to the present.* London, UK: The Women's Press.

Foucault, M. (1990). *The history of sexuality.* New York: Vintage.

Frye, M. (1983). *The politics of reality.* Freedom, CA: The Crossing Press.

Jagose, A. (1996). *Queer theory.* New York: New York University Press.

Janson, G. R. (2002). Family counseling and referral with gay, lesbian, bisexual, and transgendered clients: Ethical considerations. *The Family Journal, 10,* 328-333.

Jones, S. L. (1980). *Family therapy: A comparison of approaches.* Bowie, MD: R. J. Brady Co.

Kerr, M. (1988). Chronic anxiety and defining a self. *The Atlantic Monthly, 279*(5), 35-58.

Kinsman, G. (1996). *The regulation of desire: Homo and hetero sexualities.* Montreal, Canada: Black Rose Books.

Leslie, L. A. (1988). Cognitive-behavioral and systems models of family therapy: How compatible are they? In N. Epstein, S. Schlesinger, E. Stephen, & W. Dryden (Eds.), *Cognitive-behavioral therapy with families* (pp. 49-83). New York: Brunner Mazel Publishers.

McCandish, B. (1987). Against all odds: Lesbian mother family dynamics. In F. W. Bozett (Ed.), *Gay and lesbian parents* (pp. 23-36). New York: Praeger.

Minuchin, S. (1974). *Families and family therapy.* Cambridge, MA: Harvard University Press.

Mullaly, R. (1997). *Structural social work: Ideology, theory, practice.* Toronto, Canada: Oxford University Press.

Nelson, F. (1996). *Lesbian motherhood: An exploration of Canadian lesbian families.* Toronto, Canada: University of Toronto Press.

O'Neil, P. (2003, November 27). Make it a crime to be gay: Alliance MP. *Vancouver Sun,* p. A1.

Payne, M. (1997). Systems and ecological perspectives. In M. Payne (Ed.), *Modern social work theory* (2nd ed., pp. 3-28). Chicago: Lyceum Books.

Ristock, J. (1993). The theory and politics of helping in feminist social service collectives. In G. Drover & P. Kerans (Eds.), *New approaches to welfare theory* (pp. 55-76). Aldershot, UK: Edward Elgar Publishing.

Rohrbaugh, J. B. (1992). Lesbian families: Clinical issues and theoretical implications, *Professional Psychology: Research and Practice, 23*(6), 467-473.

Sullivan, T. R., & Baques, A. (1999). Familism and the adoption option for gay and lesbian parents. In T. R. Sullivan (Ed.), *Queer families, common agendas: Gay people, lesbians, and family values* (pp. 79-94). Binghamton, NY: Harrington Park Press.

Vanfraussen, K., Ponjaert-Kristofferson, I., & Brewaeys, A. (2003). Family functioning in lesbian families created by donor insemination. *American Journal of Orthopsychiatry, 73*(1), 78-90.

Chapter 14

Listening to Lesbian Couples: Communication Competence in Long-Term Relationships

Colleen M. Connolly
Mary Kay Sicola

Love and partnering are considered primary sources of happiness and meaning in life, and competent communication is central in developing and maintaining a successful (Fowers, 1998) and satisfying romantic relationship (Nicotera, 1993). Communication theorists (Wood, 1999) and other social scientists (Acitelli, 2001; Tannen, 1990) emphasize communication in terms of a relational dynamic and as a gender-influenced process. This article explores the intersection of these concepts by highlighting communication styles described and demonstrated in ten long-term lesbian relationships.

How couples communicate plays an important role in therapeutic work. Without effective communication, relationships frequently fail (Nicotera, 1993). Clinicians might disagree as to the theoretical approach or choice of techniques, but few differ about how foundational good communication skills are for maintaining a successful relationship (Fowers, 1998). Couples need effective problem-solving and conflict-resolution processes to maneuver through difficulties (Walsh, 1993), and most therapists believe that acquiring communication skills is pivotal in preventing or lessening relational distress and rupture (Fowers, 1998).

Communication is about both content transmission and relationship maintenance (Walsh, 1993). The content aspect involves conveying information, opinions, and/or feelings. The relationship aspect is

doi:10.1300/5792_15

what defines the nature of the relationship, with every direct or indirect communication either affirming or challenging its integrity.

Couples of all types share many communication and relational processes. Fowers (1998) suggests that two related functions of communication are present in romantic dyads. To begin with, feelings of love are maintained through self-expression, mutual understanding of partner, and the associated emotional intimacy that results. In addition, competent communication is necessary to manage the unavoidable difficulties experienced when sharing a life together.

Walsh (1993, 1998) identifies three aspects of communication that are crucial for relational resiliency: clarity, open emotional expression, and collaborative problem solving. Clarity involves sending clear, consistent messages and clarifying any ambiguous information. Open emotional expression includes such things as sharing a wide range of feelings, mutual empathy, tolerating one's partner's differences, taking responsibility for one's own feelings and behavior, and engaging in pleasurable interactions, including humor. Collaborative problem solving relates to processes such as problem identification, brainstorming options and resources, shared decision making, conflict resolution, goal setting, and a proactive stance aimed not only at problem and crisis prevention but also toward preparation for future challenges.

Open communication is considered a hallmark of well-functioning relationships. Walsh (1993) emphasizes that couples who communicate clear rules and expectations, enjoy pleasurable activities together, share laughter and humor, and possess a range of emotional expression, including empathic responsiveness and optimism, generally fare the best.

Successful coupling, according to Olson (1993), involves an interplay among communication, closeness, and flexibility, with communication being the facilitating process that moves couples toward more closeness and flexibility. Olson measures communication as follows: empathic and attentive listening skills, speaking for oneself and not for others, self-disclosure about self and relationship, clarity, staying on topic through the use of continuity-tracking, and the affective communication aspects of respect and regard.

Self-disclosure and continuity also are considered important to Omarzu, Whalen, & Harvey (2001). They contend that mutual self-disclosure helps build a foundation of knowledge about one's partner and maintain attunement. Good communication often is sufficient to begin a relationship, but continuing to mind the relational processes is necessary to move forward successfully in relationship. According to these authors, accepting and respecting differences, reciprocity, and attributing one's partner's behavior positively also are regarded as important components of relationship satisfaction.

Communication clarity and directness between partners also are considered important features by Epstein, Bishop, Ryan, Miller, & Keitner (1993). They identify clear or masked communication wherein the message content is clearly stated or camouflaged/vague. Messages can also be direct or indirect (i.e., messages go directly to the intended target or are indirectly deflected to other people). Epstein and colleagues suggest that the two aspects are independent, which results in four styles of communication: clear and direct, clear and indirect, masked and direct, and masked and indirect. When nonverbal communication is contradictory, it masks the communication and may be a sign of indirect communication as well.

Fowers (1998) suggests that the most common communication skills advocated by therapists are nondefensive listening, active listening, self-disclosure, and editing. Editing involves making a decision between several responses and choosing the one that is most "polite" (p. 47) or might be received in the best light. Fowers suggests editing can be a conscious skill developed between partners.

Lesbian couples possess many of the same processes associated with couples of all types, but they also demonstrate distinct relational strengths and stressors. They are known for their expressivity and decision-making abilities (Kurdek, 1988). They also excel in their ability to form egalitarian relationships (Bigner, 2000; Kurdek, 1998; Laird, 1993; Toder, 1992; Zacks, Green, & Marrow, 1988) and implement effective conflict-resolution methods (Berzon, 1988; Eldridge & Gilbert, 1990; Johnson, 1990; Littlefield, 1994; Metz, Rosser, & Strapko, 1994; Slater, 1995; Toder, 1992).

Studies of lesbian couples suggest they experience more relationship satisfaction than other couples (Metz et al., 1994; Ossana, 2000; Scrivner & Eldridge, 1995; Zacks et al., 1988), but some research indicates female couples are at greater risk of the relationship ending than gay males or different-sex couples (Blumstein & Schwartz, 1983; Kurdek, 1998). Why might this be so?

Couples who experience social isolation and homophobia often interpret brief periods of conflict as serious relational problems, and many lesbian couples only recognize they have reached a point of transition when the relationship is disrupted (Berzon, 1988; Slater, 1995). Moreover, couples who are isolated and lacking necessary resources and information about the unique nature of lesbian couplehood often interpret stresses and brief periods of conflict as serious problems rather than normal developmental transitions inherent to all couples (Berzon, 1988; Toder, 1992). Of course, same-sex female couples face not only the burdens of homophobia, as do gay male couples, but also confront the additional stressors associated with navigating within a sexist culture (for example, see Brown, 1995).

Although different stressors may confront male-male, female-female, and different-sex couples, all dyads appear to most frequently argue about similar issues. Kurdek (1994) surveyed gay ($N = 75$), lesbian ($N = 51$), and heterosexual ($N = 108$) couples and found that all couples rank ordered the two most frequently argued-about matters as intimacy issues (affection and sex) and power issues (demands, equality).

Regardless of the longevity of the relationship, the high self-reported relational satisfaction among lesbian couples may result from, and be reflected by, their interpersonal communication patterns. Lesbian couples employ discourse strategies associated with communication competence. For example, according to Metz and colleagues (1994), female couples experience more optimistic and positive patterns of conflict resolution than other types of couples. They studied 108 couples, with an equal match of thirty-six lesbian, gay, and heterosexual couples. When conflict in the relationship occurred, lesbian women typically were more distressed, asserted more constructive behavior, experienced a perception of greater resolution effort from the other partner, and reported less physical and verbal aggression by the partner than heterosexually partnered women.

Metz and colleagues (1994) posit that these factors might influence the higher relationship satisfaction reported by the couples in their study. They also suggest that lesbian couples "may give more priority to their relationships because they are without equivalent social supports, share a common 'coming out' experience, or may feel less role bound" (Metz et al., 1994, p. 305) than traditional couples.

Susan Johnson (1990) conducted a nationwide study of long-term lesbian couples and noted the importance of communication. In Johnson's study, couples also related therapy, the natural progression of time, forgiveness, and individual growth as important in their conflict resolution.

Glenda Littlefield (Littlefield, 1994; Littlefield, Lim, Canada, & Jennings, 2000) qualitatively explored common themes and processes with sixteen long-term lesbian couples. The role of intimacy, including spending time together, physical contact, and discussion time, remained important to conflict management for the couples in Littlefield's (1994) study. Her lesbian couple participants expressed emotional satisfaction within the relationship and stressed the importance of communication and shared decision making. Based on the couples in her study, Littlefield posits:

> Individual needs became secondary to relationship needs when dealing with conflicts or problems. The patterns of conflict resolution reflect a respect for individual opinions and needs with an ultimate goal to find solutions that will enhance their relationship quality. (Littlefield, 1994, p. 90)

General trends in clinical work and research emphasizing strengths, as opposed to deficit-based assessments and analyses, can have "profound implications" for lesbian couples (Laird, 1996, p. 566). Scholars have called for descriptive studies on the strengths associated with lesbian couples (Bradford, Ryan, & Rothblum, 1994; Laird, 1993, 1994, 1996; Zacks et al., 1988). The primary author of this chapter responded to this invitation by initiating a study on strength and resiliency in long-term lesbian couples (Connolly, 1999). This chapter represents a focused portion of that larger study.

METHODS

The research methods used in this study were feminist-based ethnography and phenomenology: phenomenological in the sense that it looked at the experiential structure and essence of these couples' lives, and ethnographic in looking at the couples situated contextually in their culture (Patton, 1990). Feminist ethnography by nature involves the documentation of women's lives, the understanding of their lives through their own perspective, and the conceptualization of the meaning they place on behavior within their social context (Reinharz, 1992). Couples were located through personal and professional contacts and participant referral. These techniques are frequently used when seeking "invisible" populations (Reilly & Lynch, 1990). Participants emerged quickly, and ten couples with relationships ranging from ten to twenty-four years were interviewed. The average length of relationship was eighteen years. The women were between the ages of thirty-four and sixty. Every woman had some college education and some had advanced degrees. All were dual-career couples, although two women had recently retired from their full-time careers.

These couples were viewed as authorities in their own lives (Rogers, 1993) and subsequently were conceptualized as co-researchers (Olesen, 1994) and collaborators (Punch, 1994). The research allowed for design flexibility (Patton, 1990; Rubin & Rubin, 1995) to allow for adapting, changing, and redesigning as necessary (Janesick, 1994). Participants guided the interview process, which was continued until no new themes emerged (Glaser & Straus, 1967; Rubin & Rubin, 1995), suggesting we attained "theoretical saturation" (Glaser & Straus, 1967, p. 61).

Initial interviews, which lasted between 1.5 hours to approximately 3 hours in length, provided rich data in broad topic areas. The interviews were transcribed, pseudonyms assigned, and data analyzed. A second interview allowed an opportunity for verification and expansion of existing themes (Giorgi, 1985; Hoshmand, 1989).

Striving for shared meaning and mutual understanding are important in the interview process (Fontana & Frey, 1994). Language can be "scrutinized—'unpacked,' not treated as self-evident, transparent, unambiguous—during the interview itself as well as later, in the analysis of interview transcripts" (Riessman, 1993, p. 32). This coconstructed meaning-making remains particularly important when talking with a population in which culture is embedded in the language (Rubin & Rubin, 1995), such as with this sample.

In communicating the results, we attempt to use the couples' own words as often as possible in the hopes that it will provide the reader a closer experience with the participants (Rogers, 1993). In addition, this chapter adapted analysis notations used by Kogan and Gale to assist the reader (Kogan & Gale, 1997; Sacks, Schegloff, & Jefferson, 1974). We employ the following transcription notes: (.) and (..) to indicate pauses in increasing length; [ ] for clarifying or summarizing information; CAPITALIZED words to signify those words spoken with added emphasis; and ( ) to symbolize clarifying information such as laughter.

The larger study's focus was on strength and resiliency (Connolly, 1999; Connolly, in press). Communication competence emerged as a theme, but it was outside the parameters of reporting within the larger study, as were the couples' descriptions of love (Connolly, 2004).

RESULTS

The couples described three themes associated with communication competence. Conveying meaning is primary to all communication. These couples conveyed meaning through a process that employed application of communication skills learned during the relationship and use of explicit definitions with a steadfast exploration of feelings. Second, these couples employed conflict-resolution strategies, including the conscious avoidance of contemptuous communication and the use of negotiation. Last, they stayed empathically attuned, attending to nonverbals and respecting individual differences.

We note at the outset that these couples valued communication and viewed it as a learned process, one that evolved over time and increased understanding of self and partner. All the couples attributed communication to their relational success.

Gloria and Hillary shared a relationship for almost twenty years. Gloria referred to communication as "vital" to relational success, or, as Hillary stated, it is the "backbone" of their relationship.

Some referred to learning from prior failed relationships to communicate differently in the current one. For example, Kate said that in prior relationships she was accustomed to the pattern of "don't talk about it and hope it will go away. Because if you talk about it, it will damage the relationship." Lynn, her current partner of over twenty years, had to "teach" her over the years that that method was not "the best way to make [their relationship] work."

The couples also learned how important timing was to the communication process. Kate and Lynn provided the example of becoming better "at gauging (.) how long to let each other kind of think it through and THEN start talking, as opposed to one being ready and the other one not being ready" to talk. Timing was especially important, either with issues that emotionally affected one or both in the partnership or when their feelings, whether positive or less-than-positive, were not in sync. In addition, the couples described their need to surmount communication differences by creating a shared meaning: What exactly did they mean by what they said?

Shared Meaning

The couples developed definitions and used clarifications to reduce the inherent ambiguity in language. This process, in turn, seemed to increase understanding. The following descriptions are reflective of the oft-repeated theme of attention to meaning.

Gloria and Hillary joked that they did not approach it as, "Here's my list of definitions, where is yours?" However, some words needed clarification and a more clear definition, and they gave an example using the word "monogamy." This dyad felt it was imperative to continue a dialogue: Did they mean the same thing when saying, "I want a monogamous relationship"? Hillary and Gloria wanted to create an understanding of what was "behind the words" and develop a "commonness of language" with each other.

> HILLARY: I don't know how people DO live with one another without really trying to listen and hear what's BEHIND what's being said . . . You can say things that you think means something, but if the other person is interpreting it in a different way or reading it through different eyes in some way, the words themselves can be very deceptive. So there has to be sort of an underlying understanding of base points.

Martha and Nelda, partnered for ten years, worked to avoid leaping to conclusions and passing judgments upon each other. "One of our strong points is we're willing to say, 'Now, what do you mean when you say that?' and not just kind of jump to conclusions." They consciously resisted imposing value judgments, seeking clarity with questions such as, "Now, why are you doing this," and "What's making you do it," and "Here's what I think." Increased understanding helped avoid conflict, but when conflict did arise, the couples evidenced strategies for effective resolution.

Conflict Resolution

Two subthemes of conflict resolution emerged from the data: conscious avoidance of contemptuous communication and strategic negotiation strategies. Notably, when the couples mentioned conflict, they repeatedly spoke of rejecting contemptuous discourse.

Avoiding Contempt

Contemptuous discourse is marked with sarcasm, put downs, name calling, mockery, hostile humor, and nonverbal communication such as eye rolling, glaring, and dismissive gestures (Gottman & Silver, 1994; Wilmot & Hocker, 2001). These long-term couples provided several examples of avoiding communication of contempt.

Hillary reflected that early on she and Gloria both were engaging in the "tearing down, nitpicky stuff that wasn't fun. It was put in the GUISE of humor, but it wasn't funny." When they "stepped back" and looked directly at the situation and overtly expressed their needs, humor proved more positive and relationally enhancing.

Two couples provided clear examples of direct and immediate responses that effected change in communication patterns. Lynn remembered back to "early on in the relationship." Kate did "something" and Lynn made "some sort of really sarcastic cutting remark back to her." Kate looked at Lynn and said, "Don't talk to me in that tone of voice." Lynn laughed in the interview and admitted: "Ah, and so I didn't."

Gloria spoke about an earlier phase in their relationship. She and Hillary had developed a negative communication pattern, where they would just "pick, pick, pick" at each other. Hillary made the consequences clear if their "sniping" type of communication continued.

> GLORIA: [W]hat Hillary did one night was said, "Look, I REALLY don't like that. And if you are going to do it, I don't want to be around you." And it's like, "Oh, well, THAT's an easy choice. I won't do it" (Gloria laughed).

The couples also spoke of a broader, unambiguous, and intentional communication process. Some described fair fighting practices. Kate and Lynn worked to never "throw zingers," or "fight unfairly" or "dirty." They tried "stick to the issues" and made it clear that their fight was not the relationship or commitment but rather the issue at hand. Martha felt she and Nelda were particularly "good about not trying to push each other's buttons" in an effort to "control the other person." By strategically avoiding contemptuous communication, these couples used language to manage or minimize conflict.

The couples' communication emphasized the opportunities that often accompany a conflict. Gloria valued getting things out in the open and avoiding what she called "closeted resentments." In her opinion, talking openly with Hillary created an environment that preempted issues that would "come back and haunt" them; they would not be "rehashing things that (.) were over and done with long ago [as a result of] harboring resentments."

Two couples used the words "domino effect" and explained their attempts at avoiding it. For example, Nelda and Martha each "forces the other one to discuss" problems. Otherwise, "you just create something else," which can have a "domino effect," and damage the relationship. The couples described their resolution of conflict through direct and unambiguous communication, including setting clear communication limits and using the process of negotiation.

Negotiation

In addition to the subtheme of avoiding contempt, the process of negotiation for conflict resolution surfaced in all interviews. All couples described regular negotiation strategies they used to either move through a relational impediment or to settle a dispute. Crafting the communication process took a lot of "very CONSCIOUS negotiating," according to Gloria.

Julie and Ingrid had been together about fifteen years. Julie noted that because they are equal partners, "it *is* a negotiation every step of the way." Ingrid does not "just surrender to me and go, 'Oh, you go ahead and decide.'"

The couples had to routinely negotiate daily tasks and activities within their same-sex household. Carol and Deborah provided an example of a negotiation process that resulted from each woman carrying forward her own mother's tradition in household tasks. They had been a couple for almost twenty years.

> CAROL: We had been together for a number of years, and all of a sudden (.) Deborah told me I was folding the towels wrong

> (Deborah chuckled). And I am like, "What do you mean 'wrong'? You know, where does it say there is a right way? You know, I am folding like my mother folded them." Deborah responded, "This is the right way, and this is how MY mother did it." Deborah then explained why it was easier or better to do it her mother's way.

Carol conceded that Deborah's way "was much easier" so Carol ultimately gave in: "Okay, fine, you win."

Elise and Fran, coupled for more than twenty years, used humor to negotiate daily chores. They employed the game of "paper/scissors" to determine "who's going to get the water, you know. Who's going to lock up? Whatever. Who's going to answer that phone call?" Elise laughed as she said, "It works." Other times, they negotiated routine activities in an instrumental way. They made a "list" of things that needed doing and then would alternately "pick" and choose the areas they would commit to complete.

Other processes emerged. The point of disagreement might be significant to only one partner, "so it's not that big of a deal to give in," as Lynn suggested. Some spoke of the need to "back off" certain topics that were more important to the other partner. Olivia and Peg, partnered for over fifteen years, described that if "somebody has a strong emotion about it, if you are able to (..) defend it, the other person usually acquiesces."

Quincy and Roberta, who had been coupled for over twenty years, described a similar process. Quincy made the majority of the decisions in the relationship. Roberta kept things "kind of hidden" unless it was "really, really important" to her, at which point she was "not shy about speaking up." Quincy then felt "free" to more frequently make decisions, recognizing that if something "bumps up against" an area of importance to Roberta, she would speak up. Because it happened infrequently, Quincy typically would concede on those points or activities.

Several couples overtly stated they sometimes solved problems by "agreeing to disagree" on the topic. Alice and Barbara had been together for almost fifteen years. Alice summed it up when she said, "[Barbara and I] agree on so many things, that the things we don't agree on . . . we just agree to disagree. I mean, it's okay. And I'm not going to convince [Barbara] and she's not going to convince me."

Teri described what she learned about being individuals within relationship, boundaries, compromise, and longevity as she approached her twenty-fifth anniversary with Sheryl:

> [Y]ou have to allow each of you to be individuals. And you all are never going to agree on some things. You're going to agree on some things. And there are some things you're just never going to agree on because you're individuals. . . . The only reason people have a relationship is they compromise. They compromise on decisions, they compromise on things that they do. Ah, and somewhere in there in order to maintain your individuality, you all have to draw that line somewhere and somehow that's got to be communicated either through learning as you live together [or learning] just how far to push it.

The coresearchers also explained very overt strategies for anticipating, delineating, and inviting conflict resolution. For example, Barbara early on declared, "Here I am. If there's something you don't like that you can't live with, get it out." Her partner, Alice, responded:

> It wasn't, "Here's the list and you have to abide by it." But it was, "Here—here are things that I have found out about myself over the years that are necessary, preferable. You know, some things are negotiable. There's a few that aren't. Uh—you know, we have to talk about these things before we even know if we are going to go anywhere."

Empathic Attunement

The couples described the relational satisfaction they achieved by attending empathically to each other and respecting differences each person brought to the relationship. How they achieved this empathic connection seemed to be based on two things: awareness of and attention to both verbal and nonverbal communication, and accessing and utilizing their diverse approaches rather than fighting against them.

The words of two couples stand out as representative of the group. Martha stated, "You've got to let the other person know you appreciate what they are doing, and it is important to you and it touches you." Also, Barbara spoke of empathy and acceptance:

> There's more than just understanding that needs to go on, because it's not really sometimes important that you understand but it's important that you have empathy and (..) acceptance that that person feels that way, whether you understand it or not.

Attention to Nonverbals

Couples referred to ways in which they would be "reading each other's minds" and experiencing a comfortable "knowing" of their partner. Couples frequently described nonverbal communication as a strong point of their interpersonal skills. Peg described the importance of "caring gestures" and "the appreciation things."

During the initial interview, Hillary and Gloria demonstrated attention to nonverbals and an intuitive knowledge of partner when Gloria, noticing Hillary was cold, presented Hillary with a sweater.

> HILLARY: I was thinking it was going to be seventy degrees today. Thank you. I haven't identified it to the point to do anything about it obviously. . . . Thank you. Thank you. Oh, it's wonderful. I always said we can both go deaf. It's perfectly fine. We say the same things at the same time together anyway, so all we have to do is sit across the room and nod at one another and carry on a conversation (Hillary laughed).

Respecting Differences

The couples referred to another process: learning to honor differences and recognizing that those differences ultimately led to strength within the relationship. Hillary noted, it really took "two VERY diverse approaches to make things work" in the relationship. Peg contended that she and Olivia knew a lot about each other, what their "strengths and weaknesses" were, and how they "complement" each other. "We are real aware of it and real conscious and we talk about it."

The women also seemed aware of how unique family of origin dynamics impacted their relational lives; they were two individuals who came from different families, and each had her own unique communication patterns and processes. Alice and Barbara provided an example of communication variations stemming from their families of origin. Alice noted, "[Barbara's] family never talks to each other. Mine, if I have a hangnail, I call both of my sisters." Barbara shared that her family did not "talk constantly" like Alice's family; they talked when there was something to say. When Barbara visited Alice's family home, she felt as if she had to "take a number to talk" and "be able to listen to six conversations at a time." Two unique models of communication converged within this relationship.

Gloria and Hillary would "joke" about Gloria "having to talk everything to death." Hillary came from a family "that never really discussed anything" and particularly not "about anything personal." The dyad diligently worked against this dynamic when forming and maintaining their relationship.

Fran and Elise talked about how complementary their likes and dislikes were when approaching tasks. They only realized the differences when Elise suggested they each go into separate rooms and list what they "like to do" and what they "don't like to do" and then compared the lists. The couple expressed how "amazing" it was, in that the results turned out to be "the very opposite." Understanding these differences could work *for* them, they changed their approach to tasks.

Many of the couples spoke of one partner who was more open and communicative, and the beneficial effects of this on the relationship. For instance, Carol admitted Deborah was "more open" and "more aware of when we need to talk," sometimes having to "drag things out" of her. In addition, they related different styles of expressing and processing anger. Deborah had "a very quick temper" and Carol tended "to stay madder longer." These differences worked to their advantage in keeping the communication open.

Hillary contended that one within the relationship "has to be able to take the risk to force the conversation," something that she "would not ever do." Hillary reacted to conflict similarly to ways her family had responded. She "avoided conflict," and part of what Hillary needed was something that "Gloria's been able to contribute." Hillary needed "somebody who would push and say, 'Oh, no, we're not going to ignore this. We are not going to pretend it didn't happen. We are going to talk about it and we are going to do it now.'"

DISCUSSION

It is axiomatic that effective communication is fundamental to successful romantic relationships. How couples achieve effective communication, however, is a more elusive concept. Examining the discourse strategies employed by successful long-term couples revealed some clues to effective communication between romantic partners, especially where those relationships had flourished without the support typically provided by cultural, religious, and legal institutions. From the couples' spoken words, we have identified three themes contributing to communication competence: shared meaning, conflict resolution, and empathic attunement.

All the couples emphasized the value of communication to their relational success, describing it variously as "vital," "the backbone," and "important." These couples spoke of their relational communication as a process sufficiently flexible to allow for individual difference and lessons learned along the way. We found their spoken words reflected a lived experience in which language explores, constructs, and conveys meaning.

For purposes of this chapter, we conceptualize communication as the ongoing, interactive process whereby these couples convey meaning. The ability to convey meaning is integral to successful communication, and the inability to communicate successfully contributes to feelings of depression, frustration, and anxiety (Baumeister & Leary, 1995; Bolger & Eckenrode, 1991). Many individuals and couples find themselves in counseling where a therapeutic goal becomes improving the ability to convey meaning. In her research on language use in the therapeutic setting, Kathleen Warden Ferrara (1994) discovered the repeated use of jointly constructed metaphor between therapist and client and noted the power of conveying meaning: "To be fully human is to experience the joint construction of reality" (p. 168).

Given the role of conveying meaning to successful communication, perhaps we should not be surprised to find that these long-term couples repeatedly identified and emphasized the importance of shared meaning. Their strategies for developing, as one put it, "a commonness of language" provided guidance to this practice.

To decrease the ambiguity inherent in language, one couple constructed definitions where meaning was clearly shared (such as the meaning of monogamy). As one woman put it, she had to "listen and hear what's BEHIND what's being said." Similarly, another described "looking behind the words." Yet another concluded, "One of our strong points is we're willing to say, 'Now what do you mean when you say that?'"

Although the couples identified the importance of communication and described it as a learned process, they evidently did not assume they shared meaning. Instead, they used language to identify, define, construct, and convey meaning.

Put another way, we suggest that these long-term lesbian couples used language as a tool to craft understanding, if not agreement. This attention to shared meaning ultimately contributed to relational success. We surmise that this helped reduce conflict by minimizing language ambiguity and thwarting faulty attributions.

These couples were not without conflict, however. Instead, they revealed strategies for negotiating and managing conflict and emphasized the positive aspects of conflict, such as avoiding resentments and identifying problems.

In recent decades, scholars have conceptualized conflict as a dynamic that occurs between interdependent parties (Wilmot & Hocker, 2001) and emphasized win-win solutions (Fisher, Ury, & Patton, 1991). These concepts surfaced as lived experience throughout the data on orientation to conflict and methods of resolution.

All couples spoke of negotiation and compromise within their relationships, oftentimes in terms of household chores. Both partners appeared invested in the manner and methods of running the household. One couple described a conflict over folding the laundry, with each advocating the style used by her mother.

Unlike different-sex couples, the division of household chores was not influenced by gender-proscribed norms or expectations. In addition, although the women suggested that this created feelings of equality within the relationship, it was not without effort. "It IS a negotiation every step of the way," stated one woman.

These couples spoke of strategies for dividing up the household work: a game, paper/rock/scissors; making a to-do list and alternately picking items; and allocation according to strong likes or dislikes. In other areas of conflict, the partners acquiesced based on the importance the other placed on the issue. Several couples suspended dialogue when it appeared positions were intransigent; they simply agreed to disagree.

Also evident was the conscious process of avoiding contemptuous communication. Contempt involves statements or nonverbal behaviors that put oneself in an elevated position from one's partner and often includes put-downs, sarcasm, and ridicule (Gottman & Silver, 1994; Wilmot & Hocker, 2001). Gottman (Gottman & Silver, 1994; Gottman, 1998; Wilmot & Hocker, 2001) describes contempt as one of the "four horsemen of the apocalypse" (criticism, defensiveness, stonewalling, and contempt), and when these horsemen ride in, the end is near. The women in this study rejected the use of, in their words, "fighting unfairly," "sarcasm," "sniping," "pick, pick, picking," or "throw[ing] zingers."

Occasional attempts at contemptuous communication were met with statements such as, "Don't talk to me in that tone of voice," or "I REALLY don't like that. And if you're going to do it, I don't want to be around you." Instead of communicating contempt, the women tried to fight fairly and not push each other's buttons in an effort to control the other person.

We characterize the final area of communication competence among these long-term couples as empathic attunement. The couples described relational satisfaction from attending empathically to their partners and respecting each other's individual differences. By empathic attunement we refer to these characteristics, as well as the couples' descriptions of mind reading and attention to nonverbal communication. Given that most meaning is conveyed through nonverbal communication (Mehrabian, 1981) and that women are more adept at accurately decoding nonverbal cues than are men (Rosenthal & DePaulo, 1979), perhaps female couples have inherent advantages in this aspect of communication.

One woman emphasized the importance of accepting her partner's feelings whether she understood them or not, another woman described conveying appreciation, and yet another spoke of "the appreciation things." The couples identified and demonstrated nonverbal communication as an interpersonal strength. During an interview, one woman noticed her partner was cold and presented her with a sweater. Another spoke of the importance of "caring gestures."

Mind reading was frequently reported and also described as a comfortable knowing of one's partner. The couples used the term to describe understanding what the partner was thinking as opposed to making inaccurate assumptions. "We say the same things at the same time," one woman stated, joking that they could both go deaf and still know what the other was saying and thinking.

Last, the couples referred to a process of learning to honor individual differences from a strength-based perspective. The couples specifically identified differing communication styles as strengths, oftentimes in terms of one partner who was more open or expressive or one who insisted on discussing important but uncomfortable topics. These couples utilized their diverse approaches rather than fighting against them.

Julia Wood (1999) has identified the role of gender influences on communication orientation. She describes a continuum between instrumental (masculine) communication styles and relational (feminine) speech communities, where instrumental communicators use language to convey information to the listener and relational speakers use language to attend to the relationship between the speakers. Deborah Tannen (1990) has dubbed this difference report talk versus rapport talk.

Listening to lesbian couples provides an opportunity to examine discourse strategies and language orientation among romantic partners who were both raised in feminine (relational) speech communities. Our data suggest individual communication-orientation differences within the couples (one partner was often described as more "open" and communicative) and across the sample. However, we find the data insufficient to assess the applicability of, or placement on, the instrumental-relational paradigm.

CONCLUSION AND RECOMMENDATIONS

These ten couples made one point clear: they talk! Further, they both had the desire and capacity to do so. Conflict is bound to arise in relationships of any length. It becomes important for clinicians and couples alike to measure relational success not by an absence of conflict, but, rather, by the couple's ability to manage and resolve the conflict. Avoiding conflict leads to dysfunctional dynamics that can undermine the relationship and place it at risk of sustained dissatisfaction and/or disruption (Walsh, 1993).

The distinguishing communication feature in resilient families is their ability to manage conflict well, which requires an ability to tolerate open disagreement (Walsh, 1993). Lesbian couples experience ongoing and routine stressors across the lifespan due to their sexual orientation (Slater, 1995), and open communication and effective problem solving are particularly important when couples must cope with prolonged stressors or sudden crises (Walsh, 1993). Oftentimes, couples wait until problems or difficulties arise rather than working preemptively to keep potential problems averted (Simpson, Ickes, & Oriña, 2001).

Lesbian women enter romantic relationships in an environment of sexism, heterosexism, and homophobia. Avoiding the internalization of negative societal messages misappropriates energies from personal and relational growth. The failure to guard against internalization of negative societal messages can result in a bankrupt self-esteem, which undermines all human development. What might be seen as part of life for the same-sex couple, such as self-censoring and carefully chosen words, can permeate the relationship and generalize to other areas of life (Falco, 1996). These coresearchers described communication skills developed within a cultural context of discrimination, prejudice, and gender socialization.

Laura Brown (1995) posits that maneuvering lesbian identity in an oppressive context is not paralleled in many other adult developmental tasks. Therefore, couples frequently enter relationships unprepared for the societally induced stressors, and they often encounter unexpected issues *because* they are entering into relational territories.

Both partners within a same-sex couple have been socialized in very similar patterns and therefore possess variations of the same benefits and deficits of that gender-role socialization (Brown, 1995). Brown contends that the salient feature of a lesbian couple, being composed of two women, is the richest strength and the greatest difficulty of the relationship. Therapists must remain cognizant of the fact that they are working with "a female gender-role development multiplied by two" (Brown, 1995, p. 280).

It remains important for therapists to evaluate the degree of stressors resulting from societal oppression and assess the couple's gender-role socialization and its impact on that particular female-female relationship. Another critical area to explore is the individual and dyadic communication competence. Couples can have capacity and skill but lack the motivation to maintain that particular relationship. This type of couple often self-selects out of the relationship, either through discussion or in response to a relational crisis. Other couples have the motivation to create an enduring relationship with the partner but fall short in the capacity and skill to do so. The results of this study can be particularly helpful in this latter case, whether working individually, dyadically, or with the family.

Relationships need continued maintenance to sustain satisfaction (Acitelli, 2001). The coresearchers appeared to have high levels of what Linda Acitelli (2001) refers to as relational awareness and relational identity. Relational awareness involves a focusing of attention between partners and about the couple as an entity. Both thinking and talking *within* the context of the relationship and *about* the relationship are important forms of relationship maintenance that heighten relational awareness. Couples with a strong relational identity, such as the participants in this study, keep their relationship in tacit awareness and they view the world through a relational lens.

Acitelli (2001) argues that relationship talk is a function of gender and relational status, a position that this study's results certainly bolster. Acitelli made the distinction of strategic (planned and/or conscious) and routine (unplanned and/or automatic) maintenance strategies. She notes research suggesting that women value paying attention to relationships more than men, and that women can view relationship talk as "a routine part of everyday conversation" (p. 159), thereby maintaining and enhancing the relationship by attending to it.

However, communication can be productive and nonproductive. It appeared that over time, the couples in this study learned or grew to understand the importance of productive conversation to maintain their relationship successfully. Patterson and Schwartz (1994) suggest that lesbian couples are more likely to skirt issues, they may be hesitant to interrupt and challenge their partners once conflict is engaged, and often "rehash the issues to the point of weariness" (p. 19). Therapists must consider these points to work effectively with this population. Resolution time may be longer. More time might be needed for women to share feelings, feel heard, express disagreement, and find a fair resolution.

Bianca Murphy (1994) reminds us of the differences and diversity in same-sex couples. She refers to three therapeutic dilemmas facing clinicians. First, although we must recognize and value differences, it is imperative not to ignore ways in which couples of all types are similar. Second, in an effort to learn more about lesbian couples and distinguish them from heterosexual couples, we must not obscure the variation among these couples. Third, we must remember that two unique individuals make up a couple. When working with lesbian couples, we must resist the assumption of similarity in relational capacities based on each partner's gender socialization, as it can obscure our ability to see individual differences and intervene appropriately.

The coresearchers appeared to successfully create safety to communicate authentically. They crafted their skills, proactively eliminated or reduced ineffective communication, and amplified effective communication. These dyads worked toward speaking the same language, while at the same time remaining individuals and respecting differences.

This study increases understanding of communication competence in lesbian couples. However, it has far wider implications. The couples described many communication skills that clinicians would hope to see in all romantic relationships, which should prove useful when working with couples of all types.

Furthermore, Brown (1999) suggests that a therapeutic goal would be to help couples of all types move *toward* more characteristics of same-sex couples, with a therapeutic outcome of couples approximating a well-functioning lesbian couple. Looking beyond the heterosexual paradigm facilitates an expanded notion of what constitutes healthy couple functioning, broadening understanding to all couples.

The nature of this qualitative research design allowed for areas of analysis to emerge from the data instead of being predetermined from the outset. Listening to long-term lesbian couples revealed three areas of communication competence, which we categorize as attention to meaning, conflict resolution, and empathic attunement. No doubt these areas overlap and influence one another, and future research could explore the effect of these characteristics on relational success. In addition, we believe data from same-sex couples offer opportunities to further explore gender-based communication theories.

These well-functioning lesbian couples succeeded in long-term relationships despite the lack of support, if not overt hostility, from cultural, religious, and legal institutions. The ways in which they achieved communication competence provide guidance to all romantic couples. However, the data are limited in that they were derived from middle-aged, well-educated women, almost all of whom were white, living in the same part of the country. We encourage future research designs to reflect the diversity within the lesbian population.

It has been observed that meanings are in people, not in words. These women did not assume their partners interpreted words the same way they did. By recognizing meaning as a relational construction, they used language as a tool to move closer to shared understanding. Conflict resolution energies were invested in disputes less encumbered by misperceptions and faulty attributions. Not surprisingly, they had a positive conflict orientation, described how relational disputes brought issues to the table, reduced resentments, and produced constructive results. Undoubtedly contributing to this positive view and successful management of conflict was the explicit rejection of communicating contempt by avoiding name-calling, dismissive gestures, and sarcasm.

These couples remained empathically attuned and valued their relational connection. They described the importance of giving and receiving messages of acceptance and appreciation and viewed individual differences as contributing to relational strength. The spoken words of these well-functioning, long-term lesbian couples reflect communication orientations and discourse strategies that would be beneficial to all who seek to create and sustain healthy relationships.

REFERENCES

Acitelli, L. K. (2001). Maintaining and enhancing a relationship by attending to it. In J. H. Harvey & A. Wenzel (Eds.), *Close romantic relationships: Maintenance and enhancement* (pp. 153-168). Mahwah, NJ: Erlbaum.

Baumeister, R. F., & Leary, M. R. (1995). The need to belong: Desire for interpersonal attachments as a fundamental human motivation. *Psychological Bulletin, 117*(3), 497-529.

Berzon, B. (1988). *Permanent partners: Building gay and lesbian relationships that last.* New York: E. P. Dutton.

Bigner, J. J. (2000). Gay and lesbian families. In W. C. Nichols, M. S. Pace-Nichols, D. S. Becvar, & A. Y. Napier (Eds.), *Handbook of family development and intervention* (pp. 279-298). New York: John Wiley & Sons.

Blumstein, P., & Schwartz, P. (1983). *American couples: Money, work, sex.* New York: William Morrow.

Bolger, N., & Eckenrode, J. (1991). Social relationships, personality, and anxiety during a major stressful event. *Journal of Personality and Social Psychology, 61*(3), 440-449.

Bradford, J., Ryan, C., & Rothblum, E. D. (1994). National lesbian health care survey: Implications for mental health care. *Journal of Consulting and Clinical Psychology, 62*(2), 228-242.

Brown, L. S. (1995). Therapy with same-sex couples: An introduction. In N. S. Jacobson & A. S. Gurman (Eds.), *Clinical handbook of couple therapy* (pp. 274-291). New York: Guilford Press.

Brown, L. S. (Speaker). (1999). *Feminist couples therapy* [Video Recording, IAMFC Distinguished Presenter Series, No. 79722]. Alexandria, VA: American Counseling Association.

Connolly, C. M. (1999). Lesbian couples: A qualitative study of strengths and resilient factors in long-term relationships (Doctoral dissertation, St. Mary's University, 1998). *Dissertation Abstracts International, 59*(7-A), 2358.

Connolly, C. M. (2004). Lesbian couples: A qualitative look at long-term love. *Journal of Couple and Relationship Therapy, 3*(1), 13-26.

Connolly, C. M. (in press). A qualitative exploration of resilience in long-term lesbian couples. *The Family Journal: Counseling and Therapy for Couples and Families.*

Eldridge, N. S., & Gilbert, L. A. (1990). Correlates of relationship satisfaction in lesbian couples. *Psychology of Women Quarterly, 14*(1), 43-62.

Epstein, N. B., Bishop, D., Ryan, C., Miller, I., & Keitner, G. (1993). The McMaster model: View of healthy family functioning. In F. Walsh (Ed.), *Normal family processes* (2nd ed., pp. 138-160). New York: Guilford Press.

Falco, K. L. (1996). Psychotherapy with women who love women. In R. P. Cabaj & T. S. Stein (Eds.), *Textbook of homosexuality and mental health* (pp. 397-412). Washington, DC: American Psychiatric Press.

Ferrara, K. W. (1994). *Therapeutic ways with words.* New York, NY: Oxford University Press.

Fisher, R., Ury, W., & Patton, B. (1991). *Getting to yes: Negotiating agreement without giving in.* New York: Penguin Books.

Fontana, A., & Frey, J. H. (1994). Interviewing: The art of science. In N. K. Denzin & Y. S. Lincoln (Eds.), *Handbook of qualitative research* (pp. 361-376). Thousand Oaks, CA: Sage.

Fowers, B. J. (1998). Psychology and the good marriage: Social theory as practice. *American Behavioral Scientist, 41*(4), 516-541.

Giorgi, A. (1985). Sketch of a psychological phenomenological method. In A. Giorgi (Ed.), *Phenomenology and psychological research* (pp. 8-22). Pittsburgh, PA: Duquesne University Press.

Glaser, B. G., & Strauss, A. L. (1967). *The discovery of grounded theory: Strategies for qualitative research.* Chicago: Aldine Press.

Gottman, J. M. (1998). Psychology and the study of marital processes. *Annual Review of Psychology, 49*(1), 169-197.

Gottman, J. M., Silver, N. (1994). What makes marriage work? *Psychology Today, 27*(2), 38-43, 68.

Hoshmand, L. (1989). Alternate research paradigms: A review and teaching proposal. *The Counseling Psychologist, 17*(1), 3-79.

Janesick, V. J. (1994). The dance of qualitative research design: Metaphor, methodolatry, and meaning. In N. K. Denzin & Y. S. Lincoln (Eds.), *Handbook of qualitative research* (pp. 209-219). Thousand Oaks, CA: Sage.

Johnson, S. E. (1990). *Staying power: Long term lesbian couples.* Tallahassee, FL: Naiad Press.

Kogan, S. M., & Gale, J. E. (1997). Decentering therapy: Textual analysis of a narrative therapy session. *Family Process, 36*(2), 101-126.

Kurdek, L. A. (1988). Relationship quality of gay and lesbian cohabiting couples. *Journal of Homosexuality, 15*(3/4), 93-118.

Kurdek, L. A. (1994). Areas of conflict for gay, lesbian and heterosexual couples: What couples argue about influences relational satisfaction. *Journal of Marriage and the Family, 56*(4), 923-934.

Kurdek, L. A. (1998). Relationship outcomes and their predictors: Longitudinal evidence from heterosexual married, gay cohabiting, and lesbian cohabiting couples. *Journal of Marriage and the Family, 60*(3), 553-568.

Laird, J. (1993). Lesbian and gay families. In F. Walsh (Ed.), *Normal family processes* (2nd ed., pp. 282-328). New York: Guilford Press.

Laird, J. (1994). Lesbian families: A cultural perspective. In M. P. Mirkin (Ed.), *Women in context* (pp. 118-148). New York: Guilford Press.

Laird, J. (1996). Family-centered practice with lesbian and gay families. *Families in Society, 77*(9), 559-572.

Littlefield, G. D. (1994). Common threads and themes involved in long-term lesbian relationships (Doctoral dissertation, Texas Woman's University, 1993). *Dissertation Abstracts International, 55*(2-A), 394.

Littlefield, G. D., Lim, M.-G., Canada, R. M., & Jennings, G. (2000). Common themes in long-term lesbian relationships. *Family Therapy, 27*(2), 71-79.

Mehrabian, A. (1981). *Silent messages: Implicit communication of emotions and attitudes* (2nd ed.). Belmont, CA: Wadsworth.

Metz, M. E., Rosser, B. R. S., & Strapko, N. (1994). Differences in conflict-resolution styles among heterosexual, gay, and lesbian couples. *Journal of Sex Research, 31*(4), 293-308.

Murphy, B. C. (1994). Difference and diversity: Gay and lesbian couples. *Journal of Gay & Lesbian Social Services, 1*(2), 5-31.

Nicotera, A. M. (1993). The importance of communication in interpersonal relationships. In A. M. Nicotera & Associates (Eds.), *Interpersonal communication in friend and mate relationships* (pp. 3-5). Albany: State University of New York Press.

Olesen, V. (1994). Feminisms and models of qualitative research. In N. K. Denzin & Y. S. Lincoln (Eds.), *Handbook of qualitative research* (pp. 158-174). Thousand Oaks, CA: Sage.

Olson, D. H. (2003). Circumplex model of marital and family systems. In F. Walsh (Ed.), *Normal family processes* (3rd ed., pp. 514-548). New York: Guilford Press.

Omarzu, J., Whalen, J., & Harvey, J. H. (2001). How well do you mind your relationship? A preliminary scale to test the minding theory of relating. In J. H. Harvey & A. Wenzel (Eds.), *Close romantic relationships: Maintenance and enhancement* (pp. 345-356). Mahwah, NJ: Erlbaum.

Ossana, S. M. (2000). Relationship and couples counseling. In R. M. Perez, K. A. DeBord, & K. J. Bieschke (Eds.), *Handbook of counseling and psychotherapy with lesbian, gay, and bisexual clients* (pp. 275-302). Washington, DC: American Psychological Association.

Patterson, D. G., & Schwartz, P. (1994). The social construction of conflict in intimate same-sex couples. In D. D. Cahn (Ed.), *Conflict in personal relationships* (pp. 3-26). Hillsdale, NJ: Erlbaum.

Patton, M. Q. (1990). *Qualitative evaluation and research methods* (2nd ed.). Newbury Park, CA: Sage.

Punch, M. (1994). Politics and ethics in qualitative research. In N. K. Denzin & Y. S. Lincoln (Eds.), *Handbook of qualitative research* (pp. 83-97). Thousand Oaks, CA: Sage.

Reilly, M. E., & Lynch, J. M. (1990). Power-sharing in lesbian partnerships. *Journal of Homosexuality, 19*(3), 1-29.

Reinharz, S. (1992). *Feminist methods in social research.* New York: Oxford University Press.

Riessman, C. K. (1993). *Narrative analysis.* Newbury Park, CA: Sage.

Rogers, A. G. (1993). Voice, play, and a practice of ordinary courage in girls' and women's lives. *Harvard Educational Review, 63*(3), 265-295.

Rosenthal, R., & DePaulo, B. M. (1979). Sex differences in accommodation in nonverbal communication. In R. Rosenthal (Ed.), *Skill in nonverbal communication: Individual differences* (pp. 68-103). Cambridge, MA: Oelgeschlager, Gunn & Hain.

Rubin, H. J., & Rubin, I. S. (1995). *Qualitative interviewing: The art of hearing data.* Thousand Oaks, CA: Sage.

Sacks, H., Schegloff, E. A., & Jefferson, G. (1974). A simplest systematics for the organization of turn-taking for conversation. *Language, 50*(4), 696-735.

Scrivner, R., & Eldridge, N. S. (1995). Lesbian and gay family psychology. In R. H. Mikesell, D. Lusterman, & S. H. McDaniel (Eds.), *Integrating family therapy: Handbook of family psychology and systems theory* (pp. 327-344). Washington, DC: American Psychological Association.

Simpson, J. A., Ickes, W., & Oriña, M. (2001). Empathic accuracy and preemptive relationship maintenance. In J. H. Harvey & A. Wenzel (Eds.), *Close romantic relationships: Maintenance and enhancement* (pp. 27-46). Mahwah, NJ: Erlbaum.

Slater, S. (1995). *The lesbian family life cycle.* New York: The Free Press.

Tannen, D. (1990). *You just don't understand: Women and men in conversation.* New York: William Morrow.

Toder, N. (1992). Lesbian couples in particular. In B. Berzon (Ed.), *Positively gay: New approaches to gay and lesbian life* (pp. 50-63). Berkeley, CA: Celestial Arts.

Walsh, F. (1993). Conceptualization of normal family processes. *Normal family processes* (2nd ed., pp. 3-69). New York: Guilford Press.

Walsh, F. (1998). *Strengthening family resilience.* New York: Guilford Press.

Wilmot, W. W., & Hocker, J. L. (2001). *Interpersonal conflict* (6th ed.). New York: McGraw-Hill.

Wood, J. T. (1999). *Gendered lives* (3rd ed.). Belmont, CA: Wadsworth.

Zacks, E., Green, R., & Marrow, J. (1988). Comparing lesbian and heterosexual couples on the Circumplex Model: An initial investigation. *Family Process, 27,* 471-484.

Index

doi:10.1300/5792_16